EVIDENCE AND BURDEN OF PROOF
UNDER THE FOREIGN SOVEREIGN IMMUNITIES ACT, 1976

A Practical Guide for Business Lawyers and Government
by Dr. Pierre F. Walter, Esq.

ISBN 978-1-453631-84-3

About Dr. Pierre F. Walter, Esq.

http://drpfw.info

Contact Information Dr. Pierre F. Walter, Esq.

publisher@sirius-c-publishing.com

Quotation Suggestion

Pierre F. Walter, *Evidence and Burden of Proof under the Foreign Sovereign Immunities Act, 1976: A Practical Guide for Business Lawyers and Government*, Newark: Sirius-C Media Galaxy LLC, 2010

CONTENTS

INTRODUCTION

Litigating under the FSIA 1976

The present book is a procedural guide for business lawyers and government counsel who have to deal with affairs litigated under the *Foreign Sovereign Immunities Act, 1976 (FSIA)*.

The essential problem in those trials is to find appropriate criteria for the *determination of the burden of proof*, both in matters of jurisdictional immunities of foreign states, and with regard to judgment enforcement and executional measures regarding the property of foreign states. To begin with, I had to validate or reject one possible guideline for finding the burden of proof, the so-called *rule-and-exception principle*, as it was used as a drafting technique in the FSIA 1976.

In fact, initially, because of sovereignty, there is a natural rule of *general jurisdiction* for United States over all of its territory. This presumption of jurisdiction was on first sight reversed by the general rules of immunity contained in the FSIA. However, after a thorough examination of the rule-and-exception principle and the drafting technique, I abandoned this pathway, for it led to quite arbitrary results. Subsequently I found that the only way to safely attribute the burden of proof in sovereign immunity litigation is by finding out in detail what really is the content of the new *restrictive immunity doctrine*.

Specifically, the following questions had to be tackled in the course of this study on the United States' *Foreign Sovereign Immunities Act, 1976*:

▸ 1/ Is the new restrictive immunity doctrine a new rule of international law, or is it only a limitation of the former absolute rule of sovereign immunity?

▸ 2/ Does this new doctrine of restrictive immunity, supposed it exists, only grant sovereign immunity to foreign states when the activity in question was of a public, governmental character, thus restoring as it were the original rule of unlimited jurisdiction of the forum state over all of its territory?

▸ 3/ Who bears the burden of proof for the facts that determine the granting or the denial of immunity; who bears the 'immunity risk' or the ultimate burden? And this burden, what does it consist of? And what happens in a *non liquet* situation? Is there any presumption *in dubio pro immunitatem* or *in dubio contra immunitatem*?

▸ 4/ How is evidence submitted in sovereign immunity litigation? How is *prima facie* evidence submitted to the court?

▸ 5/ Who bears the burden of proof in case an organism of the foreign state, but not the foreign state, is the defendant in the trial? Is the burden of proof different in such a case?

▸ 6/ What about the allocation of the burden of proof in cases that involve not jurisdictional immunities but an execution into property belonging to a foreign state? In other words, are the rules different for immunity from execution? If yes, does that mean that the burden of proof also is different?

▸ 7/ Where to find the facts to be proved in litigations that involve foreign sovereign immunity?

> 8/ Which means of proof are usually submitted in sovereign immunity litigation, or more generally put, which kind of evidence is allowed?

United States district courts curtailed down the lawmaker's progressive effort quite a bit, and rendered the statute by far more conservative than it looked on first sight. What the courts did was to tailor that new restrictive immunity to the needs of the litigation practice, while carefully respecting international law. To say, the courts took a rather *protective attitude* toward the preservation of sovereign immunity in cases where it seemed Congress wanted to grant a total license to (unlimited) jurisdiction - provided of course that *minimal contacts* were established. In fact, American jurisprudence has virtually nullified a literal interpretation of the *House Report* on the question of the *burden of proof in a non liquet situation,* by the highest court. I refer to the Supreme Court ruling in *Verlinden B.V. vs. Central Bank of Nigeria.*[1]

This was quite a corrective tone set in the land after the joyful lawmaker *seemed to see sovereign immunity as but a residual concept.* Furthermore, American district courts and the Supreme Court established something like a *catalog of sensible areas* that will remain the hard core of sovereignty even in the future, and where the new restrictive immunity doctrine has lost its reformatory spirit.

The question if this catalog of *sensitive political and governmental matters* that shall remain untouched by the restrictive immunity doctrine can be considered as a *standard of international law* is a topic vast and important enough for a further study.[2]

The FSIA contains two general rules, one for immunity from jurisdiction, §1604, and one for immunity from execution, §1609. These rules are each followed by exceptions, §§1605, 1606, 1607 and §§1610-1611. Immunity is granted only when one of the exceptions applies. This is also called the *rule and exception principle.* §1330(a) entangles the competence *ratione materiae* of the court, also called original jurisdiction or subject matter jurisdiction, with the decision about immunity, which means that in practice that court is competent to rule over the case only when an exception to immunity applies, and thus when the immunity claim of the foreign state has been denied.[3]

From *subject matter jurisdiction* is to distinguish *personal jurisdiction*, §1330(b), which requires the affirmation of subject matter jurisdiction, §1330(a) plus *service of process*, according to §1608 of the Act.[4] Thus, sections 1330(a),(b), 1608 and 1605-1607 of the FSIA are all interwoven to a point that in *Maritime International Nominees Establishment (MINE) v. The Republic of Guinea*, the court speaks about 'the Act's interlocking provisions governing the separate issues of subject matter jurisdiction, sovereign immunity, and personal jurisdiction'.[5]

This is how the FSIA entangles substantive law and procedural law, and this is why the whole matter is so tricky! It's also tricky for the judges because this drafting technique requires the court to state about the whole question of immunity *before entering the trial,* because without pronouncing itself about its competence, the court is not legally in state to rule over the matter. But the trick is that for affirming its competence, the court must affirm one of the exceptions, §§1605-1607 of the FSIA.

How does that work in practice? There is case law that elucidates the matter. In *Upton v. Empire of Iran*[6], the court stated:

> **Upton v. Empire of Iran**
>
> The Immunities Act thereby creates an identity of substance and procedure; that is, it requires the court to examine the underlying claim in light of the immunity exceptions set forth in sections 1605-1607 whenever a jurisdictional sovereign immunity defense is interposed.[7]

Other precedents clarify that the House Report's idea that foreign sovereign immunity was an *affirmative defense* cannot be taken literally but has to be interpreted in the light of valid international law, which requires the court to state about the immunity claim *sua sponte*, and not depending on the pleadings.

CHAPTER ONE

Evidence Brief

Introduction

This preliminary chapter hopefully leads to a better understanding of my later explanations in matters of evidence and the burden of proof in foreign sovereign immunity litigation. I shall provide an outline of the general principles of the law of evidence, primarily for those lawyers and law practitioners who have, like myself, received their primary law education within the continental legal system and are thus little familiar with the particularities of Anglo-American civil procedure.

The term evidence has been defined by Tayer, *A Preliminary Treatise on Evidence (1898)* and by Wigmore, *A Treatise on the Anglo-American System of Evidence in Trials at Common Law (1981)* as:

Tayer

All legal means, exclusive of mere argument, which tend to prove or disprove any matter of fact, the truth of which is submitted to judicial investigation.[8]

Wigmore

Evidence, then, is any matter of fact that is furnished to a legal tribunal otherwise than by reasoning or a reference to what is noticed without proof as the basis of inference in ascertaining some other matter of fact.[9]

Jurisdiction and Competence

Cappelletti & Perillo state in *Civil Procedure in Italy (1965)*, that 'the term jurisdiction is much used and misused'.[10] I shall clarify what jurisdiction means, and what *competence* is about. It is true that there is a certain ambiguity with regard to the term jurisdiction; this term is often used for *actually denoting the competence of a court* for ruling a certain case.

An example for the use of the term jurisdiction when actually denoting competence is to be found in the *United States Foreign Sovereign Immunities Act of 1976*. In §1330 FSIA, the conditions are enumerated under which a court possesses competence *ratione materiae* et *ratione personae* (subject matter jurisdiction and personal jurisdiction) over a foreign state.

To begin with, international law talks about *immunity from jurisdiction* and not about immunity from competence. Immunity from jurisdiction is an exception to the generally unlimited jurisdiction of a forum state over the whole of its territory. Hence, the competence of the court depends on the denial of immunity; in other words, the affirmation of the judicial jurisdiction of the forum state is a *conditio sine qua non for the admission of competence*.

In this manner, two problems that are considered generally distinct among law practitioners are in reality intertwined and entangled because of the decisive dichotomy *immunity vel non*.

Fact

Fact in Anglo-American civil procedure, means *'whatever is the subject of perception and consciousness'.*[11] The present study is only concerned with the proof of facts, while generally in litigation rights may have to be proven as well, especially in the case when those rights have been acquired under a legal system different from the one of the forum state.[12]

Facts subject to proof are those that are 'facts in issue' and 'facts relevant to the issue', or else 'facts probative to an issue'.[13] The main facts in issue are those that the plaintiff must prove in a civil action if he is to win, and those that the defendant must prove in order to establish a defense. It is either substantive law or adjective law, that is procedural law, which determines those facts, or in the words of Phipson and Elliot:

> **Phipson and Elliot**
>
> It is not the law of evidence's business to say what those facts are in any particular case. They are determined by the substantive law or by the proceedings.[14]

In the particular case of this study, the question which law is applicable is a little more tricky, for not only national law is to be considered, but also international law. As a result, the facts in issue are those derived from both national law and international law. To give an example, §1605(a)(2) FSIA enumerates exceptions from a general rule of immunity, §1604, which represent each a potential fact in issue in any sovereign immunity litigation:

- action is based upon a *commercial activity carried on in the United States*;

- action is based upon an *act performed in the United States in connection with a commercial activity of the foreign state elsewhere*;

- action is based upon an *act outside the territory of the United States in connection with a commercial activity of the foreign state elsewhere and that act causes a direct effect in the United States*.[15]

Or let us look at §1603(d) which defines the term 'commercial activity' as either a *regular course of commercial conduct* or a *particular commercial transaction or act.*

The State Immunity Act 1978 of the United Kingdom is still more precise in this respect. It states in its §3(3):

> **§3 (3)**
> In this section 'commercial transaction' means -
> (a) any contract for the supply of goods or services;
> (b) any loan or other transaction for the provision of finance and any guarantee or indemnity in respect of any such transaction or of any other financial obligation; and
> (c) any other transaction or activity (whether of a commercial, industrial, financial, professional or other similar character) into which a State enters or in which it engages otherwise than in the exercise of sovereign authority;

Thus, under the FSIA 1976, a particular commercial transaction may be a fact in issue. By the same token, under the STIA 1978, a contract for the supply of goods and services is a fact that when it is proven will lead to a denial of foreign sovereign immunity and thus will be constituent for the affirmation of jurisdiction over the foreign state.[16]

Burden of Proof

The term burden of proof in Anglo-American law is distinct from the terms *'charge de la preuve'* or *'fardeau de la preuve'* in French law[17], *'Beweislast'* in Germanic legal systems[18], *'carga de la prueba'* in Hispanic legal systems[19], *'ónus da prova'* in Portuguese and Brazilian law[20], or *'onere della prova'* in Italian law.[21] To begin with, in France, article 1315 of the Code Civil states for the proof of a debt or the payment of a debt:

§1315 Code Civil

Celui qui réclame l'exécution d'une obligation doit la prouver. Réciproquement, celui qui se prétend libéré, doit justifier le paiement ou le fait qui a produit l'extinction de son obligation.

Regarding Canada while the French version of the bilingual text of the *Uniform Evidence Act, Livre II, Règles Générales de Preuve, Titre I* speaks of *fardeau de la preuve*, this notion is not identical with the term *fardeau de la preuve* or *charge de la preuve* in continental law. Canadian law, as already mentioned above, follows the Anglo-American evidence law system, while in Québec the French translation of the English term *burden of proof* does not reflect the legal content of this notion. It is just what it is, a translation.[22]

Austrian and Swiss civil procedure and evidence law is strongly influenced by German civil procedure law and rules of evidence.[23] Federal evidence law is to be applied when the juridical matter in question is one of federal law; if however the facts at the basis of the case are those of a relationship that is ruled by Cantonal law, the civil procedure rules of that Canton are to be applied for the case. As to federal law, see for example Art 8 ZGB.[24]

Despite these apparent differences, it is nonetheless possible to derive common parallels from the different notions of the *onus probandi*. For example, like with the Anglo-American notion of the burden of proof, there is a dual nature to be noted also with the continental notions of the burden of proof. To be true, there are generally two distinct notions, a *subjective* or affirmative burden and an *objective* burden that is also called burden *strictu senso*. The subjective burden or affirmative burden of proof is called '*Beweisführungslast*' or '*subjektive Beweislast*' in German civil procedure[25], '*charge de la production des preuves*' in French civil procedure[26], '*carga de la afirmación de la prueba*' in Spanish civil procedure[27] and '*onere della prova*' in Italian civil procedure.[28] The objective burden of proof is called '*Beweislast*' or '*objektive Beweislast*' in German civil procedure[29], '*risque de la preuve*' in French civil procedure[30], '*carga de la prueba*' in Spanish civil procedure[31] and 'onere della prova' in Italian civil procedure.[32] Italian civil procedure law does not seem to make this difference as for both notions the same expression, *onere della prova*, is used. However, Cappelletti and Perillo, who have done an in-depth comparison of the Italian notion of *onere della prova* and the Anglo-American term burden of proof, conclude:

> **Cappelletti & Perillo**
> The rules governing the burden of proving a fact are intimately related to the rules governing the burden of alleging a fact. As a general rule, the party who has the burden of pleading also has the burden of proof.[33]

The affirmative burden is applied to the pleadings and establishes a certain order in the probatory procedure; according to that order, the burden shifts from one party to the other. However, the objective burden of proof is not related to the production of evidence, but decides the litigation in case of a *non liquet*, that is, an irresolvable doubt regarding any fact in question: the party who carries the objective burden, then, loses the case. This means, practically speaking, that the objective or legal burden enables the judge to render a verdict in a case where the truth cannot be found. It's the applicable substantive law that attributes the objective burden, which is why Lord Denning's expression *legal burden* is particularly fit for denoting this burden. It's also correct to denote this burden as the *ultimate burden*, as it does not shift.

These similarities admitted, it would be simplistic to use any of the terms for the *onus probandi* from any of the continental legal systems synonymously with the Anglo-American term burden of proof.

> **Cappelletti & Perillo**
> In Anglo-American law, the term burden of proof is used to describe two different burdens. (…) In the Italian non-jury system, this distinction does not exist. Italian law is concerned only with the risk of non-persuasion. Even in the Italian system, however,

the question whether the burden of proof has been met is considered in two stages. Unless the panel decides to hear the evidence itself or to remand the case to the examining judge for the further taking of evidence, the examining judge decides when to close the proof-taking stage, thus preventing the introduction of further evidence.[34]

The difference has to be seen as a result of the different ways to litigate. Anglo-American civil procedure is an *adversary system* where the parties from the start maintain antagonist positions, and it's a system that works with a jury, and not just a single judge or three judges. James & Hazard note:

James & Hazard

A leading characteristic of the Anglo-American procedural system is its adversary nature. In civil disputes it is generally up to the parties, not the court, to initiate and prosecute litigation, to investigate the pertinent facts, and to present proof and legal argument to the tribunal. The court's function, in general, is limited to adjudicating the issues submitted to it by the parties on the proof presented by them, and to applying appropriate procedural sanctions upon motion of a party.[35]

In any case, for the present study this controversy is not of importance as only Anglo-American statutes are to be examined, for which the Anglo-American law of evidence is to be applied. In fact, because of the particular nature of the adversary litigation system and its bestowal of judicial cognition upon both judge and jury[36], evidence law in general, and the rules of the burden of proof, in particular, have a much higher importance under common law than in continental law. Fortunately, the subject has been elucidated by high rank legal scholars and a sheer enormous amount of case law. Phipson on Evidence cites about 8000 precedents, Wigmore even 16000!

It is to note that statutory regulations on civil procedure seldom contain rules of evidence or a precise allocation of the burden of proof, as for example the UK's Civil Evidence Acts of 1968 and 1972[37], or South Africa's Civil Proceedings Evidence Act No. 25 of 1965[38]. This is systemically sound because the burden of proof is determined by the applicable substantive law, not civil procedure regulations.

There are however presumptions to be found in American civil procedure laws, in the rules No. 301 of the Federal Rules of Evidence (28 U.S.C.A.) and in the Uniform Rules of Evidence, 13 U.L.A. Civ. Proc. 227. A detailed regulation of evidence rules was worked out by the American Law Institute and was inserted in the *Model Code of Evidence (1942)*. Similar rules are to be found in the California Evidence Code.

Regarding Canada, the Uniform Evidence Act[39] contains not only very detailed provisions regarding the burden of proof, but it also bears the advantage that it's drafted in a truly bilingual manner (English/French).[40]

The general rule is that the judge adjudicates about legal questions, while the jury decides about the facts[41], but there are several exceptions to this rule. In addition, it has to be seen that more and more litigations are held without a jury; the judge is said to take over the two functions in one person.[42] However, in principle, the particularities and rules of the burden of proof have not changed for that reason. Phipson & Elliott write:

Phipson & Elliott

Now the trial is usually before the judge alone, the two separate functions remain. The judge performs them both, but he must take care to keep them separate. [43]

It is important to remember that Anglo-American evidence law has been coined by the particularity of the jury trial, and that is why the strict separation of the functions of judge and jury even applies when the judge decides alone. In the United States, the *Federal Rules of Evidence* detail the evidence procedure in federal jurisdiction. These rules, interestingly, also do not make a distinction between trials with or without jury, as they implicitly hold that for the latter category of trials, the judge performs both functions.[44] However, the question does not need to be deepened in this study as foreign sovereign immunity litigation is trialed without jury.

The main difficulty in understanding the Anglo-American concept of the burden of proof results from the fact that the term has more than one meaning.[45] It was only at the end of the 19th century that, with the classical monograph of J. B. Tayer, *A Preliminary Treatise on Evidence (1898)*, the legal profession began to build awareness about the need to clarify the matter. James & Hazard note:

> **James & Hazard**
>
> The term burden of proof is used in our law to refer to two separate and quite different concepts. The distinction was not clearly perceived until it was pointed out by James Bradley Thayer in 1898. The decisions before that time and many later ones are hopelessly confused in reasoning about the problem. The two different concepts may be referred to as
>
> (1) the risk of non-persuasion, or the burden of persuasion or simply persuasion burden;
>
> (2) the duty of producing evidence, or simply the production burden or the burden of evidence.[46]

The two burden have to be distinguished[47]; they are called principle burdens.[48] So far there is unanimity in the literature; on the details, however, the literature greatly vacillates. Cross distinguishes further between provisional and ultimate burdens[49] and between shifting burdens and rebuttable presumptions.[50]

Sometimes even a third burden is added, that is called the burden of pleadings[51], while in reality this burden is a consequence of the legal burden. And Phipson to add on a forth burdens, the burden of establishing the admissibility of the evidence.[52] In fact, the admissibility of proof by the judge is of high importance in the adversary trial as lay persons are going to decide about the evidence; as a result, it is crucial which evidence is admitted and which is refused by the judge, whose role is to supervise the trial game with his 'legal eye', as juries can be rather unpredictable in their verdicts. But apart from this rather fancy expansion of the system, most authors and the overwhelming number of precedents admit a dualistic system with two principle burdens.[53] These principle burdens are:

(1) The persuasive burden, legal burden or risk of non-persuasion of the jury[54];

(2) The evidential burden, burden of adducing evidence or duty of producing evidence to the judge.[55]

The presentation of evidence is a highly regulated and orderly ritual. It starts with the party who bears the evidential burden to address their proof to the judge. The judge decides if a *prima facie case* has been made, and then instructs the jury to pronounce the final decision regarding the evidence offered by both parties. This is often expressed in the terms that the parties have to 'pass the judge and convince the jury'.[56] It's in that moment that the *persuasion burden* comes to play its decisive role.[57]

The Evidential Burden

There is a special relationship between the expressions *evidential burden, prima facie evidence* and *standard of proof.* The party that bears the persuasive burden has the right to begin with presenting evidence to the judge, and as a general rule, the evidential burden follows the persuasive or legal burden.[58] As in principle the legal burden is on the plaintiff, it's the plaintiff who usually begins to produce evidence.[59] For every single issue, evidence is thus produced.[60] The judge considers the evidence in the light of the applicable *standard of proof* and decides if a *prima facie case* was established.[61] Cross writes that the concept of the evidential burden[62] is the product of trial by jury and the possibility of withdrawing an issue from that body.[63] See also the *California Evidence Code (1965)* which stipulates:

California Evidence Code (1965)

§110. 'Burden of producing evidence' means the obligation of a party to introduce evidence sufficient to avoid a ruling against him on the issue.

The American Law Institute's Model *Code on Evidence (1942)* explains:

Rule 1. ...

(2) 'Burden of producing evidence of a fact' means the burden which is discharged when sufficient evidence is introduced to support a finding that the fact exists.[64]

In fact, the notion is unknown in continental law systems, and for good reason. It only makes sense in the adversary trial system and when a jury decides about the facts[65]; the judge's function is in so far one of controlling[66] and instructing the lay persons composing the jury.[67] The burden of producing evidence is not an obligation or a duty; it simply represents a *risk*: the risk to not being able to produce evidence satisfactory to the court.[68]

The judge considers the evidence submitted by the parties and decides if

▸ (i) the evidence has met the standard of proof; or

▸ (ii) the evidence has not met the standard of proof.

The judge considers *all evidence*, not only the one submitted by the party that bears the evidential burden. This means that the party who bears the onus of proof can profit from proof submitted by the adversary. Cross and Wilkins write:

Cross & Wilkins

Although we speak of one party 'bearing' the burden of proof, or the burden of adducing evidence, it must be remembered that he may be able to rely on those parts of his adversary's evidence which are favorable for him.[69]

When a *prima facie case* was made by the party who bears the evidential burden, and the judge decides that the evidence meets the applicable standard of proof, this has basically three consequences:

▸   (i) the burden of proof is discharged;

▸   (ii) the burden shifts to the other party;

▸   (iii) the fact is proven if the other party cannot discharge their burden.[70]

The standard of proof regarding the evidential burden is not a matter that the judge must instruct the jury about; only the persuasive burden is. This is so simply because the judge alone renders this decision. Cross and Wilkins (1980) explain about the standard of proof for prima facie evidence that it necessitates *'a finding that the fact is proved if the evidence is uncontradicted'.*[71] It flows from the principle of *fair trial* that each party must have the possibility to contradict the evidence submitted by the other party. Consequently, when one party discharges their evidential burden, the other party gets the burden. This can be imagined as one party 'inheriting' the burden form the other party, or that the burden is 'passed' from one party to the other within the litigation game.[72]

This also has been called the *shifting* of the evidential burden[73], while it has to be seen that the persuasion burden never shifts. The 'shifting' is of course a juridical metaphor; the pretended 'movement' of the burden is in reality the idea of an equitable partition of the trial risk. Eggleston writes:

Eggleston
It is often said that although the legal burden of proof remains throughout the trial where it was at the beginning, the evidential

burden may shift from one party to the other. All this really means is that as a case proceeds, one party or the other will produce evidence that, if it remained unchallenged, would entitle the party producing it to a decision in his favour. In this sense he can be said to have shifted the burden of proof to the other party.[74]

Another result that flows out from this system is that when a prima facie case was not refuted or 'rebutted'[75], the fact is considered to have been proven. The court has no obligation to arrive at this conclusion, but there is a high probability that the court decides on the lines of an uncontradicted prima face case.[76]

The only case a judge is obliged to render a verdict in a particular way is when a statute puts up a general rule that contains a *legal presumption*. In case the presumption was not rebutted, the judge's verdict must follow the general rule stipulated in the statute. Similarly, when the prima facie evidence was not meeting the applicable standard of proof, the judge must render a decision adverse to the burdened party.[77] In this case, one could also speak of the risk of producing evidence satisfactory to the court was realized against the party who was charged with it. At the beginning of the trial, the evidential burden is with the party who bears the persuasive burden.[78] As *Cross on Evidence (1979)* puts it:

Cross on Evidence

As a general rule, the burden of adducing evidence is borne by the party who bears the burden of proof.[79]

When the evidential burden is discharged, it is said to shift to the other party. Because of this assumed shifting of the evidential burden, and because it is temporarily with one and then the other party, it is also called provisional burden. Lord Denning explains in *Brown v. Rolls Royce Ltd.*:

Brown v. Rolls Royce Ltd. (Lord Denning)
My Lords, the difference between the judges of the Court of Session turned to the onus of proof. (…) The difference of opinion shows how important it is to distinguish between a 'legal burden', properly so called, which is imposed by the law itself, and a 'provisional' burden which is raised by the state of the evidence.[80]

As only at the start of the trial the two burdens are united, at any other point in time during the trial a test has to be effected for the determination of who bears the evidential burden. This test has been inserted in various statutes; here is the one provided by the *California Evidence Code*:

California Evidence Code
§550 Party who has the burden of producing evidence
(a) The burden of producing evidence as to a particular fact is on the party against whom a finding on that fact would be required in the absence of further evidence.[81]

It is noteworthy in this context that also Nigeria's Evidence Act details in §136:

§136 Evidence Act of Nigeria
(1) In Civil cases the burden of first proving the existence or nonexistence of a fact lies on the party against whom the judgment of the court would be given if no evidence were produced on either side, (…)
(2) If such party adduces evidence which ought reasonably to satisfy a jury that the fact sought to be proved is established, the burden lies on the party against whom judgment would be given if no more evidence were adduced; and so on successively, until all the issues in the pleadings have been dealt with.[82]

The Persuasive Burden

We have already seen that the term *burden of proof*, in the sense to encompass both evidential and persuasive burden, and the term *standard of proof* are to be distinguished according to their different functions.[83]

The standard of proof, as we have already seen in our discussion of the evidential burden, is the measure for assessing a certain proof being *adequate and sufficient* for proving a certain fact. Generally put, standard of proof is thus a measure for the adequateness of the proof presented. All evidence must meet a certain standard to be adequate, to be sufficient; as a result, all evidence has to be evaluated by the judge for meeting the standard of proof applicable in the particular litigation.

This is a very important function of the judge and it's because of this function that the saying is that for a litigation to win, you have to pass the judge; the next step, then, convincing the jury is the final or ultimate burden. For example, if a good lawyer on the defendant's side, who wants to avoid the unpredictable verdict of a jury, can convince the judge that the evidence presented by the plaintiff is insufficient for meeting the standard of proof, the trial will end here, and it will be ended not by the jury, but by the judge. The verdict will be that the plaintiff was not able to establish a *prima face case* for his allegations.

It is to be noted that for establishing a *prima face case*, the standard of proof in Anglo-American evidence law is lower than, for example, in German law where the conviction of the judge is required.[84] The standard of proof that is sometimes also called 'quantum of proof', in fact requires only a preponderance of probability.[85] As a general rule, the standard of proof is a preponderance of probability.[86] *Cross on Evidence (1979)* speaks of three standards of proof in the American evidence law; if this standard differs from what is recognized as standard of proof in British law, is however not explicated by the author.

Cross on Evidence

Three standards of proof appear to be recognized in the United States, proof by 'clear, strong and cogent' evidence laying midway between proof on a preponderance of probability and proof beyond reasonable doubt.[87]

A fact is proved when the proof submitted by one party has a surplus of probability over the proof submitted by the other party, or, in the words of Lord Denning '... if the evidence is such that the tribunal can say we think it more probable than not'.[88] On the other hand, when the probabilities are equal, the fact is not proven.[89]

In case of a *non liquet*, a situation where it's impossible for the judge to make a finding of the fact, it's the persuasion burden that as it were renders the decision: the party that bears the persuasion burden will lose the trial. Finding of a fact means 'determining that its existence is more probable than its non-existence'.[90]

Like the evidential burden, the persuasive burden is always related to a particular issue or fact; that is why we have to distinguish the facts that are at the basis of the action, and those at the basis of the defense. However, this distinction is often simplified when its about the facts that are constituent for the action. For example, Lord Edmund Davis states in the case *Chapman v. Oakleigh Animal Products, Ltd* that 'the golden rule is that the onus of proof is on the plaintiff'.[91]

Presumptions are particular in that they link several facts, generally two, as the *Model Code on Evidence (1942)* stipulates in its Rule 701:

Model Code of Evidence

(1) *Basic Fact*
Basic fact means the fact or group of facts giving rise to a presumption.
(2) *Presumption/Presumed Fact*
Presumption means that when a basic fact exists the existence of another fact must be assumed, whether or not the other fact may be rationally found from the basic fact. Presumed fact means that fact which must be assumed.[92]

Presumptions influence the burden of proof, however, only the evidential burden; they do not shift the persuasion burden.[93] Rule 301 of the Federal Rules of Evidence, applicable for proceedings in United States federal courts, stipulate this expressly:

Federal Rules of Evidence
Rule 301. Presumptions in General in Civil Actions and Proceedings
In all civil actions and proceedings not otherwise provided for by Act of Congress or by these rules, a presumption imposes on a party against whom it is directed the burden of going forward with evidence to rebut or meet the presumption, but does not shift to such party the burden of proof in the sense of the risk of nonpersuasion, which remains throughout the trial upon the party on whom it was originally set.

The persuasive burden represents, for the party that bears it, the *risk of nonpersuasion*[94], which is the risk of not being able to convince the trier of fact[95] of a certain alleged issue in trial. It is distinct from the evidential burden in that it never shifts. This is why the persuasive burden is also called fixed burden of proof.[96] It always stays with the party that bears it due to the applicable substantive law[97] or the pleadings.[98] For this reason, it also is called *ultimate burden*, while we have seen that the evidential burden is a provisional burden. The reason why this burden does not shift is to see in its *procedural function*; it is not related to the production of evidence but enters the stage after all evidence has been produced: it then allows to render a clear verdict in favor of one party. Cross and Wilkins write:

Cross & Wilkins
The burden of proof is crucial when all evidence is in. It makes itself felt at a later stage than the burden of adducing evidence.[99]

The rule is *ei qui affirmat non ei qui negat incumbit probatio.*[100] That means the one who affirms a fact, be it positive or negative, must prove it, and not the one who contests the fact.[101] In this simple rule, there are contained actually three different principles:

▸   (1) The one who affirms a fact must prove it;

▸   (2) The one who contests a fact is not obliged to prove his negation of the fact;

▸   (3) The one who affirmatively contests a fact must prove his affirmative defense.

It is both logical and reasonable to put the burden of proof on the party that invokes a right as a lawful consequence of certain alleged facts.[102] This is in the general case the plaintiff[103] or the party that would lose the trial if there was no evidence in court.[104]

Regarding sovereign immunity, the question who bears the burden of proof for the facts that are decisive for sovereign immunity to be granted is a *procedural question*; from this question has to be distinguished who in the trial bears the burden of proof regarding the applicable *substantive law*. If, for example, the plaintiff sues a foreign state as a consequence of a commercial contract with that state, two different questions regarding the burden of proof have to be asked. The first question regards the contract itself, on which the action is based. The facts that establish this contract have to be proved by the plaintiff. The second question is who bears the burden of proof for the defense of immunity for jurisdiction, which is a question pertaining to adjective law.

The existence of such a contract would establish both the material right of the plaintiff and the procedural right to pursue a legal action against the foreign state party of that contract, because of the denial of sovereign immunity in such a case. We can thus talk about a material and a procedural burden of proof, which in this case coincide, but which also may not coincide.

The burden of proof for the affirmation of a fact also encompasses the burden of proof for the negation of a fact, also called *burden of dis-*

proof, if the party who bears the burden of proof alleges the nonexistence of a fact, or its negation. This is to say that the burden of proof is something functional in a trial, and not dependent on the nature of the allegations.[105]

This also can be demonstrated by an example. In all statutes on foreign sovereign immunity, the conditions under which courts may exert jurisdiction over foreign states are enumerated as exceptions from a general rule of immunity. Hence, if immunity is a defense, the foreign state would bear the burden of proof for the facts the are at the basis of the immunity claim. This is the basic rule put up by the United States *Foreign Sovereign Immunities Act, 1976*. But the result of such a construct feels strange: the foreign state would have to disproof all the numerous exceptions in the statute for establishing his claim for immunity. This would put a heavy onus on foreign states in trials involving foreign sovereign immunity. However, the drafting technique of the statute seems to suggest this outcome. Hence, if sovereign immunity is to be considered as an affirmative defense, the foreign state would clearly bear the burden of proof for the facts that are at the basis of the immunity defense. This is the application of the general rule of evidence that affirmative defenses need to be proven by the party who invokes them.

But the question here, which is a question not of procedural law, but of international law, is if sovereign immunity *really* is to be considered as an affirmative defense only because of the drafting technique of the statutes on foreign sovereign immunity? Affirmative defenses need to be specially pleaded in order to be taken in consideration by the court.[106] As a result the burden of proof lies on the defendant.[107] However, this cannot be true because sovereign immunity has to be considered by the court *sua sponte*. While in the *House Report* to the FSIA 1976, it is explicated that sovereign immunity was an affirmative defense, this construction is in contradiction with international law, as it would render sovereignty an illusory concept.

As a result, later jurisprudence, especially, from the United States Supreme Court, made it clear that *sovereign immunity has to be consid-*

ered by the courts sua sponte and therefore cannot be construed as an affirmative defense because such a construction would be in violation of international law. The legal materials to the FSIA 1976 insofar contain an error and cannot be taken literally.[108]

In principle, however, it is true that in all cases except affirmative defenses, the burden of proof is on the plaintiff. In addition, it has to be noted that the burden of proof is on the party who adds a new element to the pleadings.[109]

And to recapitulate it, the evidential burden follows the legal burden insofar. Interestingly so, even for affirmative defenses, the evidential burden follows the legal burden, but that situation both burdens are not on the plaintiff but on the defendant for establishing the affirmative defense.[110]

CHAPTER TWO

Assessment of the Burden of Proof

The initiative to insert a passage in the *House Report*[111] that gives some guidance on the difficult problem of the *burden of proof* came from the Committee on International Law of the Association of the Bar of the City of New York.[112]

The Burden of Proof Rule

New chapter 97 of title 28, United States Code, starts from a premise of immunity and then creates exceptions to the general principle. The chapter is thus cast in a manner consistent with the way in which the law of sovereign immunity has developed. Stating the basic principle in terms of immunity may be of some advantage to foreign states in doubtful cases, but, since sovereign immunity is an *affirmative defense* which must be specially pleaded, the burden will remain on the foreign state to produce evidence that a foreign state or one of its subdivisions, agencies or instrumentalities is the defendant in the suit and that the plaintiff's claim relates to a public act of the foreign state - that is, an act not within the exceptions in sections 1605-1607. Once the foreign state has produced such *prima facie evidence* of immunity, the burden of going forward would shift to the plaintiff to produce evidence establishing that the foreign state is not entitled to immunity. The ultimate burden of proving immunity would rest with the foreign state.

In several leading cases, American District Courts have principally affirmed the allocation of the burden of proof the way the House Report proposed it. In *Arango v. Guzman Travel Advisors Corp.*, the court stated:

Arango v. Guzman Travel Advisors Corp

The burden of establishing the applicability of this immunity naturally lays with the one claiming it.[113]

In *Verlinden B.V. v. Central Bank of Nigeria*, the district court held:

Verlinden B.V. v. Central Bank of Nigeria

The Act retains sovereign immunity as a defense, to be raised by the defendant.[114]

In *De Sanchez v Banco Central de Nicaragua*, the court explained:

De Sanchez v. Banco Central de Nicaragua

First, as is true for all the other exceptions under the FSIA, the burden of demonstrating that the claim does not fall within §1605(a)(2), i.e. the burden of proof that immunity exists, is upon the foreign state.[115]

In *Matter of Sedco, Inc.*, the court ruled:

Matter of Sedco, Inc.

Once a basis for jurisdiction is alleged, the burden of proof rests on that foreign state to demonstrate that immunity should be granted.[116]

In *Transamerican S.S. Corp. v. Somali Democratic Republic*, the court held:

Transamerican S.S. Corp. v. Somali Democratic Republic

In accordance with the restrictive view of sovereign immunity reflected in the FSIA, the burden of proof in establishing the in-applicability of these exceptions is upon the party claiming immunity.[117]

The wording of the legislative materials is not without ambiguities. The main problem comes from the fact that the court, as a general rule, is obliged to decide *sua sponte* about the affirmation of subject matter jurisdiction. This brings about an obvious contradiction between 28 U.S.C. §1330(a) and §1605(a)(w) FSIA which links together subject matter jurisdiction and sovereign immunity, on one hand, and the construct of sovereign immunity as an *affirmative defense* which would have to be specifically pleaded. The contradiction here is that to construe a defense under 1605(a)(2) as a *conditio sine qua non* for jurisdiction would rule against the general principle that courts have to state about their jurisdiction *before* examining the subject matter of the case.

The United States Supreme Court decided this important question in *Verlinden B.V. v. Central Bank of Nigeria*[118]; in that case, the foreign state did not enter an appearance to assert an immunity defense. The Supreme Court ruled that in such a case a district court still must determine that immunity is unavailable under the FSIA, as this is a condition for the court's jurisdiction.[119] Hence, the wording of the *House Report* that sovereign immunity is to be considered as an affirmative defense cannot be taken literally.

More clearly even stated the Court of Appeal of the 7th Circuit, in *Frovola v. Union of Soviet Socialist Republics*[120] that the statement of the *House Report* is not accurate in this point. Because the absence of sovereign immunity was a prerequisite to subject matter jurisdiction, the question of immunity would have to be considered by a district court even though the foreign country whose immunity is at issue not entered an appearance.[121]

The most interesting leading case that modified the statement of the *House Report* is *Alberti v. Empresa Nicaraguense de la Carne*.[122] Here, an expropriation was at the basis of the claim. The conditions under which expropriation had been effected by the Nicaraguan government could not be clarified in the litigation. This was however a decisive question under §1605(a)(3) FSIA which denies sovereign immunity if the expropriation had been done in violation of international law.

The court held that the foreign state was *not obliged to disproof all the immunity exceptions* enumerated in sections 1605 to 1607 of the Act, but only the ones the plaintiff invoked in support of his allegation that immunity had to be refused. It would be a waste of time, argued the Court of Appeal, to require of the foreign state such a detailed and complicated proof, whereas it would be relatively easy for the plaintiff to assert the particular exception on which he bases his claim. As a result, the foreign state could limit its evidence production on the assertion that the activity which gave rise to the claim, was of a public, governmental nature.

Alberti v. Empresa Nicaraguense de la Carne

Accordingly, we believe that the purposes of the act will best be served by requiring that the defendant demonstrate that the suit relates to a governmental act of the foreign state being sued, and then placing the burden of identifying the relevant exception by affidavit or otherwise upon the plaintiff.[123]

This leading case has been discussed by *Monroe Leigh, Esq.,* from *Steptoe & Johnson*, legal advisor to the State Department at the time the FSIA was drafted. Mr. Leigh insists on the wording of the *House Report* passage.[124] However, after the Supreme Court decision in the Verlinden case and considering the ambiguities in the wording of the *House Report*, it seems that the Alberti precedent serves better the practice and is more reasonable as to a functional fair play in the evidence procedure, than the strict and inflexible rule established in the *House Report*.

As to a future international law standard on the allocation of the burden of proof in sovereign immunity litigation, a skilled observer of international law knows that the construct of sovereign immunity as an *affirmative defense* would not be accepted by the international community. However, the Alberti standard might be a solution that could be accepted internationally. This seems also to be the general tenor in the international law literature. For example Julia B. Brooke, writes in her article *The International Law Association Draft Convention on Foreign Sovereign Immunity: A Comparative Approach*:

Julia B. Brooke

A strict interpretation of the second element would impose an onerous burden on the foreign state, since the statutory exceptions are numerous, complicated, and often ambiguous. As a result, courts tend to focus on the ability of the foreign state to disprove the particular exception asserted by the plaintiff.[125]

We can thus conclude that under the FSIA, the general rule that the plaintiff bears the burden of proof for personal jurisdiction, minimal contacts, service of process and the prerequisites of a default judgment were not changed.

CHAPTER THREE

Some Intricate Procedural Questions

Subject Matter Jurisdiction

The *Foreign Sovereign Immunities Act* is the only statute that grants jurisdiction of the United States judiciary over foreign states, which has been confirmed by case law. For example, in *Argentine Republic v. Amerada Hess Shipping Corp.*[126], the United States Supreme Court held that the FSIA provides the sole basis for jurisdiction over a foreign state in American courts. We have seen already that we have to distinguish between the court's *subject matter jurisdiction*, and *personal jurisdiction*. Here, I would like to look again at this procedural question, focusing on the problem of the burden of proof. This means that we need to have a detailed regard on the interplay of *subject matter jurisdiction, §1330, minimal contacts, §§1605(a)(2), 1605(a)(5)*, and *service of process, §1608*:

> **Title 28, Part IV, Chapter 85, §1330**
>
> (a) The district courts shall have original jurisdiction without regard to amount in controversy of any nonjury civil action against a foreign state as defined in section <u>1603 (a)</u> of this title as to any claim for relief in personam with respect to which the foreign state is not entitled to immunity either under sections 1605–1607 of this title or under any applicable international agreement.
>
> (b) Personal jurisdiction over a foreign state shall exist as to every claim for relief over which the district courts have jurisdiction under subsection (a) where service has been made under section <u>1608</u> of this title.
>
> (c) For purposes of subsection (b), an appearance by a foreign state does not confer personal jurisdiction with respect to any claim for relief not arising out of any transaction or occurrence enumerated in sections 1605–1607 of this title.

There are several tricky points to observe regarding the affirmation of jurisdiction under the FSIA. First, it has to be seen that the FSIA entangles sovereign immunity and subject matter jurisdiction in that the denial of immunity is a condition for jurisdiction. This leads logically to the strange construct that the court has to clarify the whole quite complex sovereign immunity matter at the very onset of the trial, as it's a condition for its jurisdiction or competence, and it goes without saying that the court has to do this *sua sponte*.

Second, as I have already pointed it out that there are terminological difficulties regarding the expressions *jurisdiction*, as it is used in the FSIA, and the term *competence*. There is no doubt, however, that section 1330 FSIA speaks of jurisdiction, but *means* competence - and *not*, for example, minimal contacts. Equally, the statute uses the terms subject matter jurisdiction and personal jurisdiction instead of subject matter competence and personal competence.

Finally, it must be seen that section 1330(b) is a *federal long-arm statute* that subjects foreign states to the territorial jurisdiction of the United States under the condition that due process regulations are strictly followed, which means that there must be minimal contacts between the facts in issue and the territorial scope of the United States of America.[127]

Personal Jurisdiction

The next question that comes up is who bears the burden of proof for personal jurisdiction? The question was asked in *Wyle v. Bank Melli of Teheran, Inc.*[128], and the court clearly comes to the conclusion that the burden of proof for personal jurisdiction follows the general principle, that is, the burden for the facts pertaining to personal jurisdiction rests with the plaintiff:

Wyle v. Bank Melli of Teheran

The legislative history makes clear what the foreign state must prove to establish immunity; that the challenged action is that of a foreign state in its public, noncommercial capacity. The burden of proving the existence of an otherwise actionable (if not barred by sovereign immunity) activity or act within the United States or having a direct effect in the United States would obviously remain with the plaintiff. Simply because the foreign state must plead and prove certain facts necessary to establish its immunity does not mean that the normal burden of proving subject matter and personal jurisdiction is reversed.[129]

Minimal Contacts

There is an abundance of literature and case law regarding the particular requirements of minimal contacts for the assertion of subject matter jurisdiction in the United States.[130] With regard to the burden of proof of the minimal contacts for jurisdiction to be established, the district court, in *Tigchon v. Island of Jamaica*, held:

Tigchon v Island of Jamaica

Plaintiff correctly notes that once a basis for jurisdiction is alleged, the burden of proof rests on the foreign state to demonstrate that immunity should be granted. However, plaintiff has not alleged the minimal facts necessary in order to establish a basis for jurisdiction.[131]

A comparison of the FSIA's federal long-arm statute, §1330(b), with the New York Civil Practice Law, §301, the famous *doing business clause*, shows clearly that the onus can only be with the plaintiff:

> **Beacon Enterprises v. Menzies**
>
> As plaintiff, Beacon bore the ultimate burden of proving the court's jurisdiction by a preponderance of evidence.[132]

In this context, Rules 4(d)(7) and 4(e) of the Federal Rules of Civil Procedure are to be observed. They state that the competence of a federal court against any non-resident defendant goes only as far as the applicable long-arm statute of the forum state.

Service of Process

The next criterion for affirming personal jurisdiction under §1330(b) FSIA is service of process according to §1608 FSIA.[133]

Regarding the burden of proof, the *House Report* contains an explanatory statement only with regard to admiralty actions.[134]

> **H. R. Report No. 94-1487**
>
> ' ... the plaintiff must also be able to prove that the procedures for service of process under section 1608(a) or (b) have commenced ...'[135]

For actions under 'ordinary' procedural law, not this passage of the legal materials applies, but Rule 4(g) of the *Federal Rules of Civil Procedure*.[136]

> **Rule 4(g) Federal Rules of Civil Procedure**
>
> The person serving the process shall make proof thereof to the court promptly and in any event within the time during which the person served must respond to the process.[137]

Default Judgment

Section 1608(e) FSIA rules the default judgment against a foreign state:

§1608(e)

(e) No judgment by default shall be entered by a court of the United States or of a State against a foreign state, a political subdivision thereof, or an agency or instrumentality of a foreign state, unless the claimant establishes his claim or right to relief by evidence satisfactory to the court. A copy of any such default judgment shall be sent to the foreign state or political subdivision in the manner prescribed for service in this section.

Section 1608(e) of the Act rules default judgments against foreign states; a default judgment can be rendered only if the plaintiff delivers conclusive proof to the court. This clause is filed after *Rule 55(e) Federal Rules of Civil Procedure* which applies for default judgments against the United States as the defendant.[138] This proof is *stricter* than the one required in Rule 55(a) for the 'ordinary' default judgment where it's enough that the defendant didn't enter an appearance.[139] Section 1608(e) FSIA requires even more than that; it requires that the plaintiff also proves his claim with regard to the applicable substantive law. This is so because §1330(a) links the question of subject matter jurisdiction with the applicability of one of the exceptions in sections 1605-1607 to the general rule of sovereign immunity.

This leads to the interesting constellation that, regarding the default judgment, according to section 1608(e) FSIA, the foreign state is *not* obliged to make a prima facie case of immunity first; the burden is entirely on the plaintiff regarding all the procedural and substantial facts at issue in the action. This is logical, by the way, as the foreign state didn't enter an appearance and in such a constellation typically doesn't produce any evidence. For the similar provision in *Rule 55(e) Federal Rules of Civil Procedure*, the precedent *Giampaoli v. Califano*[140] stated that as the plaintiff has the right to begin with producing evidence, it's upon the plaintiff to make the prima facie case, whereupon the evidential burden 'shifts to the government'. This shows that the ultimate burden here is clearly with the plaintiff.

This shows also that the FSIA did not absolve from the general rules of evidence that impose the burden of proof for the court's jurisdiction upon the plaintiff.

This is both valid for the legal burden and the evidential burden. It's always the plaintiff who bears the evidential burden for the facts regarding service of process.[141]

This section is drafted after Rule 55(e) of the Federal Rules of Civil Procedure which refers to a default judgment against the United States as a defendant party.

It is obvious that these provisions are more severe than the ordinary default judgment, that is, Rule 55(a) of the Federal Rules of Civil Procedure, where it is sufficient that the defendant party has failed to plead or otherwise defend itself. It is rather a matter of common sense that the plaintiff bears the burden of proof for the prerequisites of the default.

In the case of 1608(e) FSIA, this is a *quite severe burden* since the plaintiff must practically prove his entire claim by evidence satisfactory to the court, not only his title, but also the conditions of competence. This means that the plaintiff must prove, by a preponderance of probability, the applicability of one of the exceptions of sections 1605, 1606 or 1607 FSIA.[142]

Foreign State and Agency or Instrumentality of a Foreign State

§§1603(a)(b) FSIA

28 U.S.C. §1603. Definitions
For purposes of this chapter—
(a) A 'foreign state', except as used in section 1608 of this title, includes a political subdivision of a foreign state or an agency or instrumentality of a foreign state as defined in subsection (b).
(b) An 'agency or instrumentality of a foreign state' means any entity—
(1) which is a separate legal person, corporate or otherwise, and

(2) which is an organ of a foreign state or political subdivision thereof, or a majority of whose shares or other ownership interest is owned by a foreign state or political subdivision thereof, and

(3) which is neither a citizen of a State of the United States as defined in section 1332 (c) and (d) of this title, nor created under the laws of any third country.

(c) The 'United States' includes all territory and waters, continental or insular, subject to the jurisdiction of the United States.

(d) A 'commercial activity' means either a regular course of commercial conduct or a particular commercial transaction or act. The commercial character of an activity shall be determined by reference to the nature of the course of conduct or particular transaction or act, rather than by reference to its purpose.

(e) A 'commercial activity carried on in the United States by a foreign state' means commercial activity carried on by such state and having substantial contact with the United States.

28 U.S.C. §§1332(c),(d)

(c) ... a corporation shall be deemed a citizen of any State by which it has been incorporated and of the State where it has its principle place of business ...

(d) The word 'States', as used in this section, includes the Territories, the District of Columbia, and the Commonwealth of Puerto Rico ... '.

We have already seen previously in this study that according to the *House Report* and federal case law that the burden is upon the foreign state to prove that the conditions of §§1603(a),(b) are fulfilled.[143]

The problem was already subject of the precedent *Jet Line Service, Inc. v. M/V Marsa El Hariga*.[144] The plaintiff seized the Libyan steamship *M/V Marsa El Hariga* for indemnifying himself for discharging the raw oil from this ship.[145] The owner of the vessel, the *General National Maritime Transportation Company (GNMTC)* from Libya, claimed immunity from jurisdiction alleging it was neither a citizen of the United States under §1603(b)(3) FSIA nor created under the law of a third country, nor else an 'organ' of the Libyan government in the sense of

§1603(b)(2) FSIA. This point was a fact in issue as the plaintiff expressly contested the fact that GNMTC fell under §§1603(a),(b).

Hence, the burden of proof was upon the GNMTC for these facts; it presented two affidavits by the Chargé d'Affaires of the Libyan embassy in Washington D.C. that certified the status of the GNMTC and the ownership of the vessel.

The court stated that the burden was upon GNMTC for proving the conditions of its immunity claim and that the affidavits were proper proof and had to be evaluated accordingly.[146] In addition, it is interesting to see that the court did not limit the inquiry to the mere evaluation of these affidavits but referring to *Carey v. National Oil Corporation*[147], found from that precedent that the GNMTC was a '*wholly-owned Libyan entity which has succeeded the General Maritime Transport Organization in 1970*'. It is important to see that despite the burden of the foreign state to produce *prima facie evidence* for their immunity claim, the district courts will nonetheless inquire *sua sponte* about these facts, if there is more information available in the records presented at court. This was also important here in this case because the second affidavit did not fulfill the formal requirements for being evaluated as *adequate proof*, but was nonetheless appreciated by the court in its quality of a 'simple statement'. More importantly, the court held: 'Moreover, there is authority for the view that a court may take judicial notice of an entity's sovereign character.'[148]

Now, in such a situation, there is a certain ambiguity as both ideas cannot be true at the same time. Either the burden is upon the foreign state to demonstrate a basis for their immunity claim or there is no such burden because the court must consider all those facts *sua sponte*. So if the latter is the case, why then the whole plot about the burden of proof? This doesn't seem to make any sense, and the court obviously was conscious of that and elaborated:

Jet Line Service, Inc. v. M/V Marsa El Hariga

Consequently, unlike the situation in Pan American Tankers Corp. v. Republic of Vietnam, 291 F.Supp. 49 (S.D.N.Y. 1968), where the record was devoid of any facts probative as to whether two corporate defendants were 'creatures of the Republic of Vietnam', 291 F.Supp. at52, this Court is able to find that defendant has produced such prima facie evidence of immunity and that plaintiff, then faced with the burden of going forward, has failed to produce evidence establishing that sovereign immunity should not be granted.[149]

Pan American Tankers Corp. v. Republic of Vietnam[150] was an arbitrage action under the Federal Arbitration Act, 9 U.S.C. §§4, 8 (1964) against the Vietnamese government and two Vietnamese companies resulting from navigation contract. The plaintiffs alleged breach of contract by the fact that the Vietnamese government didn't allow them to discharge the cement from their ships. Vietnam claimed foreign sovereign immunity. The court referred to the *House Report* that construes sovereign immunity as an *affirmative defense*; in addition, the court explained, Vietnam could have claimed immunity directly with the State Department, and that in that case the suggestion of the American government would have been conclusive for the court. However, Vietnam had not done that nor had the Vietnamese government offered any evidence to the fact if the two defendant companies were agencies or instrumentalities of a foreign state under §§1603(a)(b) FSIA.

Now, this is really one of the rare cases where at the end the court stays with a non liquet situation. Contrary to an older precedent, *Puente v. Spanish National State*[151] that was still ruled before the restrictive immunity doctrine was applied in the United States, the court stated in the present case:

Pan American Tankers Corp. v. Republic of Vietnam

Since the Republic of Vietnam has asserted this plea, which is in the nature of a defense, it would appear to have the burden of proving its privilege of immunity. It is hereby ordered that the defendant The Republic of Vietnam submit such affidavits and other proofs as it may deem supportive of its plea of sovereign immunity. (...) Should the Republic of Vietnam succeed in establishing at least a prima facie case to sustain its plea, the Court may order an evidentiary hearing to further develop the record, on the motion of either party, unless the essential facts are clearly set forth and not disputed.[152]

In addition, this case clarifies that the court is obliged to find out *sua sponte* about the governmental character of an agency or instrumentality of a foreign state *only if there are significant indices to be found in the pleadings served to the court by the parties.*

Pan American Tankers Corp. v. Republic of Vietnam

Because the Court must have 'full development of the facts' in order to dispose of the legal issues, ..., the papers to be submitted by both parties should be based on specific facts and events succinctly stated and not accompanied by generalized conclusions.[153]

The court thus appreciated the proof submitted by GNMTC, admitting it to be an organ of the Libyan government under §§1603(a),(b) FSIA and concluded it was adequate enough to establish a *prima facie case* of immunity.[154] Hence, the judge saw the burden of going forward with evidence, or evidential burden, shifting to the plaintiff.

Subsequent case law confirmed that the burden is upon the foreign state to demonstrate that the conditions of §§1603(a),(b) FSIA apply. In *S & S Machinery Co. v. Masinexportimport (MASIN)*[155] the appeal was filed by MASIN, a Romanian company, and the Romanian Bank for Foreign Commerce and was about the seizure by S & S of property the defendants maintained in the United States, as well as about the issuing of certain letters of credit. The defendants had not waived their immunity from execution.

Before the Court of Appeals stated about the question of a possible immunity waiver, it examined the juridical nature of both the Romanian Bank and MASIN.

The Legal Status of Romanian Bank

Regarding the Romanian Bank, the court found the situation clear-cut in the sense that it was an agency or instrumentality of a foreign state.[156] For arriving at that conclusion, the judge was scrutinizing also the Romanian law; such judicial exam of foreign law is rendered necessary under the terms of §§1603(a),(b) and was confirmed by the legal materials.[157] Thus the court considered, in particular, Article VII of the Romanian Constitution which clearly states that all banks are state property.[158] The court then concluded:

> **S & S Machinery Co. v. Masinexportimport (MASIN)**
> This evidence alone is sufficient to prove that Romanian Bank is a state-owned instrumentality established to serve the state's foreign trade goals.[159]

In addition, the court considered the proof submitted and came to conclude that Romania had established a *prima facie case* of immunity under section 1603 and that, as a result, the evidential burden had shifted to the plaintiff. However, S & S failed to discharge this burden.

> **S & S Machinery Co. v. Masinexportimport (MASIN)**
> S & S failed to rebut any of this persuasive evidence, arguing instead that more was required to prove agency or instrumentality status. We disagree. Convincing and uncontroverted evidence established that the Bank is but a cat's paw of the Romanian government - an instrumentality owned and controlled by the state.[160]

In *First National City Bank v. Banco Para El Comercio Exterior de Cuba (BANCEC)*[161], the United States Supreme Court has stated several important principles that apply in similar cases against organisms of foreign states.

In 1960, the defendant was created by the Cuban government as an autonomous credit institution for facilitating foreign trade operations, and was established as a full juridical person. The facts at issue are quite complicated and I will report here only the conclusion of the Supreme Court regarding what the court calls a 'presumption of independence' in favor of organisms of foreign states when they have been properly created and invested with legal person status. In such a case, the Supreme Court ruled, the presumption is rebutted only if the foreign state can be shown to have used its responsibility under international law in a fraudulent manner, so as to benefit of sovereign immunity in front of a United States tribunal.

The Legal Status of MASIN

As to MASIN, the plaintiff argued that already the presumption of state property as it exists in all socialist jurisdictions should give rise to the conclusion that MASIN was an agency or instrumentality of the Romanian state.[162] However, taking reference to the case *Edlow International Co. v. Nuklearna Elektrarna Krsko*[163], S & S concluded that the state property presumption is not to be considered as adequate proof under section 1603 as there were well also in socialist economies entities that are distinct from the state.[164] The court held that Edlow was not standing against their ruling, as there was additional evidence.

S & S Machinery Co. v. Masinexportimport (MASIN)

We may assume for present purposes that there is essentially private entities operating within socialist economies. This does not alter our holding that the district court correctly concluded that MASIN is an agency or instrumentality of the state. For unlike 'Edlow', where only the presumption of state ownership was relied upon, MASIN established its status as a state-owned and state-controlled trading company with specific evidence.[165]

We can thus conclude that according to this precedent, a legal presumption as it was existent in socialist regimes at the time, is not per se an adequate proof for the governmental status of a foreign state's organism under section 1603(b) FSIA. If the governmental status of the foreign organism is not contested by the plaintiff, the proof can be acquitted by affidavit or even a statement delivered to the court by an accredited official of the foreign state. If, however, the plaintiff contests such proof, additional evidence is needed. It is difficult to say how severe this burden is as in the case discussed here, all the proof one can possibly imagine was delivered satisfactorily to the court.[166]

As to the obligation of judges to examine foreign law under section 1603 FSIA, it is important to note that the American judge is not obliged to take notice *sua sponte* of foreign law. Common law considers foreign law as a fact that must be pleaded and proved. This is still the case in the United Kingdom. However, in the United States, there was a certain development of the law with the introduction, in 1966, of Rule 44.1 Federal Rules of Civil Procedure.

Rule 44.1 Federal Rules of Civil Procedure

A party who intends to raise an issue concerning the law of a foreign country shall give notice in his pleadings or other reasonable written notice. The court, in determining foreign law, may consider any relevant material or source, including testimony, whether or not submitted by a party or admissible under the Federal Rules of Evidence. The court's determination shall be treated as a ruling on a question of law.

The determination of foreign law is thus considered as a *legal question* with American district courts. Nonetheless, a district court will take notice of foreign law only if the question has been submitted to the court in the pleadings by the party 'who intends to raise an issue concerning the law of a foreign country'. This means that this party in so far bears the burden of proof regarding the particularity of foreign law that it wants to apply to their favor.[167]

The question of how severe the standard of proof is was more clearly outlined in *O'Connell Machinery Company, Inc. v. M/V Americana*[168] where addition proof was lacking, except an affidavit of an employee of the Italian embassy in Washington D.C. that swore to the effect that the ship M/V Americana belonged to *Italian Line*, an agency or instrumentality of the Italian state. While in S. & S. Machinery, the proof was conclusive, here the court considered the sole affidavit as adequate proof for establishing the *prima facie case* of sovereign immunity.

O'Connell Machinery Company, Inc. v. M/V Americana

Plaintiff next argues that insufficient proof has been presented to support defendant's contention that Italian Line is an 'agency or instrumentality' of the Republic of Italy. We have before us, however, the affidavit of Gerardo Carante, 'Counselor of Commercial Activities of the Republic of Italy' and 'Chief Officer of the Commercial Office at the Embassy of the Republic of Italy', describing the ownership of Italian Line. This affidavit, executed on the letterhead of the Italian Embassy in Washington, states that the majority of the shares of Italian Line is owned by FINAMARE, a 'subdivision of the *Istituto per la Ricostruzione Industriale (IRI)*', a government entity which coordinates the management of Italian government enterprises. IRI's annual budget and plans, in turn, are approved by a member of the Italian Cabinet and, ultimately, submitted to the Parliament. (…) In our view, this establishes that Italian Line is, indeed, an 'agency or instrumentality of a foreign state', as defined in 28 U.S.C. §1603(b).[169]

In two other precedents that equally concerned admiralty actions and the *pre-judgment attachment* of vessels, the burden of proof under section 1603 was scrutinized in all detail. These actions were pending in front of different district courts but concerned the same parties, *Outbound Maritime Corporation v. P.T. Indonesian Consortium of Construction Industries (ICCI)*.[170] Why there were two different actions between the same parties is simply the result of the plaintiff, a corporation founded under New York law and that acts as a 'non vessel owning carrier (NVOCC), claiming damages for breach of an orally concluded contract, having seized two different vessels belonging to ICCI, one within the district of New York, and the other within the district of Maryland.

In the case *Outbound I*, the evidence defendant was submitting was deemed insufficient by the court, for two reasons.

Credibility of the Affidavit

The affidavit did not reveal the facts upon which the nationalization of ICCI was based and the court ruled:

Outbound I

As an affirmative defense however the entity claiming the protection of the statute has the burden of demonstrating, inter alia, that it falls within the statutory definition of a 'foreign state' or that it constitutes an entity 'a majority of whose shares or other ownership interest is owned by a foreign state.' 28 U.S.C. §1603. Once a defendant presents prima face evidence of this, the burden shifts to the plaintiff to demonstrate that the Act does not apply.[171]

So this criterion could be called the 'credibility' of the affidavit, which in the present case, as it seems[172], limiting itself to simply stating that ICCI was fully owned by the Indonesian government.

Formal Requirements Regarding the Affidavit

The second criterion that is critical for the affidavit is that it has to be submitted by an official of the foreign state, which in the present case was not adequately effected.

Outbound I

In this case, ICCI bears the burden of producing evidence to establish its claim of sovereign immunity. At the December 8, 1983 hearing, defendants presented only the affidavit of an officer of ICCI and translated version of a May 5, 1983 Indonesian Presidential Proclamation purportedly nationalizing ICCI. The affidavit merely states in conclusory terms that ICCI is wholly owned by

> the Republic of Indonesia. I cannot credit the affidavit of the officer of ICCI since it does not state the underlying facts of nationalization nor is it made by an official of the Republic of Indonesia on whose behalf defendants seek to invoke immunity.[173]

This is not a new element; it was already considered and stated upon in the before-mentioned precedents *O'Connell Machinery* and *S & S Machinery*. However, the judge in the present case also found an additional affidavit inadequate that was rendered by the Consul General of Indonesia to the United States.

Outbound I

I directed counsel to submit competent evidence of the claim of sovereign immunity which necessarily would include the Proclamation, its effective date and further evidence of the interest of the Republic of Indonesia in ICCI. In response, counsel has submitted the affidavit of the Consul General of the Republic of Indonesia sworn to on December 9, 1983 which now forms the only support for defendants' claim of immunity. This affidavit simply is not enough. (...) The translation of the asserted Proclamation contains numerous handwritten corrections and is not authenticated. While I intentionally withheld this decision to give defense counsel every opportunity to submit competent evidence of the May 5th Proclamation, counsel has produced nothing but this poor copy, which is so bad that the effective date of the Proclamation, i.e., the date of payment by the Republic of Indonesia to the private shareholders, is not clear. As such, I cannot place much evidentiary value on the proffered submission.[174]

The judge cited the precedents *Victory Transport Inc. v. Comisaría General de Abastecimientos y Transportes*[175] and *Civil Aeronautics Bd. v. Alitalia-Linee Aeree Italiane*.[176] These two affairs however only confirm that under the absolute sovereign immunity doctrine, a governmental organism of a foreign state could claim immunity only directly to the State Department. The second possibility, that is, to raise the immunity claim directly in front of the tribunal, was reserved to the foreign state itself, or the ruler of the foreign state.[177] That is why the Court of Appeals, in the case Victory Transport, did not judge the affidavit of the Spanish Consul in New York as adequate proof:

Victory Transport

A consul is supposedly clothed with authority to act for his government only in commercial matters. Since nothing in the record indicates that the Spanish Consul was specially authorized to interpose a claim of sovereign immunity, the affidavit was plainly insufficient.[178]

The reason for this meticulous formal handling of the proof submission is that it must be conclusive for the court that not the person who renders the affidavit is the authority that claims immunity, but *implicitly the foreign state itself*. Hence, there must be some substance for the court to see that the foreign official was acting within the scope of his governmental functions when submitting the affidavit, and not just within the scope of his commercial functions. In the *Civil Aeronautics* suit, the defendant Italian airline 'Alitalia' could address the immunity claim only directly to the State Department, not to the court.

On first sight, these requirements seem to be exaggerated and they may generally contradict to the case law that I was discussing above. But such a general view cannot render an adequate picture of the proof situation in each and every of these precedents. Thus, the regard here must be rather careful and detailed; the answer cannot be given as a general statement. What can be said is that '... statements of foreign officials ... have been accorded great weight in determining whether an entity is entitled to claim the protection of the FSIA.[179]

This means only that the official character of the witnessing functionary of the foreign state plays a *certain role* in the appreciation of the evidence; this is however not enough. Besides the affidavit itself must appear clear, precise, conclusive and credible, by and large, so as to convince the court that it is the foreign state itself that is really the owner or controller of the foreign organism that claims immunity in front of the court. This, then, is what the court found in the *Outbound I* case.

Outbound I

The affidavit in itself is confusing. It recites that part of defendant ICCI was privately owned but apparently that arrangements were made to transfer all private interest to the government. It is unclear whether this transfer was ever effectuated. It is unclear when it was done, if ever. The defendant JV is not even mentioned.[180]

While, generally speaking, in all these precedents, we can see a judicial appreciation of the general submission procedure for proving elements of §1603, that is, per affidavit, the judge in *Outbound I* has ostensibly esteemed insufficient the content of the submitted consular affidavit. What is perhaps still more astonishing is that the judge also found the quality of the offered prove being inadequate. He concludes the judgement:

Outbound I

The means of raising a claim of sovereign immunity is fairly well known. 48 C.J.S.2d Intern'l Law §52 (1981), 45 Am.Jur. 2d §54 Intern'l Law (1969). The failure of the counsel for the defendants to submit anything from the United States Department of State or the Indonesian Embassy is simply amazing. Under the circumstances, I find that the single affidavit presented in support of defendant's claim of immunity is simply insufficient to make out a prima facie case of sovereign immunity.[181]

In view of the precedents, this judgment delivers a clear guideline as to the quality of the proof submitted in these cases; it makes very clear that such proof is not just 'a simple formality' for foreign organisms to get rid of for being granted sovereign immunity in front of American tribunals. I would even go as far as saying that this judgment lets us see that American district courts *really take serious the burden of proof situation* and thereby make it rather difficult to foreign organisms to slip in the veil of a 'governmental garment' so as to be immune from responsibility as a result of their commercial transactions with private traders. In plain English, the proof to be delivered here must be precise, clear, convincing and authoritative enough to let recognize it's not just fake, but that the real actor behind the organism on the international stage is the foreign state, and *only* the foreign state.

The District Court of Maryland only at first sight contradicted this conclusion in the case of *Outbound II*.[182] The plaintiff alleged that the defendants have failed to prove the applicability of the FSIA, that is, that ICCI was owned by the Republic of Indonesia. However, the court esteemed the proof as adequate and sufficient.[183] The interesting thing now is that we have a totally different proof situation in front of the Maryland court, which allows us to get a feel for the standard of proof required under section 1603(b).

To begin with, the court examined an affidavit of the General Consul of Indonesia in New York, and concluded:

> **Outbound II**
>
> The court finds that the evidence submitted establishes that defendants are 'an agency and instrumentality of a foreign state' as defined in §1603(b). Courts that have considered the sufficiency of proof required to establish foreign sovereign status under the FSIA have concluded that 'statements of foreign officials ... have been accorded great weight in determining whether an entity is entitled to claim the protection of the FSIA. (...) Outbound submits no evidence to rebut the persuasive evidence submitted by defendants.[184]

In fact, Outbound claimed litispendence because of the affair pending in front of the New York court. They thought that this would foreclose the Maryland court to state about the action. The court rejected the argument of *res judicata* however with the argument that the New York court judgment would not be a 'final judgment' in the pending affair. In such a case the *res judicata* rule doesn't apply.[185] Regarding the more important question of the quality of the proof submitted to the court, the Maryland court did not need to doubt in the same way as the New York court, because the affidavit submitted was long, clear, precise and detailed.

Outbound II

In addition, the proof before this court appears to be different than that before the New York court. In its opinion, the New York court noted that the affidavit of the Consul did not mention the defendant, Jv. 575 F.Supp., at 1224. The affidavit before this court states at page 2 'JV is a joint venture entered into by ICCI. (...) ICCI owns a majority of the ownership interest in JV. Similarly, the New York court noted that while arrangements apparently were made to transfer all private interests to the government, the affidavit was 'unclear [as to] whether this transfer was ever effectuated.' Id. Yet, the affidavit before this court states: 'The transfer of shares directed in the regulation was effected on June 11, 1983, by payment to the private shareholders of the amounts each paid in to ICCI.' Affidavit at p. 2. Finally the New York court indicated that the translation of the Presidential Proclamation before the court 'contains numerous handwritten corrections and is not authenticated ...' and further commented that the copy received by the court was so poor 'that the effective date of the Proclamation ... is not clear.' Id. The document before this court is entitled 'Regulation of the Government of the Republic of Indonesia Number 19 Year 1983', it does not contain any handwritten corrections, the copy is quite clear, and article 5 of the regulation dealing with the effective date of its enactment quite clearly shows May 5, 1983 as the date of enactment. (...)[186]

As to the quality of the witness, the court stated against the distinction that was made in *Outbound I*, between a General Consul, and an Ambassador, of the foreign state:

Outbound II

Further, the New York court's reference to the failure of counsel for defendants to submit anything from the United States Department of State or from the Indonesian embassy does not appear significant to this court. First, the legislative history of the

FSIA clearly indicates that the Act was intended to withdraw the executive branch from involvement with claims of immunity and place responsibility for such determinations with the judiciary, 'thereby reducing the foreign policy implications of immunity determinations and assuring litigants that these often crucial decisions are made on purely legal grounds and under procedures that insure due process. (…) In this court's view, an affidavit from the Indonesian consulate is no less an official document than an affidavit from the Indonesian embassy, and is not thereby entitled to any less weight. Also, the cases cited by the New York court in support of its finding that the affidavit of the Consul General was insufficient proof are all pre-FSIA cases, where different procedures were required to claim and be granted sovereign immunity.[187]

The court thus rejected the argument that there was a difference in quality between an affidavit rendered by the consulate rather than the embassy of the foreign state. This verdict is indeed covered by the precedents that, regarding the quality of the witness, held that it's enough that that person is an *official* of the foreign state's government. Also this ruling finds a confirmation in Rule 902(3) of the Federal Rules of Evidence. This rule also only talks about 'any foreign official' and states in addition:

Rule 902(3) Federal Rules of Evidence

A final certification may be made by a secretary of embassy or legation, consul general, consul, vice consul, or consular agent of the United States, or a diplomatic or consular official of the foreign country assigned or accredited to the United States.[188]

Besides, it is interesting to note that in *Gray v. Permanent Mission of the People's Republic of the Congo to the United States*[189] the permanent mission of a foreign state to the United Nations was recognized as a 'foreign state' under section 1603(a) and not as an 'agency or instrumentality of a foreign state' under section 1603(b). The district court held that 'indeed it is hard to imagine a purer embodiment of a foreign state than the state's permanent mission to the United Nations.'[190]

This distinction is of high practical value because service of process, under section 1608, is different for foreign states, one one hand, and agencies and instrumentalities of foreign states, on the other. It is for this reason that the legal materials note under section 1603(a) FSIA the fact that for organisms of the foreign state, section 1608(a) is not applicable.

Conclusion

The proof of the conditions of §§1603(a),(b) of the Act is upon the foreign state and its agencies and instrumentalities to make a *prima facie case for sovereign immunity*, that is, that it's a foreign state or an agency or instrumentality thereof under the provisions of that section.

For discharging this burden, the foreign state or its organism must present *prima facie evidence* that is adequate enough to meet the applicable *standard of proof*. After that has been done, the evidential burden shifts to the plaintiff for proving that one of the exceptions to foreign sovereign immunity applies under the FSIA. This proof can be delivered in the following ways:

▸   by rebutting the prima facie case;

▸   by proving the conditions of an exception to immunity, §§1605-1607, 1610, 1611 FSIA.

Regarding the means of proof, it's primarily the *affidavit* that has been utilized in practice for meeting this requirement; exceptionally it may be a simple statement rendered by an official of the foreign state that could be held sufficient for proving the governmental character of the organism in question.

As to the content of the affidavit, as I said above, the applicable case law cannot be generalized because of the complexity of the issue.

As all proof, such an affidavit must appear clear, without contradictions, precise, logical, conclusive and credible to the court for meeting the standard of proof required under section 1603.

For avoiding unnecessary risks, the foreign state is advised to not just simply state that the organism was a public and governmentally functional entity of the foreign government, but detail the facts that show this to be true. When this proof has been delivered satisfactorily to the court, the evidential burden shifts to the plaintiff to either rebut the *prima face case* by, for example, a *responsive affidavit*.[191] In addition, it has to be seen that the presumption of state property that is generally true for socialist regimes, as an isolated form of proof, is not to be considered as *adequate and sufficient* to meet the standard of proof under section 1603(b).

CHAPTER FOUR

Solving Evidence Problems under the FSIA

Rule-and-Exception Construction

The *Foreign Sovereign Immunities Act 1976* is construed in a particular fashion. It poses for each of the immunities first an immunity rule, and thereafter a long list of exceptions. The rule for jurisdictional immunities is stated in section 1604 of the FSIA:

> **Title 28, Part IV, Chapter 97, §1604**
> Subject to existing international agreements to which the United States is a party at the time of enactment of this Act a foreign state shall be immune from the jurisdiction of the courts of the United States and of the States except as provided in sections 1605 to 1607 of this chapter.[192]

The major questions to ask at this point of the present study are:

▸ (i) Which are the facts that each party in a sovereign immunity litigation must allege?

- **Note**: This question is about the incidence of the *Evidential Burden*.

▸ (ii) Which party carries the immunity risk in case the evidence in court is not sufficient to make a decision, when thus the litigation results in a non liquet situation?

- **Note**: This question is about the incidence of the *Persuasive or Legal Burden*.

To begin with, and as I have shortly outlined it early in this study, the FSIA does not contain any provision regarding the burden of proof; but there is a quite detailed explanation to be found in the *House Report*, under section 1604:

H.R. Report No. 94-1487

New chapter 97 of title 28, United States Code, starts from a premise of immunity and then creates exceptions to the general principle. The chapter is thus cast in a manner consistent with the way in which the law of sovereign immunity has developed. Stating the basic principle in terms of immunity may be of some advantage to foreign states in doubtful cases, but, since sovereign immunity is an affirmative defense which must be specially pleaded, the burden will remain on the foreign state to produce evidence that a foreign state or one of its subdivisions, agencies or instrumentalities is the defendant in the suit and that the plaintiff's claim relates to a public act of the foreign state - that is, an act not within the exceptions in sections 1605-1607. Once the foreign state has produced such prima facie evidence of immunity, the burden of going forward would shift to the plaintiff to produce evidence establishing that the foreign state is not entitled to immunity. The ultimate burden of proving immunity would rest with the foreign state.[193]

This passage suggests that foreign sovereign immunity under the FSIA has been construed as an *affirmative defense*. This construction would entail a particular procedural consequence. Sovereign immunity would need to be *specifically pleaded* for the court to take into consideration. Further, the persuasive burden, or immunity risk, would be on the foreign state as defendant of the action. This would further entail, as the evidential burden at the start of the trial coincides with the persuasive burden, that the foreign states has the right to begin with producing evidence. Thus, the foreign state would need to show that -

▸   (i) it is a foreign state under 1603(a),(b) FSIA;

▸   (ii) the action in question was of a public, governmental character.

After the production of such *prima facie evidence*, the evidential burden would shift to the plaintiff to demonstrate that one of the exceptions to foreign sovereign immunity applies. If the plaintiff cannot show satisfactorily to the court that an immunity exception applies, the court would have to grant immunity to the foreign state by applying the general rule (§1604). As I pointed out already in the general introduction to the law of evidence, the court is not obliged to follow the prima facie evidence, however in case of a general rule in a statute, as it is the case in the FSIA with sections 1604 and 1609, the general rule has a decisive impact on the weight of probability. In such a case, the judge is well obliged to resort to the general rule in any situation of doubt. The *House Report* recognized this general principle to be true for the FSIA, stating that ' … the basic principle in terms of immunity may be of some advantage to foreign states in doubtful cases …'.

If, on the other hand, the plaintiff succeeds to prove that an exception to foreign sovereign immunity applies, the court is obliged to deny immunity to the foreign state. And if, already at the start of the trial, the foreign state is not able to make a *prima face case* for sovereign immunity, the court is obliged to reject the immunity claim. In this latter case, the plaintiff will not have anything to prove procedurally, but well of course regarding the applicable substantive law.

The House Report Evidence Rule

As I have briefly pointed it out already in my evaluation on the *House Report,* the incidence of the burden of proof that was explained in the legal materials is highly ambiguous in several respects. Before the United States Supreme Court stated on this important point, district courts seemed to be bewildered by the daring construction of foreign sovereign immunity as an *affirmative defense* and, confused, explained that this could not be true. Courts declared that in contradiction to the statement in the *House Report*, they had to rule about the immunity question *sua sponte*, as a legal necessity within the court's stating about their competence, right at the start of the trial.

This reasoning was correct, so the clear statement in the legal materials to the very contrary gave rise to a hefty debate both in case law and in the international law literature. And this confusing situation rested for several years.

Needless to add that this controversy was not conducive to my having a good time with writing my doctoral thesis; it was a major matter of confusion and upset, to be true, and I had nobody to ask what was the way to go. I had to find my way out of the maze.

In 1979, three years after the enactment of the FSIA, in *Behring International Inc. v. Imperial Iranian Air Force (IIAF)*, the question was addressed, for the first time, in an *obiter dictum* by the District Court of New Jersey.[194]

The plaintiff, an American company, was seizing property owned by IIAF as a consequence of not being paid for certain services rendered to IIAF. While the defendant did not expressly claim immunity from jurisdiction, but only immunity from the prejudgment attachment of their property[195], the court ruled about this point concluding that immunity from jurisdiction had to be denied. In a note, the court briefly explained the burden of proof situation:

Behring International Inc. v. Imperial Iranian Air Force (IIAF)

Under the Immunities Act, sovereign immunity is an affirmative defense which must be specifically pleaded. The burden is upon the foreign state to 'produce evidence at its claim of immunity'.[196]

The ambiguity comes from the fact that generally courts have to state *sua sponte* about their competence at the start of the trial.[197] In fact, the drafting technique of the FSIA and the other immunity statutes was criticized in the international law literature. The main argument was that it was of little use to put up a 'rule' of sovereign immunity, and then undermine it with so many exceptions that virtually nothing is left but a *residual concept.*

Some authors suggest that at least for jurisdictional immunities, it would have been better to state jurisdiction as the rule and stating precisely in which singular case or cases a foreign state still enjoys foreign sovereign immunity. Other authors explain that the drafting technique of the statutes simply followed the historical development of sovereign immunity, and that it had been intentional that here the statutes reflect also the legal history.[198] I have explained this already in the general introduction to the law of evidence. In fact, the obvious contradiction between §1330(a) FSIA, and the conception of foreign sovereign immunity as an affirmative defense was eventually giving rise for the United States Supreme Court to clarify this point.

In the first precedent, *Verlinden B.V. v. Central Bank of Nigeria*[199], the Supreme Court stated in a note:

Verlinden B.V. v. Central Bank of Nigeria

The House Report on the Act states that 'sovereign immunity is an affirmative defense that must be specially pleaded'. H.R. Rep. No. 94-1487, at 17. Under the Act, however, subject matter jurisdiction turns on the existence of an exception to foreign sovereign immunity, 28 U.S.C. §1330(a). Accordingly, even if the foreign state does not enter an appearance to assert an immunity defense, a District Court still must determine that immunity is unavailable under the Act.[200]

In more recent precedents, the question was elucidated in still more precise terms. Taking reference to the Verlinden precedent, the Appeal Court of the 7th Circuit, in *Frovola v. Union of Soviet Socialist Republics*, explained:

> **Frovola v. Union of Soviet Socialist Republics**
> The FSIA begins with the presumption that foreign states are immune from suit, subject to specific exceptions. (...) Furthermore, a district court lacks jurisdiction of a suit against a foreign country until it is determined that the defendant does not have immunity. (...) Thus, the statement in the legislative history that sovereign immunity is an affirmative defense which must be pleaded and proven by the party asserting it, H.R. Rep. No. 1487, at 17, 1976, U.S. Code Cong. & Adm. News at 6616, is not entirely accurate. Because the absence of sovereign immunity is a prerequisite to subject matter jurisdiction, the question of immunity must be considered by a district court even though the foreign country whose immunity is at issue has not entered in appearance.[201]

In reality, the question is of much a theoretical nature because only rarely a sovereign immunity litigation resulting in a non liquet came up where the court had to rule about the immunity question without sufficient evidence, and thus according to the incidence of the burden of proof. This is why the courts could limit their arguments at repeating the principle in obiter dicta that more or less copied the *House Report* reasoning on the burden of proof in sovereign immunity litigation under the FSIA.

As I have explained it in the introductory chapter on civil procedure and the rules of evidence, in principle it is the plaintiff who bears the burden of proof for competence *ratione materiae* (subject matter jurisdiction), and here the FSIA obviously has put this old rule upside-down, imposing the foreign state with the burden of proving its immunity claim satisfactorily to the court.[202] But the question is if international law does not put a limit here on the national law maker?

To begin with, a highly interesting precedent was set by the Appeal Court of the 7th Circuit in *Alberti v. Empresa Nicaraguense de la Carne*.[203] In this case, the court stated about the incidence of the burden of proof for an expropriation; the conditions under which this expropriation was undertaken could not be entirely clarified from the evidence in court.

As to the facts, Nicaragua expropriated the plaintiff of his shareholder rights at Empresa without paying an indemnity, and thereafter acted within these shareholder rights in managing the company. As a response, the plaintiff indemnified himself by ordering products from Empresa that he did not pay. Thus, the question came up if the expropriation was *in violation of international law* under §1605(a)(3) FSIA.

> **§ 1605. General exceptions to the jurisdictional immunity of a foreign state**
>
> (a) A foreign state shall not be immune from the jurisdiction of courts of the United States or of the States in any case—
> (3) in which rights in property taken in violation of international law are in issue and that property or any property exchanged for such property is present in the United States in connection with a commercial activity carried on in the United States by the foreign state; or that property or any property exchanged for such property is owned or operated by an agency or instrumentality of the foreign state and that agency or instrumentality is engaged in a commercial activity in the United States;

Right at the start of the trial, the court stated on the incidence of the burden of proof:

> **Alberti v. Empresa Nicaraguense de la Carne**
> It is uncontested that defendants bear the burden of establishing their immunity from this suit; therefore, the only issue is whether they have met this burden.[204]

In accordance with the *House Report*, the court stated that the foreign state has to make a prima facie case on two elements: 'that it is a foreign state under the definition employed in FSIA, and that the claim relates to a public act'[205] Once this evidence was submitted, the general rule of immunity in section 1604 would have the effect of a *presumption of immunity in favor of the foreign state* that the plaintiff had to overcome if he is to win; and he had to do this by proving that one of the exceptions applies.[206]

In the present case there was no doubt as to Empresa being an organism of a foreign state under §§1603(a),(b) of the Act. It was thus only the question of the activity in question was a governmental or public one, that the court had to rule about. This gave rise to the scrutiny of the burden of proof. The judge took the *House Report* as a point of departure and reasoned that a public act was 'an act not within the exceptions in section 1605-1607'[207]

However, the judge reasoned that this would practically imply that the foreign state had to disprove all the exceptions that the Act contains, for having immunity being granted, and that such a situation could not what the legislator had in mind when drafting the FSIA. It would require of the foreign state an almost impossible task to refute all the exceptions under the Act, while it would be relatively easy for the plaintiff to indicate on which exception he relies.

In addition, it would be a sheer waste of time and resources to require from the foreign state such an amount of evidence when it was so easy for the plaintiff to arrest his claim on the specific exception or exceptions that he holds applicable. The court implied with this reasoning of course that the judge in sovereign immunity litigations should consider only the exceptions that the plaintiff invokes, and not all exceptions.

From the foregoing, we have learnt that district courts must state about their competence *sua sponte*, so they have to consider all possible exceptions from foreign sovereign immunity. And insofar the reasoning in the Alberti case cannot be entirely accurate. It is accurate as to its end result however: the court came to the conclusion that for making the *prima face case* of foreign sovereign immunity, the foreign state could present evidence that by and large, in a general manner, shows that the activity in question was public or governmental, and that it was then the plaintiff's task to see how he can win by proving the applicability of one of the exceptions to the general rule of §1604.

This is nothing new, however, and was already current practice in former precedents. Julia B. Brooke briefly summarized that foregoing case law in her article on the ILA draft convention, and came to concluding on the lines of the Alberti precedent, while affirming that this was more or less the current practice in matters of handling foreign sovereign immunity in United States federal courts.[208]

Julia B. Brooke

Second, the defendant state must demonstrate that the activity complained of does not fall within one of the exceptions set out in sections 1605 to 1607 of the Act. A strict interpretation of the second element would impose an onerous burden on the foreign state, since the statutory exceptions are numerous, complicated, and often ambiguous. As a result, courts tend to focus on the ability of the foreign state to disprove the particular exception asserted by the plaintiff.[209]

After these reflections about the burden of proof, the court concluded that the foreign state could limit its production of evidence to demonstrating, in a general manner, that the act in cause was governmental, and that it could further limit it to the specific exception(s) the plaintiff invokes.

Alberti v. Empresa Nicaraguense de la Carne

Accordingly, we believe that the purposes of the act will best be served by requiring that the defendant demonstrate that the suit relates to a governmental act of the foreign state being sued, and then placing the burden of identifying the relevant exception by affidavit or otherwise upon the plaintiff.[210]

I have already noted previously that in a case note, Monroe Leigh, Esq., the acting legal advisor of the State Department at the time of the enactment of the FSIA strongly criticized the Alberti precedent.[211] Mr. Leigh, from Steptoe & Johnson in Washington D.C., whom I have met back in 1985 for a discussion about my doctoral thesis, wrote in his case note:

> **Monroe Leigh, Esq.**
> The effect of this protective measure is to place both the responsibility for producing evidence and the risk of nonproduction upon the plaintiff. It should be observed that while the FSIA plan, as explained in the legislative history, may have posed some practical difficulties, the court's solution departs from the FSIA's allocation of the burden of proof to the foreign state invoking immunity. At least in this case, where there was no dispute regarding the fact of nationalization, the court effectively eliminated the foreign state's burden by requiring only a general statement by defendant to prove a prima face case of immunity.[212]

While I have briefly mentioned that discussion above, I will now discuss this interesting point more in detail. In fact, there are three allegations being made in Mr. Leigh's statement:

▸ (1) The interpretation of the *House Report* regarding the burden of proof that was done by the court in Alberti resulted in raising the burden of proof on the side of the plaintiff. The latter had been charged with both the 'responsibility for producing evidence' and the 'risk of nonpersuasion';

▸ (2) The FSIA contains a rule regarding the burden of proof called by Monroe Leigh 'FSIA's allocation of the burden of proof', while he admits that the *House Report* statement 'posed some practical difficulties';

▸ (3) As there was no dispute regarding the fact of the nationalization itself, the Appeal Court, according to Leigh, reduced the foreign state's burden of proof by limiting it to a mere 'general statement'.

For the following reasons I hold Mr. Leigh's criticism for unjustified, if not erroneous regarding the principles and rules of evidence that it invokes.

Ad (1)

It was not disputed between the parties that the plaintiff bears the evidential burden after Nicaragua established a *prima facie case* of sovereign immunity regarding the nationalization. The Court of Appeal did not rule on the risk of nonpersuasion here, but only on the incidence of the *evidential burden*. The legal burden or risk of nonpersuasion comes to carry only in the moment that the plaintiff, too, has achieved to *rebut the prima facie evidence* established by the foreign state. This was however not the case. The plaintiff even failed to respond the submission of the foreign state, and remained completely inactive, let alone submitted any counter-evidence, and this despite the fact that the court asked for it. In this case, it is obvious that the *plaintiff did not rebut the prima face evidence*, and thus the legal burden never came to carry in this case.

Ad (2)

It is incorrect to state that the Act itself contained a rule of the burden of proof; there is no provision to this effect to be found in the FSIA. Regarding the legal materials, the Court of Appeals well considered the explanation given therein, but then modified the application of this explanation for the judicial practice. The judge considered the fact that immunity cannot be construed, from a procedural point of view, as an *affirmative defense*, because courts have to state about their competence *sua sponte*; abrogating this practice would have repercussions in international law and practice. As a result, the court adapted the explanation of the *House Report* to the judicial practice in matters of sovereign immunity litigation. It has to be seen that this modification that the court proposed in Alberti only regards the evidential burden, and *not the persuasive burden or risk of nonpersuasion*.

Ad (3)

That a nationalization is a public, governmental act was not even contested by the plaintiff, and this fact was admitted by Monroe Leigh in his case note. So why should Nicaragua have been obliged to prove all the details regarding this public act? It follows from litigation equity that only what is contested needs to be proved. In such a situation, to talk about the court having 'eliminated' the burden of proof of the foreign state is untenable.

To summarize, the Alberti precedent represents a sound, logical and practical adaptation of the burden of proof explanation in the *House Report* to the requirements of judicial practice and procedural equity considerations. As the court, in compliance with the overwhelming majority of international law scholars and international practice, considered a nationalization as 'a quintessential Government act'[213], the prima facie evidence that Nicaragua had submitted to demonstrate this fact was sufficient to having the evidential burden shift to the plaintiff for rebutting the *presumption of immunity* established by the prima facie case. And here is where the case ended, as the plaintiff did not even respond to the submission of the foreign state. The court held:

> **Alberti v. Empresa Nicaraguense de la Carne**
> Defendants having established a prima facie entitlement to immunity it was plaintiff's obligation to produce support for their position that a statutory exception was applicable.[214]

As I said above, the foreign state can limit its production of evidence until the plaintiff has contested the prima facie case; only in the latter case would the foreign state bear the full burden of proving that the act in question was of a public, governmental nature. But the plaintiff did not contest the prima face evidence. The court stated:

Alberti v. Empresa Nicaraguense de la Carne

It is only when the plaintiff has produced this evidence that the defendant must prove its entitlement to immunity by a preponderance of the evidence.[215]

We have seen that by and large that in sovereign immunity litigation, foreign states have the right to begin with producing evidence, and accordingly bear the *evidential burden* for their sovereign immunity claim. That means, more precisely, that the foreign state, or its organism, need to establish a *prima facie case* regarding the conditions pointed out in §§1603(a) or (b) FSIA and further, that the exceptions to foreign sovereign immunity that the plaintiff invoked, and that are enumerated in §§1605 to 1607 FSIA, do not apply. We also have seen that the general rules of evidence that require the plaintiff to prove the facts that establish *personal jurisdiction* have not been abrogated by the FSIA.

From the foregoing follows that once the foreign state has submitted prima facie evidence satisfactorily to the court, the evidential burden shifts to the plaintiff to demonstrate that an exception to sovereign immunity applies. As we have seen already in some detail, the perhaps most common exception that is invoked in sovereign immunity litigation is the so-called 'commercial activity exception', §1605(a)(2) FSIA. However, sometimes, in such a situation, when a plaintiff cannot find ground to show that the activity in question was of a commercial nature, he is well advised to try proving that the foreign state has waived their immunity. There are quite a few obvious and less obvious ways how a foreign state may have waived their immunity.

To begin with, in *Harris v. Vao Intourist, Moscow*[216], which can be considered a landmark decision as it is quoted in a series of subsequent precedents, we face exactly such a situation. The plaintiff, testamentary executor of an american tourist who was killed in a fire that ravaged the Moscow International Hotel, sued not only the hotel but also the Russian government. The judge considered a simple letter from the Soviet Ambassador sufficient for establishing a *prima facie case* in favor of the defendants. Thereby, the judge ruled, the evidential burden shifted to the plaintiff to show that an exception applies. The plaintiff invoked the waiver exception, §1605(a)(1) FSIA, but the judge concluded that 'the statutes and treaties cited by plaintiff, though indicating a capacity of the defendants to sue or to be sued at their option, do not reflect an intention to waive governmental immunity.' Accordingly, the action was rejected by the court.

In *Matter of Rio Grande Transports, Inc.*[217], the case was about a claim to exonerate responsibility for an American vessel that was colliding with an Algerian vessel. The defendant, the *Compagnie Nationale Algérienne de Navigation (CNAN)*, filed a conditional claim and answer against the American plaintiff. CNAN was recognized by the court to be an 'agency or instrumentality of a foreign state' under §1603(b), which proof was delivered by both a letter from the Algerian Ministry of Transportation and an affidavit from the Chargé d'Affaires of the Algerian embassy in the United States.[218]

The interesting question came up if the counterclaim filed by CNAN was to be considered as an *implicit waiver of sovereign immunity* under the terms of §1605(a)(1) FSIA.

After having examined a particularity in American admiralty law[219], the judge refused to admit an implicit immunity waiver with the argument that the defendant, running the risk to lose their only forum when passing the deadline stipulated in 46 U.S.C. §185 and thus for preserving substantive rights.[220] As such, the defendant only acted for preserving their rights but not implied to waive their immunity for that matter. The judge also invoked a Supreme Court precedent, *The Bremen v. Zapata-Off-Shore Co.*[221], where the case was ruled in the same manner. The defendant *Zapata*, an american company, filed a protective limitation proceeding and conditional claim, under 46 U.S.C. §185, as it is regularly done in maritime actions for limiting financial responsibility. In *Ohntrup v. Firearms Center, Inc.*[222], the explanation provided by the legal materials regarding implicit sovereign immunity waivers was interpreted and explained. The plaintiff had bought a gun from defendant which did not function correctly and as a result wounded him. Between defendant and the fabricant of the weapon, *Makina*, a Turkish company, an arbitrage agreement was concluded which the plaintiff interpreted as an immunity waiver. The court held that the contract between *Makina* and *Firearms Center* did not rule any torts committed to third parties, and therefore no immunity waiver could be construed from the arbitration clause. In addition, in *International Association of Machinists and Aerospace Workers (IAM) v. OPEC*[223], it was clarified that the only fact to have not responded timely to the action cannot be construed as an implicit immunity waiver.

Such a case is of course different from the case if a foreign state responds to the claim without however claiming foreign sovereign immunity. This is one of the clear-cut situations where the foreign state implicitly waives his sovereign immunity defense. This was already foreseen by the legal materials that state that an 'implicit waiver would also include a situation where a foreign state has filed a responsive pleading without raising the defense of sovereign immunity.'[224]

To conclude as to the general burden of proof allocation under §1605(a)(1) FSIA, we see that the situation is similar to the other exceptions in that here as well, the foreign state must begin to present evidence satisfactorily to the court by making a *prima facie case* of sovereign immunity, whereupon the burden shifts to the plaintiff to demonstrate that an express or implicit immunity waiver exists, and that this waiver was contained in any contractual relationship that he himself had with the foreign state.

For an implicit or explicit immunity waiver to be assumed under section 1605(a)(1) of the Act, there must be proof of an unconditional immunity waiver to be contained in any juridical relation between the private plaintiff and the foreign state. With respect to arbitration agreements, the plaintiff must prove that American law had been chosen to rule any dispute arising out of the agreement in order the establish the necessary *nexus* between the contract and the jurisdiction of the United States.

An implicit immunity waiver in an international treaty was only affirmed by the courts for the case that the clause in question was hinting at an *intentional abandonment of a legal right* on the side of the foreign state, defendant of the action. In any other constellation, such implicit immunity waivers were denied to be agreed upon by the parties of international treaties.

The repartition of the burden of proof that is suggested in the *House Report* and that was partially modified by federal case law, is that it's the foreign states to begin with producing prima facie evidence about two elements, first, that it is a foreign state under §§1603(a),(b) FSIA, and second, that the activity at the basis of the action had a public, governmental character. For proving the second element, the foreign state only needs to disprove any explicit or implicit immunity waiver under §1605(a)(1) FSIA that the plaintiff has invoked in its claim.

Once the foreign state has produced prima facie evidence regarding the two elements, which can by done by affidavit or otherwise, the evidential burden *shifts to the plaintiff* for proving that the alleged immunity waiver was such that it fulfilled the requirements of §1605(a)(1) FSIA.

CHAPTER FIVE

The Burden of Proof for Immunity Exceptions

The Commercial Activity Exception

§1605(a)(2) FSIA

§1605(a)(2) FSIA states that a foreign state shall not be immune from jurisdiction for any case in which the action is based upon:

> **§1605(a)(2) FSIA**
> *(Clause 1)*
> a commercial activity carried on in the United States by the foreign state, or
> *(Clause 2)*
> an act performed in the United States in connection with a commercial activity of the foreign state elsewhere, or
> *(Clause 3)*
> an act outside the territory of the United States in connection with a commercial activity of the foreign state elsewhere and that causes a direct effect in the United States.

First, of all, it has to be noted that the notions 'foreign state', 'commercial activity' and 'United States' are defined in §1603. This does not require further discussion.

> **§ 1603. Definitions**
> For purposes of this chapter—
> (a) A 'foreign state', except as used in section 1608 of this title, includes a political subdivision of a foreign state or an agency or instrumentality of a foreign state as defined in subsection (b).

(b) An 'agency or instrumentality of a foreign state' means any entity—
(1) which is a separate legal person, corporate or otherwise, and
(2) which is an organ of a foreign state or political subdivision thereof, or a majority of whose shares or other ownership interest is owned by a foreign state or political subdivision thereof, and
(3) which is neither a citizen of a State of the United States as defined in section 1332 (c) and (d) of this title, nor created under the laws of any third country.
(c) The 'United States' includes all territory and waters, continental or insular, subject to the jurisdiction of the United States.
(d) A 'commercial activity' means either a regular course of commercial conduct or a particular commercial transaction or act. The commercial character of an activity shall be determined by reference to the nature of the course of conduct or particular transaction or act, rather than by reference to its purpose.
(e) A 'commercial activity carried on in the United States by a foreign state' means commercial activity carried on by such state and having substantial contact with the United States.

The interesting legal issue involved here in this so-called *commercial activity exception* is the particular nexus required between the action or act in question, on one hand, and the commercial activity, on the other. To discuss this further in detail I found it useful to divide the statutory ruling into three separate clauses. When you read them, you see that there is a movement in the sense that the commercial activity *moves as it were farther and farther away*. When I was reading this for the first time, I had to think immediately of a passage in the *House Report* regarding §1330(b), which I discussed already earlier on:

H. R. Report No. 94-1487

(b) Personal Jurisdiction. Section 1330(b) provides, in effect, a Federal long-arm statute over foreign states (including political subdivisions, agencies, and instrumentalities of foreign states). It is patterned after the long-arm statute Congress enacted for the

District of Columbia, Public Law 91-358, section 132(a), Title I, 84 Stat. 549.[225]

In my view, the commercial activity exception of the Act uses a very similar long-arm clause here to establish the nexus or a minimal contacts provision between the action of the foreign state the litigation is about, on one hand, and the commercial activity, on the other. In clause (3), it is evident that this nexus can be a relatively feeble one, and here, the literature is all but united if such kind of 'direct effects jurisdiction' is still constitutional or not.[226] Whatever one may think about such a legislative attempt to 'force jurisdiction' into one's nation - which can be problematic under international law - the principle that is unquestioned here is that such *nexus* between the suit and the commercial activity must exist, and here the statute is clear-cut in that it requires that the action pending at court *be based upon the commercial activity* in question.

Clause 1

As to this first clause of the section, there are instructive explanations to be found in a judgment by the Court of Appeals of the 3rd Circuit, in the case *Sugarman v. Aeromexico, Inc.*[227] The plaintiff claimed damages from the mexican government, alleging he had greatly suffered from waiting for his delayed flight to the United States, in a mexican airport. The district court had recognized Aeromexico as being an *agency or instrumentality of a foreign state* under the section. What is interesting to note about the appeal judgment is that it contains a confirmation of what was to be supposed from the point of view of the burden of proof. The court clearly held that the burden is upon the plaintiff to show the necessary connectivity required by section 1605(a)(2) FSIA.[228] This ruling becomes even more clear when considering *Verlinden v. Central Bank of Nigeria*[229] where the court held that it's upon the plaintiff to identify a 'regular course of commercial conduct' or a 'particular commercial transaction or act' under this section, as well as that the activity has 'substantial contact(s) with the United States.[230]

Clause 2

This criterion was interpreted in the case *Gilson v. Republic of Ireland*[231] where the plaintiff, an American citizen, claimed damages from a commercial contract concluded with the government of Ireland, or an agency thereof. The plaintiff invoked that the government of Ireland had not fulfilled its duties under the contract, and in addition had divulged certain facts that they had to keep secret under the contract. There was no doubt as to the *commercial character* of the activity in question.[232] Hence, the Court of Appeal only stated about the necessary *nexus* between the facts at issue and the territory of the United States. Admitting as verified the facts alleged by the plaintiff[233], the Court in applying *clause 2* of §1605(a)(2) and clearly concluded that the burden for proving the minimal contacts required by the clause was upon the plaintiff.

Clause 3

The third clause of section 1605(a)(2) was subject of the precedents *Upton v. Empire of Iran*[234] and *Wyle v. Bank Melli of Teheran, Inc.*[235] The Upton suit was initiated by a woman whose husband was killed when, back in 1974, the hall of Teheran international airport crashed down. Mrs. Upton as well as two other plaintiffs was claiming damages from the Iranian government and the Iranian Civil Aerospace Department. Here also, the court affirmed that the burden of proof for the necessary *nexus* under the third clause of §1605(a)(2) is upon the plaintiff.

Upton v. Empire of Iran

Plaintiffs principally rely upon 28 U.S.C. §1605(a)(2), clause 3, as a bar to the defendants immunity. (…) The court finds that causing injury to American citizens abroad is insufficient to satisfy the requirement of the District of Columbia long-arm statute. The relatively simple statement of plaintiff's position points up the correctness of this result. They contend that 'defendant's acts caused the deaths and injuries to Americans which caused direct effects in the United States. (…) Their own language attenuates the connection between the act and the effect. (…) Inasmuch as section 1605(a)(2), clause 3, is unavailable to remove defendants' immunity under section 1605, and plaintiffs are unable to assert jurisdiction under any of the alternative exceptions to sovereign immunity, this court lacks subject matter and personal jurisdiction over these defendants by the terms of 28. U.S.C. §1330. Accordingly, the court dismisses the action.[236]

The court also ruled on the retroactivity of the FSIA which only entered in force on the 19th January 1977, and affirmed it[237], referring to *Yessenin-Volpin v. Novosti Press Agency, Tass.*[238] However, while thus two district courts have initially affirmed the retroactivity of the Act, it was later denied by the Court of Appeals of the 2nd circuit in the case *Corporación Venezolana de Fomento v. Vintero Sales.*[239] From this judgment, a retroactive application of the FSIA was generally denied by the American jurisprudence.

This becomes still more evident in *Wyle v. Bank Melli of Teheran, Inc.,* a suit that was initiated by the bankruptcy attorney of two shipment companies, the *Pacific Far East Line* (PFEL) and *Atlantic Bear Steamship Co.* (ATLANTIC), against Bank Melli from Iran, the government of Iran, an iranian shipment company (PSO)[240] and the Bank of California. The plaintiff alleged a fraudulent cooperation of the defendants with regard to a letter of credit. In fact, for the navigation of PFEL and ATLANTIC within the Bushire port in Iran, PSO required a letter of credit to be issued by Bank Melli for indemnifying eventual loss or deterioration of the cargo. PFEL offered a letter of credit to the Bank of California for indemnifying Bank Melli for the case that PSO would ask for the letter of credit. After complicated arrangements, Bank Melli claimed from Bank of California the payment of the entire amount guaranteed, pretending PSO had cashed in the letter of credit from PFEL and ATLANTIC who had violated the credit agreement. The plaintiff alleged that there was no reason for cashing the letter of credit as there was no loss or deterioration of any cargo.

With regard to the minimal contacts between the activities of PSO and Bank Melli, the plaintiff invoked the *House Report* statement where jurisdictional immunity is construed as an *affirmative defense*. He thus concludes that what is valid for the question of affirming or denying sovereign immunity, and the burden of proof regarding those facts, must equally be valid for minimal contacts.[241] Thus, the plaintiff argued that the burden of proving minimal contacts was on the defendants, but as the latter had not presented any proof to the court as a basis of their immunity claim, the plaintiff thought he had been dispensed from presenting any evidence. The court did not share the plaintiff's opinion:

Wyle v. Bank Melli of Teheran, Inc.

This argument is specious. The legislative history makes clear what the foreign state must prove to establish immunity: that the challenged action is that of a foreign state in its public, non-commercial capacity. The burden of proving the existence of an otherwise actionable (if not barred by sovereign immunity) activity or act within the United States or having a direct effect in the United States would obviously remain with the plaintiff. Simply because the foreign state must plead and prove certain facts necessary to establish its immunity does not mean that the normal burden of proving subject matter and personal jurisdiction is reversed.[242]

The burden of proof for the existence of *minimal contacts*, and implicitly, for the affirmation of subject matter and personal jurisdiction of the tribunal is thus unequivocally upon the plaintiff. The repartition of the burden of proof in the *House Report* only regards the immunity question, and did not change the general rule that the plaintiff must demonstrate and prove the facts that are establishing the competence of the court.

Expropriation in Violation of International Law

§1605(a)(3) FSIA

Introduction

This exception is a novelty in American law in that contrary to general international law principles, where all nationalizations are considered as sacrosanct in the sense that they are considered as 'quintessential government acts', the FSIA allows to sue a foreign state nonetheless when the foreign state has effected the nationalization 'in violation of international law'. One of the initiators of this exception was *Professor Louis B. Sohn*, at the time legal advisor to the State Department, when the Act was in preparation, and who was for twelve years professor of international law at Harvard University. The other person who signed responsible for the introduction of this exception is *Monroe Leigh, Esq.*, who was the acting legal advisor when the FSIA was drafted, and who was for long years a founding member of the law firm *Steptoe & Johnson* in Washington, D.C.

Section 1605 (a)(3) seems to have been drafted in analogy with the international law of torts, or *international torts*, and the responsibility of states for torts committed by one of their officials, which is called in the literature *state responsibility* or *international responsibility*.[243] In addition, there is a parallel to United States law, the so-called *Hickenlooper Amendment* to the Foreign Assistance Act of 1965.

28 U.S.C. §1605(a)(3)

(3) in which rights in property taken in violation of international law are in issue and that property or any property exchanged for such property is present in the United States in connection with a commercial activity carried on in the United States by the foreign state; or that property or any property exchanged for such property is owned or operated by an agency or instrumentality of the foreign state and that agency or instrumentality is engaged in a commercial activity in the United States; ...

The *House Report* explains for this section:

H. R. Report No. 94-1487

(a)(3) *Expropriation claims*. Section 1605(a)(3) would, in two categories of cases, deny immunity where 'rights in property taken in violation of international law are in issue'. The first category involves cases where the property is present in the United States by the foreign state, or political subdivision, agency or instrumentality of the foreign state. The second category is where the property, or any property exchanged for that property, is (i) owned or operated by an agency or instrumentality of a foreign state and (ii) that agency or instrumentality is engaged in a commercial activity in the United States. Under the second category, the property needs to be present in connection with a commercial activity of the agency or instrumentality.

The term 'taken in violation of international law' could include the nationalization or expropriation of property without payment of the prompt, adequate and effective compensation required by international law. It would also include takings which are arbitrary or discriminatory in nature. Since, however, this section deals solely with issues of immunity, it in no way affects existing law on the extent of which, if at all, the 'act of state' doctrine may be applicable. See 22 U.S.C. 2370(e)(2).[244]

We have to distinguish the different clauses in this exception, under the special focus of the repartition of the burden of proof.

Expropriation in Violation of International Law

The Court of Appeals of the 7th Circuit, in *Alberti v. Empresa Nicara-guense de la Carne*[245], a case we have already discussed earlier on regarding its important rulings on the burden of proof, is equally interesting with regard to the interpretation of the criterion 'expropriation in violation of international law', under §1605(a)(3) FSIA. As in this case, the expropriation was considered by the court to be a public, governmental act and the defendant state thus established a *prima facie case* to support its immunity claim, the fact at issue was if the expropriation had been effected 'in violation of international law'.

> **Alberti v. Empresa Nicaraguense de la Carne (7th Cir.)**
> Plaintiff's final basis for removing this case from the protection of sovereign immunity rests upon their allegation that the nationalization was in violation of international law. If this is the case then defendant's immunity is removed by section 1605(a)(3), as the remaining elements are present. To decide this issue we must determine what is required by international law to validate a nationalization and then allocate the appropriate burden of proof.[246]

The plaintiffs forwarded the view that international law required the prompt payment of an adequate compensation to the property holders. As they had not received compensation, they thought that the expropriation was in violation of international law. The defendants, by contrast, argued that international law only required that reasonable and comprehensive provisions had been enacted for a compensation to be paid.[247] While the court admitted that generally, in the international law literature, prompt, adequate and effective compensation was required to be effected by the nationalizing government, the court admitted that there was little agreement about the precise terms under which such payment must be effected in the particular case.[248] The court however rejected the argument of the plaintiffs that compensation had to be paid *before* the nationalization:

Alberti v. Empresa Nicaraguense de la Carne (7th Cir.)

We think that international law does not require payment of compensation prior to nationalization. Our position is buttressed by Congress' adoption of the 'prompt', rather than a prior or immediate, payment standard in the legislative history of 1605(a)(3). (…) Prompt payment, by definition, is made within a reasonable time *after* nationalization. As long as the expropriating nation affords property owners a means of obtaining prompt payment the dictates of international law have been satisfied.[249]

As the legal provisions in Nicaragua indeed foresaw payment of a prompt, adequate and effective compensation, the court proceeded to state on the burden of proof for this fact at issue. I will cite the entire passage of the judgment here because it exemplarily reveals the repartition of the burden of proof, and its underlying principles, under the Act, and how those principles are to be applied in procedural practice:

Alberti v. Empresa Nicaraguense de la Carne (7th Cir.)

In our opinion section 1604 requires a foreign state to establish a prima facie case on two elements: that it is a foreign state under the definition employed in FSIA, and that the claim relates to a 'public act'. Once this evidence is produced section 1604 provides a 'presumption' of immunity that the plaintiff must rebut by offering evidence that one of the statutory exceptions applies. It is only when the plaintiff has produced this evidence that the defendant must prove its entitlement to immunity by a preponderance of the evidence. Plaintiffs do not contend that defendants have failed to establish that they are both to be treated as foreign states under the FSIA. The question that remains is whether defendants have established that the suit relates to a public act. The only definition of public act appears in the suggestion in the legislative history that a public act is 'an act not within the exceptions in sections 1605-1607'. House Report at 6616. This definition, which is circular, would require a defendant to establish the inapplicability of every statutory exception. Common sense refutes this position as it would be a nearly impossible task for a defendant to refute the exceptions before the plaintiff has indicated which one is applicable or, as in this case,

> how a nationalization was in violation of international law. (...)
> Defendants having established a prima facie entitlement to im-
> munity it was plaintiff's obligation to produce support that a
> statutory exception was applicable. This they did not do; al-
> though they were not precluded from adducing affidavits. In-
> stead they failed even to respond to defendant's motion to dis-
> miss. In this situation, defendants need not disprove a claim that
> the nationalization was in violation of international law, and we
> need not consider whether their affidavit was sufficient for that
> purpose.[250]

It is interesting to examine if the same repartition of the burden of
proof exists under the act of state doctrine? There is namely an exception to the act of state doctrine contained in the *Hickenlooper Amendment* to the Foreign Assistance Act of 1965 which states that American
courts, if the president, for political reasons opposes it, are not supposed to apply the act of state doctrine, except that 'claim or title or
other right to property ... based upon (or traced through) a confisca-
tion or other taking after January 1, 1959, by an act of that state in violation of the principles of international law', 22 U.S.C. §2370(e)(2).

Referring to this provision, the district court of the district of Columbia, in the LIAMCO precedent, concluded that '[t]he president has
made no suggestion in this matter, but petitioner has failed to show
that the amendment's requirements have been met.'[251] The conditions
namely require that the expropriation was effected in violation of the
principles of international law. Hence, the court states that the petitioner 'has failed to show that the taking was in violation of international law.'[252]

The court applied thus the act of state doctrine, which resulted in
an arbitration sentence rendered in Geneva, the 12th of April, 1977, not
to be executed within the United States, notwithstanding the fact that
the court had refused to grant Libya immunity from suit. In a more recent case, *Kalamazoo Spice Extraction Company v. The Provisional Military Government of Socialist Ethiopia*[253], the district court equally strug-
gled with factual problems regarding the question if the nationaliza-

tion of plaintiff's company by the Ethiopian government was effected 'in violation of international law'. As under §§1330(a),(b) FSIA, jurisdiction requires the absence of immunity, the judge had to deal with all the factual problems regarding the exceptions from sovereign immunity, before he could state about its jurisdiction. However, before having affirmed its jurisdiction or competence, the court is impeached from entering the examination of the underlying substantive law. This vicious circle, that is a result of the strange drafting technique of the Act, was broken by the court:

> **Kalamazoo Spice Extraction Company v. The Provisional Military Government of Socialist Ethiopia**
>
> When factual issues are determinative of both the jurisdictional question and the merits, as here, a court must assert jurisdiction unless the claim is insubstantial or frivolous. (...) KAL-SPICE's claims are neither insubstantial nor frivolous. Because plaintiff has made a substantial allegation of a violation of international law, the court must assert jurisdiction.[254]

As to the burden of proof of the plaintiff with regard to a violation of international law through the nationalization in question, a *substantial allegation* was thus considered to be sufficient by the court.

The Minimal Contacts Requirements

We have already outlined the principles of due process being part of the FSIA, which is why a minimal contact or *nexus* must exist between the facts at issue, and the territorial jurisdiction of the United States. This is required by variety of the exceptions to the general rule of immunity. Here, §1605(a)(3) requires that the property (or the property exchanged for it) be present in the United States in connection with a commercial activity of the foreign state conducted in the United States, or that the property belongs, or is administered by, an agency or instrumentality of the foreign state, conducting commercial activity in the United States. This latter criterion was examined in *De San-*

chez[255], a case we discussed earlier on. The court admitted an expropriation in violation of international law regarding the refusal of *Banco Central* to pay out to Mrs. Sanchez the amount of the cheque, without the payment of a prompt, adequate and effective compensation.[256] Then the judge stressed the fact that contrary to section 1605(a)(2), the 'commercial activity' exception, §1605(a)(3) did *not* require that the property be used *in connection with* a commercial activity, when such activity was conducted by an agency or instrumentality of the foreign state:

> **De Sanchez v. Banco Central de Nicaragua**
>
> Section 1605(a)(3) … permits a court to exercise jurisdiction over the foreign state so long as the state's agency or instrumentality holds the property allegedly confiscated, or property exchanged for it, and conducts commercial activities in the United States, even if the property is not used in connection with those commercial activities.[257]

Appreciating the evidence submitted by the plaintiff, the court affirmed the existence of commercial conduct by *Banco Central* in the United States.[258] As to the burden of proof regarding those minimal contacts, we have already seen that as these criteria are substantial elements of personal jurisdiction, the burden of proof is upon the plaintiff. In the present case, the court took reference to the *Verlinden*[259] precedent and held:

> **De Sanchez v. Banco Central de Nicaragua**
>
> Although *Verlinden* approached the issue as one of personal jurisdiction, which Banco Central contends is lacking in this case, the analysis is the same because the FSIA makes the court's personal jurisdiction coterminous with its subject matter jurisdiction over the claim asserted against the foreign state. 28 U.S.C. §1330(b).[260]

In the following note, the court pursued:

De Sanchez v. Banco Central de Nicaragua

I acknowledge that Incer's testimony, standing alone, is not particularly strong evidence of the scope and nature of Banco Central's commercial activities in the United States. However, because the burden of proof of the defense of sovereign immunity is upon Banco Central, … and it has failed to present evidence rebutting Incer's testimony, I am compelled to find in favor of Sanchez on the issue. I also acknowledge that generally the burden of proof on the existence of personal jurisdiction, like subject matter jurisdiction, falls upon the plaintiff. *Familia de Boom v. Arosa Mercantil, S.A.*, 629 F.2d 1134, 1138 (5th Cir. 1980), *Product Promotions Inc. v. Cousteau*, 495 F2d 483, 490 (5th Cir. 1974), *Jetco Electronic Industries, Inc. v. Gardiner*, 473 F.2d 1228, 1232 (5th Cir. 1973). However, because the FSIA incorporates the elements of personal jurisdiction into its grant of subject matter jurisdiction, and the foreign state must bear the burden of proof that subject matter jurisdiction is lacking, a plaintiff suing under the Immunities Act is necessarily relieved from his duty to prove that the defendant foreign state is subject to personal jurisdiction of the court. Therefore, because Banco Central has failed to prove that Sanchez's claim does not arise under 1605(a)(3), its contention that personal jurisdiction is lacking is also without merit.[261]

These revelatory passages in the judgment are in obvious contradiction with the precedents, and with the conclusions I have taken further up in this study. However, the court's argument that the plaintiff was liberated from his burden of proof regarding personal jurisdiction because the Act has interwoven it with subject matter jurisdiction, is not very convincing. Because this circular schema, as a result of the drafting technique of the Act, can be broken apart, so that we can well look at the burden of proof for subject matter jurisdiction, on one hand, and for personal jurisdiction, on the other. In addition, it has to be seen that these considerations of the court were but an *obiter dictum*, not relevant for the final decision.

Even if we admit that the plaintiff has to bear the burden of proof for minimal contacts as part of personal jurisdiction, we can conclude that in the present case the plaintiff has well acquitted this burden, even though the court held it was not 'particularly strong evidence'.[262] In other words, Sanchez has well established a *prima facie case* with respect to that fact at issue whereupon the evidential burden shifted toward the defendant, Banco Central. However as the bank failed to present evidence 'rebutting Incer's testimony', the judge actually concluded that the bank failed to discharge this burden, which is why the judge was 'compelled to find in favor of Sanchez on this issue.' This is why the developments of the court regarding the burden of proof were not relevant, and just *obiter dicta*. In addition, more recent precedents overruled these considerations, that is *Alberti*[263], and *Wyle*[264] that we discussed already earlier. In *Alberti*, the Court of Appeals of the 7th Circuit, affirming the burden of proof of the foreign state for its immunity claim, modified the allocation of the burden of proof, as it was outlined in the *House Report*. The court limited the burden of proof of the foreign state to the prima facie demonstration of a public act 'and then placing the burden of identifying the relevant exception by affidavit or otherwise upon the plaintiff.[265]

After this important leading case, we can conclude that the foreign state does not bear the burden of proof for personal jurisdiction; this burden is upon the plaintiff. Hence, the burden of proof for minimal contacts is equally upon the plaintiff, including the necessary *nexus* required by §1605(a)(3). This criterion is almost identical with clause 2 of §1605(a)(2), for which the burden of proof of the plaintiff was affirmed in *Gilson v. Republic of Ireland*.[266]

Conclusion

To summarize, these precedents reveal that the burden of proof is upon the plaintiff for demonstrating the applicability of any of the criteria employed by §1605(a)(3) and that the burden of proof of the foreign state is limited to two elements, that is, that it is a *foreign state* or an *agency or instrumentality of a foreign state*, under §§1603(a),(b) and that the activity in question was of a public, governmental nature. In other words, the examination of section 1605(a)(3) regarding the burden of proof fully confirms our earlier conclusions.

The Immovable Property Exception

§1605(a)(4)

This exception from immunity is 'classical' in the sense that is existed already under the absolute immunity doctrine.[267] The refusal to grant immunity for litigations regarding property of the foreign state situated in the forum state is justified by the fact that foreign states can freely dispose where they want to locate their property, and this decision implies a voluntary submission of their property under the jurisdiction of the states where such property has been located. This could be called an implicit immunity waiver.[268] On the other hand, we could also explain this immunity exception with the consideration that the jurisdiction of a forum state is absolute in the sense that it covers all the immovable property located in its territory, without regard to who is the owner of such property.

§1605(a)(4) FISA denies immunity from jurisdiction in the case:

28. U.S.C. §1605(a)(4)

(4) in which rights in property in the United States acquired by succession or gift or rights in immovable property situated in the United States are in issue; (…)

The House Report explains for this section:

H.R. Report 94-1487

(a)(4) Immovable, inherited, and gift property. Section 1605(a)(4) denies immunity in litigation relating to rights in real estate and in inherited or gift property located in the United States. It is established that, as set forth in the 'Tate Letter' of 1952, sovereign immunity should not be granted in actions with respect to real property, diplomatic and consular property excepted. 26 Department of State Bulletin 984 (1952). It does not matter whether a particular piece of property is used for commercial or public purposes.

It is maintainable that the exception mentioned in the 'Tate Letter' with respect to diplomatic and consular property is limited to questions of attachment and execution and does not apply to an adjudication or rights in that property. Thus the Vienna Convention on Diplomatic Relations, concluded in 1961, 23 UST 3227, TIAS 7502 (1972), provides in article 22 that the 'premises of the mission, their furnishings and other property thereon and the means of transport of the mission shall be immune from search, requisition, attachment and execution.' Actions short of attachment or execution seem to be permitted under the Convention, and a foreign state cannot deny to the local state the right to adjudicate questions of ownership, rent, servitudes, and similar matters, as long as the foreign state's possession of the premises is not disturbed.

There is general agreement that a foreign state may not claim immunity when the suit against it relates to rights in property, real or personal, obtained by gift or inherited by the foreign state and situated or administered in the country where the suit is brought. As stated in the 'Tate Letter', immunity should not be granted 'with respect to the disposition of the property of a deceased person even though a foreign sovereign is the beneficiary.' The reason is that, in claiming rights in a decedent's estate or obtained by gift, the foreign state claims the same right which is enjoyed by private persons.[269]

The general allocation of the burden of proof as it is to be concluded from in the legislative history and the precedents is not just a matter of one single exception, but it principally valid for all exceptions, §§1605 to 1607 FSIA.[270] For the exception under §1605(a)(4), we can distinguish two criteria:

- the *material* criteria, 'rights in property acquired by succession or gift' and 'rights in immovable property;

- the *procedural* criterion, that is, the necessary nexus to the territorial jurisdiction of the United States, 'in the United States'.

For the *procedural* criterion, the burden of proof is clearly upon the plaintiff. For the material criteria, if we follow the precedent *Alberti*, the burden of proof is equally upon the plaintiff. Specifically for section 1604(a)(4), there is not yet any precedent that deals with the burden of proof. However, in *Matter of Rio Grande Transport, Inc.*[271], already discussed earlier in this study, the court briefly explained how to interpret the term 'immovable property'; the pleadings here indicate that the court allocated the evidential burden to be upon the plaintiff and confirmed that the burden for the material criteria in §1605(a)(4) is equally upon the plaintiff. In fact, the question was if a limitation fund for limiting naval tort responsibility also is to be considered as 'immovable property'.[272]

The Noncommercial Tort Exception

§1605(a)(5) FSIA[273]

Introduction

This exception of the Act is of particular interest because its existence cannot only be explained with the restrictive immunity doctrine, but is to be understood rather as a complementary provision to the 'commercial activity exception', §1605(a)(2) FSIA.

This exception to the general rule of sovereign immunity equally requires a *nexus* between the facts at issue and the territorial jurisdiction of the United States. The tort must have occurred in the United States.

> **28. U.S.C. §1605(a)(5)**
>
> (a) A foreign state shall not be immune from the jurisdiction of courts of the United States or of the States in any case—
> (5) not otherwise encompassed in paragraph (2) above, in which money damages are sought against a foreign state for personal injury or death, or damage to or loss of property, occurring in the United States and caused by the tortious act or omission of that foreign state or of any official or employee of that foreign state while acting within the scope of his office or employment; (…)
>   (A) any claim based upon the exercise or performance or the failure to exercise or perform a discretionary function regardless of whether the discretion be abused or
>   (B) any claim arising out of malicious prosecution,

abuse of process, libel, slander, misrepresentation, deceit, or interference with contract rights.

The *House Report* explains:

H. R. Report No. 94-1487

(a)(5) *Noncommercial torts.* Section 1605(a)(5) is directed primarily at the problem of traffic accidents but is cast in general terms as applying to all tort actions for money damages, not otherwise encompassed by section 1605(a)(2) relating to commercial activities. It denies immunity as to claims for personal in injury and death, or for damage to or loss of property, caused by the tortious act or omission of the foreign state or its officials or employees, acting within the scope of their authority; the tortious act or omission must occur within the jurisdiction of the United States, and must not come within one of the exceptions enumerated in the second paragraph of the subsection.

As used in section 1605(a)(5), the phrase 'tortious act or omission' is meant to include causes of action which are based on strict liability as well as on negligence. The exceptions provided in subparagraphs (A) and (B) of section 1605(a)(5) correspond to many of the claims with respect to which the U.S. Government retains immunity under the Federal Tort Claims Act, 28 U.S.C. 1680(a) and (h).

Like other provisions in this bill, section 1605 is subject to existing international agreements (see section 1604), including Status of Forces Agreements; if a remedy is available under a Status of Forces Agreement, the foreign state is immune from such tort claims as are encompassed in sections 1605(a)(2) and 1605(a)(5).

Since the bill deals only with the immunity of foreign states and not its diplomatic or consular representatives, section 1605(a)(5) would not govern suits against diplomatic or consular representatives but only suits against the foreign state. It is noteworthy in this regard that while article 43 of the Vienna Convention on Consular Relations of 1963, 21 UST 77, TIAS 6820 (1970), expressly abolishes the immunity of consular officers with regard to civil action brought by a third party for 'damage arising from an accident in the receiving state caused by a vehicle, vessel or aircraft', there is no such provision in the Vienna Convention on Diplomatic Relations of 1961, supra. Consequently, no case relating to the traffic accident can be brought against a member of a diplomatic mission.

> The purpose of section 1605(a)(5) is to permit the victim of a traffic accident or other noncommercial tort to maintain an action against a foreign state to the extent otherwise provided by law ... '[274]

When we dissect this provision, we can make out the following system, consisting of four distinct areas, or sets of criteria.

▸   (1) *The minimal* contacts or *nexus* between the facts at issue and the territorial jurisdiction of the United States: 'occuring in the United States';

▸   (2) *Causality*: 'caused by the tortious act or omission';

▸   (3) *Scope of Employment*: 'while acting within the scope of his office or employment.'

▸   (4) *Exception*: 'except this paragraph shall not apply to ... (A) any claim based upon ... a discretionary function ...

Minimal Contacts or Nexus

In the case *Perez v. The Bahamas*[275], the plaintiff claimed damages from the government of the Bahamas for the fact that his son was hurt by a gun shot fired from a patrol boat of the Bahamian naval police. The accident occurred less than half a mile off Great Isaac Bay in the Bahamas. The decisive question regarding §1605(a)(5) FSIA was the scope of the term 'in the United States' under the definition of §1603(c).[276] In fact, this provision grasps a part of governmental activity that doesn't fall under the 'commercial activity' exception, which is unequivocal under its terms. The court clearly stated that it is upon the plaintiff to prove the applicability of the noncommercial torts exception:

Perez v. The Bahamas

Plaintiff advances two interpretations in an effort to place event 'in the United States' for jurisdictional purposes. (...) The injury complained of, then, did not occur 'in the United States', and the exception in section 1605(a)(5) does not operate to remove The Bahamas' immunity from jurisdiction. Plaintiffs have failed to show how The Bahamas fits into any of the exceptions to the immunity granted to all foreign states by the FSIA. Accordingly, the court lacks jurisdiction over this action...[277]

This precedent was confirmed by the cases *McKeel v. Islamic Republic of Iran*[278] and *Olsen by Sheldon v. Government of Mexico*.[279] In the McKeel case, the Court of Appeals of the 9th Circuit stated on the appeal of hostages taken in the American embassy in Iran; the appeal was directed against the ruling of the district court that rejected the plaintiff's claims against both the United States and Iran. The suit was in particular about the question if the hostage taking occurred 'in the United States', §1603(c) FSIA. The court implicitly ruled that the evidential burden for this legal criterion was on the appellants.

McKeel v. Islamic Republic of Iran

Appellants argue that section 1603(c) should be interpreted to embrace 'all territory and waters' with respect to which the United States exercises any form of jurisdiction. Inasmuch as United States embassies are subject to the jurisdiction of the United States for certain purposes, appellants argue that events occuring at the embassies fall within the waiver of immunity contained in section 1605(a)(5).[280]

The same appellate court ruled even more clearly in the precedent *Olsen by Sheldon*. The suit was filed by children whose parents, prisoners held in Mexico, had been killed in the crash of a plane that had taken them from the United States to Mexico. The crash occurred during the landing on Tijuana airport, Mexico.[281] With regard to the criterion 'occuring in the United States', the court stated that it was sufficient when only a part of the tortious action was occuring in the United States:

> **Olsen by Sheldon v. Government of Mexico**
> In this case, appellants allege conduct constituting a single tort - the negligent piloting of the aircraft - which occurred in the United States. We are satisfied that appellants have alleged sufficient conduct occuring in the United States to bring this case within the non-commercial tort exception as expressed in section 1605(a)(5) and its legislative history.[282]

This line of reasoning is consistent in later case law, as for example in *Tigchon v. Island of Jamaica*[283], where the court held:

> **Tigchon v. Island of Jamaica**
> Plaintiff correctly notes that once a basis for jurisdiction is alleged, the burden of proof rests on the foreign state to demonstrate that immunity should be granted. However, plaintiff has not alleged the minimal facts necessary in order to establish a basis for jurisdiction.[284]

When I wrote my thesis, back in 1985-1987, the question who bears the burden of proof for the exceptions from sovereign immunity, as pronounced by the FSIA, was hardly ever tackled in the international law literature. In the article by Julia B. Brooke, that I mentioned earlier, the question was shortly mentioned in the notes.[285] The author defended the opinion that in certain cases, as for example the *Upton* precedent, courts tended to put the *persuasive or ultimate burden* upon the plaintiff.[286] As we have to distinguish between the question of the *jurisdiction* of the court, on one hand, and the *applicability vel non of an exception to sovereign immunity*, on the other, the author is for the least inaccurate in her article.[287] Contrary to the burden of proof regarding the basis of the sovereign immunity claim, which rests on the foreign state, the burden for proving all the facts regarding the jurisdiction of the court is upon the plaintiff. While subject matter jurisdiction is under the FSIA entangled with the question of immunity *vel non*, this is not the case for the conditions of *personal jurisdiction* where the burden if entirely upon the plaintiff. In a subsequent case that didn't concern the long-arm statute of the FSIA, but the *New York Civil Practice Law, §301*[288] which equally requires a nexus of the facts to territory of the United States; it's the famous *doing business clause*. In the case *Beacon Enterprises v. Menzies*[289], the plaintiff, a New York company filed suit against a Californian company for copyright violation.

The Court of Appeals clearly affirmed that the burden of proof for personal jurisdiction is upon the plaintiff.[290]

Causality

The causal link between the illicit action and the suffered damage is an essential criterion in the law of torts. This causal link, which links the action with the infringement of a legal right of the plaintiff, is thus part of substantive law, the law of torts. As such, the burden of proof is upon the plaintiff, as he must generally prove all the factual elements that the claim is based upon.

The FSIA does not expressly modify the underlying substantive law.[291] Thus, we have to distinguish between the evidence rules that govern the applicable substantive law from those that govern the claim of sovereign immunity. This distinction has shown to be relevant already when we examined the 'commercial activity' exception, §1605(a)(2) FSIA. The plaintiff who basis his claim upon a commercial contract with a foreign state, must prove the existence of this contract.[292] This is also valid for torts; the burden of proof is upon the plaintiff to prove the facts regarding the tort.[293]

However, there is a certain difference between §1605(a)(2) and §1605(a)(5) for in the latter section, there is an addition element, namely the *causality* requirement. But this difference does not influence the basic separation between procedural law and substantive law. Another argument confirms this result, that is, section 1605(a)(5) is drafted after the United States' Federal Tort Claims Act (FTCA).[294] This statute, which concerns tort actions against the United States government, contains literally the same causality clause, 28 U.S.C. §1346(b) FTCA.[295] As to this criterion, the burden of proof of the plaintiff has been stated in a number of precedents.[296]

Scope of Employment

The arguments brought forward under the criterion 'causality' are equally valid for this present criterion, with one distinction; here it is conceivable that the foreign state bears the burden of proof for rebutting the presumption that the tortious action was committed by the state's official or personnel 'within the scope of his office or employment'. This is so because it is obvious that the employer can much more easily prove this fact than any third party who generally ignores what exactly the professional relationship is between the foreign state as employer, and his employees. In *Castro v. Saudi Arabia*[297], that we discussed already earlier in this study, Saudi Arabia proved that the soldier had acted outside of his professional duties when he participated in road traffic as a civil person in the United States.[298] In such a case, Saudi Arabia argued, the United States government was responsible for the action.[299]

While the court held that '[t]he defendant has demonstrated that none of the exceptions in FSIA operate to deprive Saudi Arabia of its immunity from this court's jurisdiction[.]'[300], it would be erroneous to see an allocation of the burden of proof in this statement. Apart from the fact that the judge has not used the term 'burden of proof' at all, the fact that the foreign state has started to produce evidence is not enough for affirming a conclusive repartition of the burden of proof. In fact, the judge appreciated the evidence produced by the two parties; the burden of proof, as a risk of non-persuasion only comes to bear in a *non liquet* situation. We can thus admit that the only burden that was in play here was the evidential burden, and that when formulating its statement, the court had this burden in mind. However, the plaintiff did not contest the proof submitted by Saudi Arabia.[301] Thus, there was not litigation where the question of the burden of proof was to be asked, for it is to be asked only in case the evidence is contested by the other party.

A more recent precedent answers this question even more clearly. It is the case *Skeen v. Federative Republic of Brazil*[302], which concerned an assassination attempt against the plaintiff by Antonio Francisco da Silveira, Jr., the grandson of the Brazilian Ambassador to the United States. The fire was opened in front of a night club in Washington, D.C. The court held:

Skeen v. Federative Republic of Brazil

In order to invoke §1605(a)(5) in this case, plaintiff must demonstrate that da Silveira's actions were 'within the scope of his office or employment'. Section 1605(a)(5) is essentially a respondeat superior statute, providing an employer (the foreign state) with liability for certain tortious acts of its employees.[303]

Quoting the *Castro*[304] precedent, the court stated that the decision about the criterion 'scope of employment' depended on the applicable state law.[305] It is interesting to note that the judge compared the non-commercial tort exception with the Federal Tort Claims Act (FTCA) and wrote:

Skeen v. Federative Republic of Brazil

This is the choice of law rule applied under an analogous federal statute, the Federal Tort Claims Act (FTCA), which also provides for federal jurisdiction simply on the basis of the identity of the defendant, without regard to the existence of other federal issues in the case. Under the FTCA, the United States waives its sovereign immunity and accepts liability for the tortious acts of its officials committed within the scope of their employment. The statute indicates - and the courts have consistently held - that, with certain statutory exceptions, 28 U.S.C. §2680, the definition of 'scope of employment' under the FTCA must be determined by reference to state law.[306]

Applying the law of the state of Columbia, the court finally rejected the lawsuit with the argument that Silveira had acted *outside the scope of his office or employment* with the Brazilian embassy in the United States.[307] The developments of the court for §1605(a)(5) regarding the analogous federal statement indeed were leading also to an analogous treatment of the burden of proof; for under the FTCA, regarding the criterion 'scope of employment', in §1346(b) FTCA, there is general agreement that the burden if upon the plaintiff for demonstrating that the state employee had acted within the scope of his employment with the United States government.[308] It is also interesting to see that the court found the scope of responsibility under both statutes 'nearly identical'.[309]

Exception

It flows from the drafting technique of this section that the burden of proof for the exception is upon the foreign state. In general, according to statute construction, the exception of an exception recurs to the general rule. Moreover, this argument is confirmed by §§2680(a),(h) FTCA[310], analogous provision, clarifying that the exceptions from the exception are construed as affirmative defenses; accordingly, the burden of proof is upon the American government, for proving the factual elements of those defenses.[311]

There are also precedents regarding the FSIA; however, in these cases the burden of proof of the foreign state for the exceptions from the exception have not yet explicitly clarified by the judges, as this was the case for the FTCA. Nonetheless, the analogous character of both statutes in this respect is so striking that the burden of proof situation is almost certainly the same. Before we are going to discuss these cases, it should be clarified what American law understands under a 'discretionary function', §2680(a) FTCA and §1605(a)(5) FSIA? In the leading case *Dalehite v. United States*[312], the Supreme Court interpreted the term within the framework of §2680(a) FTCA. In the syllabus[313] of this decision, the long developments of the Supreme Court[314] were condensed as follows:

Dalehite v. United States (S.Ct.)

The 'discretionary function or duty' that cannot form a basis for suit under the Act includes more than the initiation of programs and activities; it also includes determinations made by executives or administrators in establishing plans, specifications or schedules of operations. Acts of subordinates in carrying out the operations of government in accordance with official directions cannot be actionable.[315]

An indication for the burden of pleading, the evidential burden, regarding §1605(a)(5) FSIA, is to be found in *Letelier v. Republic of Chile*[316], an action where the relatives of Orlando Letelier, Chile's Minister of Foreign Affairs at the time, claimed damages for the assassination of Letelier through a car bomb in the United States.[317] The district court held:

Letelier v. Republic of Chile

Subject to the exclusion of these discretionary acts defined in subsection (A) and the specific causes of action enumerated in subsection (B), neither of which have been invoked by the Republic of Chile ... [318]

The court denied sovereign immunity for Chile after having examined §1605(a)(5)(A), (B), arguing that a 'discretionary function' was not to be admitted in the present case.

Letelier v. Republic of Chile

Whatever policy may exist for a foreign country, it has no 'discretion' to perpetrate conduct designed to result in the assassination of an individual or individuals, action that is clearly contrary to the precepts of humanity as recognized in both national and international law. Accordingly there should be no 'discretion' within the meaning of section 1605(a)(5)(A) to order or to aid in an assassination and were it to be demonstrated that a foreign state has undertaken any such act in this country, that foreign state could not be accorded sovereign immunity under subsection (a) for any tort claims resulting from its conduct. As a consequence, the Republic of Chile cannot claim sovereign immunity under the Foreign Sovereign Immunities Act for its alleged involvement in the deaths of Orlando Letelier and Ronni Moffitt.[319]

In *Letelier II*[320], the court pronounced itself with regard to the evidence requirements for a *default judgment* under §1608(e) FSIA. The court's developments here are interesting for they reveal which specific requirements must be met under this section and who bears the burden of proof for the factual basis of those requirements. The court concluded that the burden of proof is upon the plaintiff and that he must thus establish 'his claim or right to relief by evidence satisfactory to the court.'

Letelier v. Republic of Chile (Letelier II)

2. Pursuant to the dictates of 28 U.S.C. §1608(e), plaintiffs have produced satisfactory evidence to establish that on or about September 21, 1976, employees of the Republic of Chile, acting within the scope of their employment and at the direction of Chilean officials who were acting within the scope of their office, committed tortious acts of assault and battery and negligent transportation and detonation of explosives that were the proximate cause of the deaths of Orlando Letelier and Ronni Moffitt. Accordingly, a judgment by default as to these claims will be entered in favor of plaintiffs and against the Republic of Chile.[321]

In a more recent precedent, *Olsen by Sheldon v. Government of Mexico*[322], which we discussed already earlier on, the court ruled specifically with regard of what it called the 'discretionary function exception', §1605(a)(5)(A) FSIA.[323]

Olsen by Sheldon v. Government of Mexico (9th Cir.)

Section 1605(a)(5)(A) provides an exception to noncommercial tort jurisdiction for claims based upon a state's discretionary function. Mexico seeks to bring the airplane crash within this exception by contending that the conduct which led to the crash was discretionary.[324]

Apart from the fact that in both these cases, the courts mentioned the advantage the foreign state has under this section, that is, to plead the 'discretionary function' as an affirmative defense, in the present case, the comparison that the Court of Appeals makes with the FTCA is relevant and important as to the allocation of the burden of proof:

Olsen by Sheldon v. Government of Mexico (9th Cir.)

The FSIA provides considerable guidance as to which sets or decisions constitute discretionary functions. Not only does the language of the FSIA discretionary function exception replicate that of the Federal Tort Claims Act (FTCA), 28 U.S.C. §2680(a), but the legislative history of the FSIA, in explaining section 1605(a)(5)(A), directs us to the FTCA. House Report at 21. To determine the scope of the discretionary function exception of the FSIA, we therefore turn to the interpretation given the similar FTCA provision.[325]

The Court of Appeals thus compared the discretionary function under the FTCA with the one in the FSIA, applying the jurisprudence referring to the FTCA to interpret the FSIA.[326] In fact, the two statutes are not only similar from an editorial point of view, but also with regard to their legislative objective. Congress' intention to model section 1605(a)(5) FSIA after the FTCA was clearly expressed in the legislative history. In addition, the case law that interprets the exceptions, §§1605(a)(5)(A),(B) regularly references precedents that were ruled under the respective provisions of the FTCA. Hence, the allocation of the burden of proof that was established under the FTCA can practically be applied to the FSIA, with regard to the factual basis of §§1605(a)(5)(A),(B) FSIA. This was confirmed by the precedents examined here, and regarding the burden of pleadings or evidential burden, with regard to the criterion of 'discretionary function'.

Conclusion

The examination of sections 1605(a)(4) and 1605(a)(5) FSIA confirms the conclusion that we have already taken earlier on in this study. The burden of proof of the foreign state for its immunity defense is limited in the sense that the foreign state, starting to produce evidence, is required to establish a *prima facie case* as a basis for its immunity claim.

Under §1605(a)(5) FSIA, the burden of proof is upon the plaintiff for demonstrating the causality link between the tortious act and that damage suffered, as well as for the criterion that the employee of the foreign state was acting 'within the scope of his office or employment'.

It follows from this framework, and the drafting technique employed in the FSIA, that the exceptions from the exception, §§1605(a)(5)(A),(B) are affirmative defenses where the burden of proof lies upon the foreign state to demonstrate the applicability of one of those exceptions. This systematic argument is confirmed by the analogous statute, the Federal Tort Claims Act (FTCA), §2680(a),(h), referenced not only by the legal materials to the FSIA, but also by federal jurisprudence interpreting §1605(a)(5) FSIA.

To summarize, the repartition of the burden of proof under section 1605(a)(5) FSIA is as follows. The plaintiff bears the burden of proof for:

▸ Minimal contacts;

▸ Causality between the tortious act and the damage suffered;

▸ The employee having acted within the 'scope of his office or employment'.

The burden of proof lies upon the foreign state for the exceptions (A) and (B) to §1605(a)(5) FSIA. With regard to §1605(a)(4), the burden of proof lies entirely with the plaintiff for proving the minimal contacts or nexus requirement, 'in the United States' and for the material criteria, 'rights in property acquired by succession or gift' or 'rights in immovable property.'

CHAPTER SIX

The Core Areas of Sovereign Immunity

Overview

In this part of the study, we shall have a more detailed regard upon the requirements that American federal jurisprudence has found to apply regarding the *prima facie case* to be established by the foreign state defendant of any action that involves foreign sovereign immunity litigation, because the foreign state has claimed such immunity. We will focus particularly upon those actions where jurisdiction was denied, and will try to classify those actions because the analysis will reveal that there are several core areas of sovereign behavior where federal courts have shown to be particularly reluctant to affirm jurisdiction under §1605(a)(2) FSIA *(commercial activity exception)*. Contrary to cases where such commercial activity was affirmed by the courts and where the judges could rely on the text of §1603(d) FSIA or the legislative history[327], the cases we are going to examine, present a different set of facts at issue.

To give the reader a clearer picture of the distinction I wish to establish, let me shortly review what we have in part already seen earlier in this study, but this time under a slightly different perspective. To begin with, the most clear-cut cases have been shown to be those actions that were dealing with what has been called the 'Nigerian cement catastrophe', both in the United States and the United Kingdom, but also in Germany and other countries.[328] American federal courts, in these affairs, have all rejected the argument submitted by Nigeria that the breach of those purchasing contracts had been effected in Nigeria's governmental authority, that is, to prevent a national economic catastrophe. The courts also have denied the alleged 'military character' of the utilization of the cement, that is, for building and upgrading the country's infrastructure. Nigeria also forwarded the view that, as the actions regularly were based upon letters of credit issued by the *Central Bank of Nigeria*, this bank, because of its governmental authority, as per se immune from all actions. This argument was overall rejected, and was actually a quite twisted one, as of course, it's not the character of the person or *persona* that acts behind the screens that is the divider under the restricted immunity doctrine, but the character of the *activity* that lies before the court and that gave rise to the action. And in all those cases, the commercial character of the purchasing contracts concluded between the Nigerian government and private merchants was affirmed by the courts - and Nigeria had to pay after all.[329]

Regarding other precedents where the commercial activity exception was affirmed, most of which I have discussed earlier on in this study, American federal courts have been particularly lucid to detect the often hidden *governmental portmanteaux* behind obvious financially lucrative business transactions conducted by foreign states, and unveiled it as a *mask* that served to hide the commercial character of those transactions. For example, in *United Euram v. U.S.S.R.*[330], the Soviet Union had rendered remunerated services within the United States under a bilateral cultural treaty, which were qualified by the court as commercial in character.[331]

Another interesting case is *Jackson v. People's Republic of China*[332], where the judge qualified bonds issued by the Chinese government for building railways in the United States, back in 1911, as commercial, despite a 'statement of interest' issued by the American government which claimed 'to set aside default judgment against China.[333]

Despite this general trend in American post-FSIA case law to interpret 'commercial activity' in a broad manner, there is a subtler effort to be made out, when one looks closely at it, to *preserve for foreign states a certain core area of governmental action* that is and shall be untouched by the restrictive immunity doctrine. These areas could be classified as follows, while they slightly overlap:

- ▸ *a) Foreign Affairs*

- ▸ *b) Interior Affairs*

  - • aa) Police and National Security Activities
  - • bb) Protection of National Resources

- *c) Budgetary Activity*

- *d) National Defense*

Foreign Affairs

Just a year after the FSIA entered into force[334], a district court rendered an important judgment mentioned earlier, *Yessenin-Volpin v. Novosti Press Agency, Tass.*[335] This interesting suit was improperly filed to the United States Supreme Court, from where the action was removed to the competent district court[336] under the terms of §1441(d) FSIA.[337] The suit was filed as a libel action for alleged defamations against the plaintiff that were published in February 1976, and thus before the FISA had entered into force, in the NOVOSTI magazines *Sowjetunion Heute*, and *Krasnaya Zvesda*, and the TASS magazines *Izvestia*, and *Sovietskaya Russiya*, that regularly circulate in the United States. As already pointed out earlier in this study, NOVOSTI and TASS were qualified by the court as *agencies or instrumentalities of a foreign state* under §1603(b) FSIA. The plaintiff invoked *clause 3* of §1605(a)(2) FSIA and the court examined if the publishing of the articles was *'based upon a commercial activity carried on in the United States by the foreign state'.*[338]

The plaintiff based his argument upon the fact that in NOVOSTI's statutes, this agency was assigned the competence to carry out various commercial tasks for the Soviet state within the United States. The court argued that it was not the status of the agency that was the decisive criterion under the Act, but solely the nature of the activity in question.[339] Consequently, the court had to decide which was actually the activity that the litigation was about, for in that case, this was *not* obvious, as in so many others.[340] The court did not deny that NOVOSTI 'does engage in commercial activity' because 'it sells articles to foreign media.'[341] But it was not that activity of the press agencies that the litigation was really about.

Yessenin-Volpin v. Novosti Press Agency, Tass.

The relevant issue in this case, however, is not whether Novosti or Tass engage in commercial activities but whether their alleged libels were 'in connection with a commercial activity'.[342]

In the following developments, the judge sustained the view that the publishing of the articles was actually a governmental activity; these rather lengthy developments can be summarized in three main arguments.

(1) The four magazines in which the alleged defamations were published, were all official publications of the Soviet state.[343] This was the result of the court evaluating the evidence submitted by the agencies, to make their *prima facie case* of sovereign immunity. The judge referred to the affidavit swearing that the header title of the journal *Sowjetunion Heute* indicated that it was a publication by the press department of the embassy of the Soviet Union in Germany, in collaboration with NOVOSTI.[344] The publication *Krasnaya Zvesda* was equally identified, in this affidavit, as being the central organ of the Soviet Ministry of Defense, and *Izvestia* turned out to be published by the Supreme Soviet of the USSR.[345] Finally, the magazine *Sovietskaya Russiya* describes itself as the organ of the central committee of the Soviet communist party, the Supreme Soviet and the Council of Ministers.[346]

(2) The second argument the court used to affirm a governmental character of the activity in question was that the libels appeared in all four publications at the same time.

Yessenin-Volpin v. Novosti Press Agency, Tass.

Thus, by collaborating in the publication of stories in these journals, Novosti, as well as Tass, was engaged not in 'commercial activity' but in acts of intra-governmental cooperation of a type which apparently constitutes much of Novosti's (and presumably more of Tass's) activity.[347]

In addition, the court underlined that this activity was not related to any contract, nor any possible arrangement with a foreign political party, as such arrangements, according to the judge, are 'commercial in most circumstances'.[348]

(3) In the third argument, a development of the first actually, but more rigorously expressed, the judge considered the 'cooperative relationship' of those four agencies, because the libels were published in

exactly the same manner in all four publications. That is why the judge saw in this kind of collaboration an intention and held that the libels were actually 'an official commentary of the Soviet government[349], 'an activity whose essential nature is public or governmental'[350] The court's reasoning was thus systematically correct in that the judge scrutinized the nature of the activity in question, under §1603(d) FSIA. For these reasons, the court rejected the actions against TASS and NOVOSTI.

Moreover, it is to be noted that the non-commercial tort exception, §1605(a)(5), discussed earlier in this study, expressly excludes libel actions. This was confirmed by the district court in the present case.[351]

The same district court, but another judge, also decided the case *Carey v. National Oil Corporation*.[352] I need to briefly relate the rather complex factual background.[353] NEPCO acquired, through a complicated network of transactions[354], raw oil from the California Asiatic Oil Company (CALASIA), which had a drilling concession in Libya. In September 1973, Libya nationalized 51% of the drilling concessions, among them CALASIA's.[355] As a result, the 'Chevron Oil Trading Company' (COT) did not fulfill its contractual obligations with PETCO, invoking the 'force majeure' clause contained in the contract. In March 1970, Libya created NOC, a state-owned company, and transferred the nationalized concessions to it.

Regarding the political background of the nationalizations, the judge painted what he called 'the petroleum picture in the Middle East'[356], a picture that was quite tainted by the outbreak of the Kippur war in October 1973, that gave rise to a total embargo of the petroleum producing countries against the United States, the Netherlands, and the Bahamas.[357] All these actions were rejected, for different motifs, but by overall affirming the jurisdictional immunity of both NOC and Libya. The court held that '[i]it is beyond cavil that these actions by Libya were not part of a commercial undertaking; rather, they were deliberate weapons of foreign policy, aimed at influencing the conduct of other nations, or at least punishing undesirable conduct.'[358]

The judge thus ruled not only about the nationalization itself, but also what relationship can possibly be seen between this governmental activity and the foreign policy of Libya. It is interesting in this context that the judge saw something like an *intentionality* here from the side of Libya to use those drastic measures as some kind of weapon. I think there can be hardly an activity by a foreign state where the *core sphere of national sovereignty* is to that point clear-cut and visible, which is why I believe the court made that very transparent in the otherwise brilliant judgment.

This somewhat 'protective' attitude of the court here regarding the core area of Libya's sovereignty means, if one agrees or not, that in the future foreign states will try to construe 'sovereign purpose' as a basis for their sovereign immunity defense, which could in principle endanger the restrictive immunity approach that the FSIA has taken. The motivation of a government, or their intentions, was not to be considered, in the first place, by §1603(d) FSIA. Even if such a motivation or intention is governmental, it is a purpose, and should not be considered, as this section clearly states that the qualification of the activity as private or governmental should be according to its nature, 'rather than by reference to its purpose.'

These are leading cases in a domain that is still on shaky ground after the enactment of the FSIA; they may signal a certain tendency in American federal jurisprudence to henceforth apply the Act rather conservatively and to give to foreign states a certain margin for forwarding subtly political motivations and intentions, when those were painting the background of the commercial activity itself.

I may for that reason, as this jurisprudence is post-FSIA, have a short look how this would look under the legal situation prior to the FSIA. The court stated in the eighth action that 'nationalization is a quintessentially sovereign act, never viewed as having commercial character' and referred to *Victory Transport Inc. v. Comisaría General de Abastecimientos Y Transportes*[359], where the Court of Appeals of the 2nd Circuit already applied, back in 1964, the restrictive theory of sovereign immunity. The appellee, a division of the Spanish Ministry of Commerce had chartered a vessel from the appellant for transporting wheat to Spain that this Ministry had purchased in the United States. Because of lacking safety in Spanish ports, the vessel was damaged. The court, considering it significant that the State Department had not filed a suggestion for granting immunity, rejected the immunity claim by reference to the *Tate Letter (1952)*, '… unless it is plain that the activity in question falls within one of the categories of strictly political or public acts about which sovereigns have traditionally been quite sensitive.' Then the court explains:

> **Victory Transport Inc. v. Comisaría General de Abastecimientos Y Transportes**
>
> Such acts are limited to the following categories:
> (1) internal administrative acts, such as expulsion of an alien;
> (2) legislative acts, such as nationalization;
> (3) acts concerning the armed forces;
> (4) acts concerning diplomatic activity;
> (5) public loans.[360]

The court further stated that the chartering of the vessel for transporting the wheat 'is not a strictly public or political act.'[361]

It is obvious that a nationalization falls under the second category of this schema. There are several reasons why for this study, I have chosen a slightly different classification. In addition, it has to be seen that the court's schema here is not complete, as foreign policy is not mentioned, and there is overlapping in that the third category could well have been merged with the first. And while a nationalization was always considered as a purely governmental act, one could imagine foreign policy regulations that could fall within the second category, and that are not nationalizations *sensu strictu*.

In addition, the fifth category is not anymore considered sacrosanct and protected. The court took reference to Jean-Flavien Lalive's article[362] who, in turn, seems to have overtaken the schema from Lauterpacht. In fact, the classification was published, for the first time, in the article by Lauterpacht, *The Problem of Jurisdictional Immunities of*

Foreign States (1951).[363] Regarding the fifth category, Lalive notes at p. 286 that 'it's a delicate question while the arguments against immunity seem to prevail in principle'. As for the United States, after *Jackson v. People's Republic of China*[364], a case I discussed in detail earlier in this study, and where the governmental character of Chinese government bonds that were emitted back in 1911 for construing railways and public buildings in the United States was clearly denied, the fifth category can be seen obsoleted in the meantime.

Interior Affairs

Police Actions

In *Perez v. The Bahamas*[365], already discussed earlier on, where the action was about a shot fired from a boat of the Bahamian naval police against the vessel of the plaintiff, the district court stated:

Perez v. The Bahamas

The commercial character of an activity is to be determined by the nature of the act or course of activity and not by reference to its purpose, 28 U.S.C. §1603. Police enforcement of Bahamian fishing law does not become commercial because it may have some commercial purpose or goal.[366]

In fact, the ultimate reasons behind police actions can be of various kinds, but the action remains an action that is by its very nature governmental and public in nature.

The other action that falls in this present category, is a case ruled by the Court of the Appeals of the 5th Circuit, *Arango v. Guzman Travel Advisors*[367], where DOMINICANA[368], the national airline of the Dominican Republic, equally a defendant of the action, had collaborating in repelling the Arango family from entering the country for a 'package tour', as they figured on a blacklist of 'undesirable foreigners'; they were forcibly placed on board the flight the Dominican flight from Santo Domingo to San Juan, Puerto Rico.[369] The judge strictly distinguished between this 'involuntary re-routing', on one hand, and the breach of the 'package tour' contract, on the other.[370] Apparently, the court stated about two different questions:

(i) the governmental character of the repulsion taken by the Dominican immigration;

(ii) the governmental character of the assistance DOMINICANA gave to this police action.

ad i)

There was no doubt for the judge as to the governmental character of the expulsion action itself, as it was carried out by Dominican immigration 'pursuant to that country's laws.'

ad ii)

This second question is way more interesting as the answer may not be as clear-cut. The judge made a fine distinction here between the normal commercial activities carried out by the airline staff, and the *exceptional aiding in the expulsion action*, where he saw the personnel being compelled to act jointly, as this was a governmental or police action where, in their quality as government employees, they had no right to refuse collaborating and thus had to give their helping hand. For that reason, the judge concluded that also DOMINICANA acted pursuant to Dominican Republic law enforcement, in that particular action. As the FSIA might not have foreseen such a case, or simply left the question open, the precedent is very important.

Actions for the Protection of Natural Resources

Under this category, there is an equally important precedent to report and discuss, *International Association of Machinists and Aerospace Workers (IAM) v. The Organization of the Petroleum Exporting Countries (OPEC)*.[371] The facts are relatively simple. The plaintiff, an international trade union, pursued OPEC for damages, arguing that OPEC's crude oil fix price policy was a violation of American antitrust laws, particularly §1 Sherman Act. I will of course not discuss in this study if that was substantially the case, as we are only interested in the procedural aspect, that is, if OPEC's fix price policy was to be considered a commercial or governmental activity.[372] With regard to OPEC's immunity claim, the court, after having reviewed the legal materials, states: 'If the activity is one in which only a sovereign can engage, the activity is non-commercial. These standards are somewhat nebulous, however, in the context of a particular factual situation.'[373]

Right at the start of his developments, the judge took a specific direction for the arguments to follow, by interpreting the 'commercial activity' criterion in the following manner:

IAM v. OPEC

It has been suggested that in determining whether to define a particular act narrowly or broadly, the court should be guided by the legislative intent of the FSIA, to keep our courts away from those areas that touch very closely upon the sensitive nerves of foreign countries. This Court agrees that this 'commercial activity' should be defined narrowly.[374]

After this point of departure, the court evaluated the nature of the activity in question, by appreciating the *specific evidence* presented, rather then ruling on a 'generalized view of the evidence'[375] and concluded:

IAM v. OPEC

From the evidence presented to this Court, it is clear that the nature of the activity engaged in by each of these OPEC member countries is the establishment by a sovereign state of the terms and conditions for the removal of the prime natural resources - to wit, crude oil - from its territory.[376]

It is of interest to have a closer look at the evidence the court was examining in this case, for it has played a decisive role for the final judgment, and the court did not take it easy to peruse it. First of all, it has to be seen that the court has stated *against the evidence rule* established in the legal materials.

IAM v. OPEC

[F]or this court to have subject matter jurisdiction the defendant must show that the activities engaged in by the defendants are 'commercial activities'.[377]

Apart from the obvious redactional error in that statement and the fact that the court can only have meant to say that the 'plaintiff must show', it is rather the foreign state defendant of the action who must establish *prima face evidence* for the fact that the activity in question had a public, governmental character. In fact, there are only two logical possibilities to resolve the burden of proof question, it's that either the burden is upon the foreign state to demonstrate that the activity in question was governmental, or the burden is upon the plaintiff to establish evidence that the activity in question was commercial. Obviously, the FSIA chose the first alternative, in that the foreign state has the right to begin with producing evidence, and the jurisprudence confirmed it over and over.

Here, the situation was awkwardly that as the court was in error about the repartition of the burden of proof, and accordingly it did not call upon OPEC to start with producing evidence that the oil price fixing activity was of a governmental nature, but in the contrary the plaintiff who presented expert evidence to the court to demonstrate that said activity was commercial in nature. However, the court rejected the experts, questioning the expertise of the experts[378], and nominated *sua sponte* two experts[379] that it gave 'complete reliance' because of their academic standing and experience.[380] This means more in detail that:

(i) the court based its decision only on the expert evidence produced by its own nominated experts, and not on the evidence of the experts that the plaintiff had proposed;

(ii) the court justified its ruling to grant OPEC immunity on the doctrine of 'permanent sovereignty over natural resources', saying that such authority was a principle of international law.

The Price Fixing Procedure

The court did a thorough examination of OPEC's raw oil price fixing procedure and considered as shown by the evidence the fact that all member states built consensus about what is called the *government take*.[381] This term designates the amount the governments obtain for each barrel of sold crude oil that is extracted within their territorial boundaries. In the beginning, the states received that take in form of a tax, later by *buyback*, amount that the drilling company had to pay. In our days, the government take is effected as a tax, through the very price fixing procedure, and by the control of the production. Within this mechanism, the price fixation was not the most important element, according to the court, but only the most popular aspect of it. This system was rather founded upon the capacity and the will of the OPEC member states to control and govern the whole process of raw oil production.[382] The court concluded:

IAM v. OPEC

The control over a nation's natural resources stems from the nature of sovereignty. By necessity and by traditional recognition, each nation is its own master in respect to its physical attributes. The defendants' control over their oil resources is an especially sovereign function because oil, as their primary, if not sole, revenue-producing resource, is crucial to the welfare of their nations' peoples.[383]

The plaintiff, quoting the *House Report*, forwarded the argument that OPEC's price fixing procedure was to be seen as a commercial activity; in this process of commercial gain in the patrimonial interest of the states was lying the primary character of the activity, which is why it had to be qualified as commercial. The court rejected this argument, stating that such a general view of the evidence at court was inappropriate and that the activity at issue had to be identified first of all:

IAM v. OPEC

While it may be true that through their activities as partial or total owners of these companies, the defendant nations do engage in commercial activities, this does not mean, and the legislative intent does not support the conclusion, that all activities, even those remotely connected with these companies, are necessarily commercial. The fact that a nation owns and operates an airline company, does not mean that all government activities regulating the use of airspace, or the ingress and egress of airplanes to and from the nation's airports, are commercial activities. Accordingly, we must look to the specific activities in which the defendants engage.[384]

A clear distinction had to be made, according to the court, between the 'proprietary' activities of the states and those that are of a governmental character. The activities of OPEC, the court held, were to be qualified as governmental by nature. The court supported this argument also by the fact that the sales conditions for the crude oil were fixated long before its extraction; for that reason a patrimonial interest could not result from it. In addition, even if one would assert such an interest, the court concluded, the governmental nature of the activities would not change, just because the modalities of how the activities were executed had changed.[385]

Standards of International Law

The court examined *Resolution 1803* of the United Nations' General Assembly and referred to a number of others.[386] But the judge did not bother about the juridical validity of such resolutions, in general, nor of Resolution 1803, in particular[387], but stated:

IAM v. OPEC

In determining whether the activities of the OPEC members are governmental or commercial in nature, the Court can and should examine the standards recognized under international law. The United Nations, with the concurrence of the United States, has repeatedly recognized the principle that a sovereign state has the sole power to control its natural resources.[388]

This a bit superficial conclusion does not really come as a surprise in this judgment that obviously was motivated by political reasons. The apodictic character of the verdict was to be seen already at the start of the judgment, when the court defined 'commercial activity' in a rather restrictive manner, looking at things in a way to be sensibly hostile to the wordings and the intention of the FSIA and its legal materials. Then, a redactional error, a wrong repartition of the burden of proof, and accordingly, a wrong manner to handle the evidential burden, the reject of the expert evidence produced by the plaintiff without giving a substantial reason for doing so, and finally the summoning of sources of international law that can be said to be controversial to this day, and that are recognized only on the basis of the political value, all this makes for a judgment that is on rather shaky ground. And yet, despite these weaknesses in the judgment itself, the subsequent jurisprudence seems to have fully accepted the direction that was taken in this leading case, and seems to bother little about the procedural details I was mentioning here.[389] This is to be explained with the sensibly political aspect of these litigations.

The Court of Appeals Judgment

The verdict was confirmed by the Court of Appeals of the 9th Circuit[390], while the question was looked at from a different legal point of view: the Court of Appeals argued it through with the *act of state doctrine* as the legal hanger, but came to the same result. This is interesting to note as the act of state doctrine is another legal construct than foreign sovereign immunity. It is namely a way of dealing with the applicable *substantial law*, not a procedural defense such as sovereign immunity. The Court of Appeals explained the difference as follows:

IAM v. OPEC (9th Cir.)

The doctrine of sovereign immunity is similar to the act of state doctrine in that it also represents the need to respect the sovereignty of foreign states. The two doctrines differ, however, in significant respects. The law of sovereign immunity goes to the jurisdiction of the court. The act of state doctrine is not jurisdictional (...). Rather, it is a prudential doctrine designed to avoid judicial action in sensitive areas. Sovereign immunity is a princi-

ple of international law, recognized in the United States by statute. It is the states themselves, as defendants, who may claim
sovereign immunity. The act of state doctrine is a domestic legal
principle, arising from the peculiar role of American courts. It
recognizes not only the sovereignty of foreign states, but also
the spheres of power of the co-equal branches of our government. Thus a private litigant may raise the act of state doctrine,
even when no sovereign state is a party of the action. (…) The
act of state doctrine is apposite whenever the federal courts
must question the legality of the sovereign acts of foreign
states.[391]

The Court of Appeals underlined the fact that the two doctrines
are independent and that the FSIA only rules the sovereign immunity
defense as a procedural handicap, but doesn't touch the act of state
doctrine. That is why the Court of Appeals validated the *motivation* of
the OPEC member states for price fixing under the act of state doctrine
because, obviously, such motivation would not be a valid criterion under the FSIA, where only the *nature* of the activity in question is to consider under §1603(d).[392] In my view, such an argument appears *construed* after all, as all those reasonings, valid as they are, were provided
by the law giver when drafting the FSIA and its legal materials, and it is
therefore a valid question, and was asked in the literature, if not the
restrictive sovereign immunity doctrine, as it is subject of the immunities act, has not substantially modified, if not overruled the act of state
doctrine? I cannot give an answer here to that interesting question
because it's outside of this research topic and thus not part of this
monograph. However, it has to be seen that this question has been
fertile and the output that followed up to *IAM v. OPEC* in the literature
is considerable.[393] However, it is interesting what the Court of Appeals
stated with regard to the sovereign immunity question:

IAM v. OPEC (9th Cir.)
While we do not apply the doctrine of sovereign immunity, its
elements remain relevant to our discussion of the act of state
doctrine.[394]

Despite the fact that the appellant contested the governmental character of OPEC's price fixing activity, the Court of Appeals limited itself to report the arguments produced by the district court, without criticizing them, but also, without approving of them. The *writ of certiorari* against the Court of Appeals judgment was rejected by the United States Supreme Court.[395] The OPEC precedent was cited in *Matter of Sedco, Inc.*[396], equally a case regarding crude oil, where the plaintiff, owner of a drilling platform, filed a suit for exoneration and limitation of responsibility resulting from an oil spill disaster against *Petróleos Mexicanos* (PEMEX), created by the Mexican government back in 1938 as a government agency responsible for the exploitation and the development of the hydrocarbon resources of that country.[397] PEMEX had used the drilling platform for effecting the extraction of crude oil and claimed sovereign immunity, and the court stated about the repartition of the burden of proof.

Matter of Sedco, Inc.

Once a basis for jurisdiction is alleged, the burden of proof rests on that foreign state to demonstrate that immunity should be granted.[398]

However, the court only ruled on questions of law, that is, the qualification of the activity in question as governmental or commercial. As in the OPEC case, the court first identified which actually was the activity that was substance of the litigation:

Matter of Sedco, Inc.

Undeniably, Pemex, as a national oil company, engages in a substantial amount of commercial activity. (...) However, this Court must focus on the specific acts made the basis of the present lawsuit in applying the FSIA. It is whether these particular acts constituted or were in connection with commercial activity, regardless of the defendant's general commercial or governmental nature that is in issue.[399]

Distinguishing the case from cases where the commercial nature of the activity was rather obvious[400], the court concluded:

Matter of Sedco, Inc.

That is to say that every act done by a foreign state which could be done by a private citizen in the United States is 'commercial activity' under §1605(a)(2). Such a world view unrealistically denies the existence of other types of governments and economic systems.[401]

After having scrutinized the precedents *Arango* and *Yessenin-Volpin*, the judge stated that the existence of a contractual relationship, even if it was not the essential denominator of the action, was often an indicator for the commercial nature of the activity.[402]

The court stated that PEMEX was totally dependent on its government shadow. For example, the drilling dates were determined long in advance by a governmental regulation[403] and PEMEX had no influence on Mexican petroleum policy, as this was made 'by higher levels of the government.'[404] Under Mexican law, PEMEX had the competence to handle information regarding natural resources and to draft programs for executing the governmental resource development policy, which is renewed and updated every six years by various ministries, and approved by the President of Mexico. In addition, there was no contractual relationship with American companies regarding the extraction of the crude oil, nor with regard to the usage of the drilling platform. Thus, the court concluded:

Matter of Sedco, Inc.

Acting by authority of Mexican law within its national territory and in inter-governmental cooperation with other branches of the Mexican government, Pemex was not engaged in commercial activity as contemplated by Congress in the FSIA when the IXTOC I well was drilled.[405]

Finally, the court, taking reference to OPEC, supported its conclusion further with the argument that also in the present case, the crude oil was a natural resource for Mexico that is why the activities in question were of a public, governmental nature.

Matter of Sedco, Inc.

The court must regard carefully a sovereign's conduct with respect to its natural wealth. A very basic attribute of sovereignty is control over its mineral resources and short of actually selling these resources on the world market, decisions and conduct concerning them are uniquely governmental in nature.[406]

The last precedent to report and discuss under the present category concerns the exportation of animals that were considered a natural resource of a country, *Mol, Inc. v. People's Republic of Bangladesh*.[407] The plaintiff, an American corporation, filed a law suit for damages against Bangladesh for breach of a licensing agreement regarding the capturing and exportation of Rhesus monkeys from Bangladesh to the United States. As Bangladesh did not enter an appearance, the plaintiff asked for a *default judgment* under §1608(e) FSIA, but the court rejection that motion with the argument that Bangladesh was immune from suit both under the sovereign immunity doctrine, and the act of state doctrine.[408]

The facts are quite interesting. Since India put an embargo on the exportation of rhesus, Bangladesh became the main exporter of these monkeys that are traded on the world market for ending up in laboratories of various kinds, for the purpose of scientific research. In 1976, the plaintiff obtained a licensing agreement from Bangladesh for capturing and exporting those monkeys; however the license was given under certain conditions. If the licensee did not act according to these conditions, Bangladesh had the right to revoke the license. In 1979, Bangladesh revoked the license, arguing the licensee had acted contrary to two conditions in the license.[409]

We have seen earlier in this study, that the burden of proof is upon the plaintiff for the conditions of a default judgment under §1608(d)

FSIA. That means a default judgment shall by rendered by a district court only if the claimant establishes his claim or right to relief by evidence satisfactorily to the court. The court argued that this severe burden of proof had political reasons, in that it was set 'to prevent unwarranted intrusions upon the diplomatic efforts of the United States by private litigants.[410] Despite the fact that the plaintiff had produced affidavits and documents in support of its motion, the judge concluded in accordance with the suggestion of the State Department, acting as *amicus curiae*.[411] The State Department had argued that the court didn't have jurisdiction over the case as the activity in question was governmental for reasons of the 'protection of natural resources of a foreign state'. Regarding *clause 3*, §1605(a)(2), that we discussed earlier in this study, the court argued:

Mol, Inc. v. People's Republic of Bangladesh

I conclude that Bangladesh's granting of a License to plaintiff in this case was not a 'commercial activity', but a sovereign act not subject to suit in the United States courts. The granting of such a license as part of a comprehensive regulation of wildlife under the police power is an action in which the sovereign power is essential. Likewise the granting of an export license, like the power to exclude imports or regulate exports in general, is a power possessed only by sovereigns, not private parties. I find that the activity in suit here is by its 'nature' sovereign activity.[412]

The plaintiff objected that the license had after all the objective to bring Bangladesh a commercial profit or material gain and that for that reason it was of a commercial nature. But the report reply that '[t]he purpose of the activity is irrelevant under the statute[.]'[413] and concluded:

Mol, Inc. v. People's Republic of Bangladesh

If I were allowed to consider the purpose of the activity, it would clearly indicate that the activity was based upon the 'public interest' as perceived by the government of Bangladesh, to conserve wildlife and establish closer control over the exportation of

Bangladeshi species. This is true even if Bangladesh receives revenue from the License. The power to tax, or to power to levy a duty upon exports or imports, is a sovereign function designed solely to bolster the fisc by generating state income; yet these activities do not thereby become 'commercial'. Even if Bangladesh's sole purpose in entering in the License was to generate revenue (and the record reveals other goals, including the conservation of wildlife and the meeting of a demand for humanitarian purposes), the granting of the License in this case was not a commercial activity.

However, the purpose of the activity, as opposed to its 'nature', is not relevant for immunity purposes. The 'nature' of the activity in suit is the regulation of wildlife. This is a sovereign activity not subject to challenge in foreign courts.[414]

The plaintiff then argued that the rhesus in question were *ferae naturae* and that therefore, Bangladesh had acted regarding these animals as any other owner of animals would behave. While the court find this argument positively 'inventive', the court rejected it with the simple reasoning that this doctrine was not applicable when matters were about governmental activities that regulate wildlife, and the capture or exportation of certain species. The very fact that the plaintiff had needed a license for doing these activities was proving that the rhesus in question were not *ferae naturae*.[415] In addition, the court argued that an exportation license as it was part of the licensing agreement was 'obviously a governmental , not a proprietary act'.[416]

Finally, the plaintiff forwarded the view that the power to control the *capture* of animals was a power every animal holder had and that for this reason, it was of a commercial nature. The court, taking reference to the OPEC precedent, concluded:

Mol, Inc. v. People's Republic of Bangladesh

The power to regulate the taking of game upon land owned by a landowner is an aspect of sovereignty, attached to land and derived from feudal precedent, which is subordinate to the State's overriding police power. It is clear that Bangladesh is acting as a sovereign in this case.[417]

It has to be seen that under the act of state doctrine, the result would have been the same. What we see here is a certain tendency in American federal jurisprudence to exclude a whole area of government activity from the possible wide scope of 'commercial activity' under §1605(a)(2) FSIA, and this area could be labeled 'the protection of natural resources of a foreign state'. While the act of state doctrine leads to the same result in these cases, the sovereign immunity defense has a particular value and should not be confounded with act of state; the two doctrines should be seen within their respective boundaries. And as the FSIA does not actually incorporate the act of state doctrine, which has been considered by some as a deficiency, the jurisprudence has effectively managed to get those sensibly political areas out of the litigation mill and thereby preserve certain core areas of sovereign activity under the provisions of the FSIA.

Budgetary Activity

Under this category we shall further discuss a precedent that we mentioned already earlier up, *De Sanchez v. Banco Central de Nicaragua*.[418] Here an American federal court had to state about an activity of Nicaragua's Central Bank.[419] The facts are quite complex. The plaintiff, a citizen of Nicaragua, emigrated to the United States in 1979, during the civil war in her country, and filed suit against *Banco Central* and *C & S Bank*, an American commercial bank. Already in 1971, the plaintiff had obtained a certificate of deposit from *Banco Nacional de Nicaragua*, a commercial bank in Nicaragua, about the amount of $150.000.

Shortly before she departed to the United States, Mrs. Sanchez asked *Banco Nacional* to pay her out the deposited amount. But as the bank had not enough dollar cash available, it asked *Banco Central*, where it maintained an account, to deliver the needed cash. Banco Central charged the account of *Banco Nacional* with an equivalent amount in cordobas, the national currency, and issued a cheque over $150.000 in favor of Mrs. Sanchez drawn on the account that *C & S Bank* had with *Banco Central*. But upon her arrival in the United States, when she wanted to cash the cheque, she got to hear that the *Banco Central* account had been closed; after that the bank argued there was some money, but not enough to cover the whole amount; finally the check was returned to Mrs. Sanchez with the imprint 'Refer to Maker'. C & S explained that because of the political troubles, all payments by *Banco Central* had been suspended according to an order by the new president of the bank, who was set in office by the revolutionary regime.

After having scrutinized the term 'commercial activity' under §1603(d) FSIA, as well as the legal materials, the court stated about the burden of proof.

De Sanchez v. Banco Central de Nicaragua

First, as is true for all the other exceptions under the FSIA, the burden of demonstrating that the claim does not fall within §1605(a)(2), i.e., the burden of proof that immunity exists, is upon the foreign state.[420]

As it was in the precedents I discussed before, the court in the present case held that the purpose of the activity in question was *irrelevant*; only the nature of the activity was subject to qualification.[421] The court considered the precedents *Arango*, *Yessenin-Volpin*, *Carey* and *Opec* and then evaluated the evidence.[422] The affidavits submitted by *Banco Central* certified for the official character of the bank.[423] The plaintiff responded to this evidence by the testimony of Dr. Roberto Incer, the former president of Banco Central under the Somoza regime who certified that the central bank has also engaged in commercial activity and that, more specifically, the issuing of the cheque had been one of those commercial activities.[424] The judgment cites a passage of the testimony:

Q. In utilizing the C & S account, was Banco Central wearing its commercial hat or its Government hat?

> A. This was just a commercial operation, a banking operation. It was not a Government function.[425]

The witness also revealed that *Banco Central* used its account with C & S bank for the payment of expenses that Nicaraguan students incur in the United States, for covering letters of credit for imports and for paying debts with C & S.

Until that point, the judgment really lets us believe, and also the evidence, that the court should have recognized the commercial character of the issuing of the cheque by *Banco Central*. But it took an almost incredible turn and twist and ended up in the contrary conclusion. First, the court declared it was not satisfied with the evidence produced, and the arguments provided here by the court are intriguing:

De Sanchez v. Banco Central de Nicaragua

The problem with regarding these statements as probative to the ultimate issue on this motion is two-fold. First, it is not enough for these witnesses merely to offer conclusory descriptions of Banco Central's general character or specific conduct. To be sure, reasonable people may disagree over the proper characterization of what Banco Central did; indeed, some commenters have concluded that the governmental/commercial dichotomy in foreign sovereign immunity law in unworkable because of the conceptual difficulties. But I can decide this motion only upon facts, and not on the basis of a government's official opinion. To the extent that these statements are simply conclusory, I must disregard them.[426]

The judge found the evidence 'too general' for conclusively demonstrating that the specific activity in question was either commercial or governmental. A part of the evidence was indeed not at all about the issuing of the cheque itself.[427] The court distinguished the case from *National American Corporation v. Federal Republic of Nigeria*[428], where the breaches of contract arising during the 'Nigerian Cement

Catastrophe' were qualified as commercial activity, while the Nigerian government had argued that the repudiations of contract had been undertaken 'for preventing a national economic catastrophe'. It was only from this point in the judgment that the real developments took off, namely with the court defining what really was the pertinent activity in question, or the pertinent question to ask:

> **De Sanchez v. Banco Central de Nicaragua**
>
> It seems clear that Banco Central is imbued with general authority over Nicaragua's financial affairs, and that on occasion it engages in commercial activities through its C & S account; neither facts decides this motion, however. Similarly, whether Banco Central acted to conserve its foreign currency supplies in a time of fiscal crisis when it ordered that Sanchez's cheque not be honored is nondispositive. Just as Nigeria acted to avoid a national catastrophe by repudiating its obligations in order to stop the flow of cement into its ports, Banco Central may be acting purely in its own sovereign interests by repudiating its debt to Sanchez. But if that debt arose from commercial conduct, as did Nigeria's, then Banco Central cannot invoke immunity against this suit.[429]

After having clearly peeled out the core juridical question, the judge looked at additional evidence and came to conclude that the issuing of the cheque, in this particular case, was a governmental act effected by *Banco Central*. It is really intriguing to see that it was the plaintiff who had submitted the evidence that ultimately was in favor of the defendant, *Banco Central*.

Let me comment here on this particularity of the American law of evidence. In principle, the judge is not impeached from appreciating evidence submitted by one part, in favor of the other. The judge is supposed to regard all the evidence in the record to prove a fact at issue, notwithstanding which party has submitted the evidence to the court. In addition, the judge can ask a witness additional questions, and here as well, it is not relevant which party has presented the witness, or expert evidence, to the court.[430]

We can admit in the present case that *Banco Central* was not able to make a *prima facie case* regarding the governmental character of the activity in question (issuing of the cheque) in order to support its immunity claim, as the judge didn't find the evidence was meeting the necessary standard of proof. The result should have been to deny immunity for the defendant. This would have been done by a so-called *directed verdict*. However, such is done by the court generally only if the other party has issued a motion for directed verdict[431], but there is agreement that that court can issue a *directed verdict* also *sua sponte*.[432] However, in the present case, the court did not pursue such action. The reason is probably the general rule of sovereign immunity contained in §1604 FSIA, taken as a 'residual presumption' of immunity for all cases where the evidence results in a *non liquet* situation.

The evidence revealed here in particular that, since September 1978, there were no foreign exchange regulations in Nicaragua, and *Banco Central* and other Nicaraguan banks, maintained accounts with American banks in order to facilitate the exchange of cordobas in dollars. Then, because of the decision of the Carter administration to freeze Nicaragua's access to the international monetary funds, Incer, the *Banco Central* president at that time, decreed a control policy for foreign exchange.[433] The witness also said that decisions regarding foreign exchange were taken 'at the highest level of Banco Central.'[434] When *Banco Nacional* asked *Banco Central* to transfer the dollars for covering the certificate of deposit of Mrs. Sanchez, it was Incer himself who had allowed the transaction.

This precedent offers the great advantage that it contains explicit passages from the witness evidence submitted to the court. As it's really a very important case, I will publish the decisive last part of the hearing hereafter:

De Sanchez v. Banco Central de Nicaragua (Hearing)

Q. Are you telling me that Banco Central was obliged to buy and sell dollars as desired by the private banks? Is that the point you are making here?

A. The Central Bank was obliged to sell dollars to the private bank when they requested for private transactions.

Q. Banco Central was required to abide by a private bank's request; is that correct?
A. Yes.

Q. So, the only requests that were not honored were those that were not permitted by law; is that right?
A. That's right.

Q. Why did you want to know about all these requests?
A. Because of the low level of foreign exchange. There was not enough to meet all the demands that were represented at that time in the Central Bank of Nicaragua.

Q. Why was Banco Central required to honor requests by private banks to buy dollars?
A. Why? Because the Central Bank - just as I say, the Central Bank has to keep a fixed exchange rate between the Cordoba and the dollar, so any excess amount - the Central Bank is obliged to keep a fixed exchange rate within the Cordoba, the national currency of Nicaragua, and the dollar, so any excess supply of dollars that were in the market and the bank did not want to acquire it, they sold it to the Central Bank and the Central Bank had to meet any excess demands that were in the market so that this exchange rate should be kept fixed.

Q. That related to both buying and selling dollars?
A. Yes.

Q. Central Bank's function is to buy and sell dollars from private banks in order to maintain a stable exchange rate?
A. That's right.

Q. I believe you told us before that you did not really concern yourself with the relationship between the private bank and the customer in the transaction that created the ned for the dollars; is that right?
A. That's right.

Q. Your sole interest was in the maintenance of the stability of the exchange rate; is that correct?
A. That's right.

Q. Is that correct?
A. That's right.[435]

The court concluded:

De Sanchez v. Banco Central de Nicaragua
From this testimony, it is clear that Banco Central was not engaged in commercial venture when it exchanged dollars for Cordobas upon the request of Banco Nacional. Clearly Sanchez was not Banco Central's customer, since her certificate of deposit was held with Banco Nacional and not with it. Banco Nacional earned no fee from the transaction, ..., and as Incer testified it was not even interested in the dealings between Banco Nacional and Sanchez, Banco Central's function in this matter - the maintenance of foreign exchange rates through regulation of foreign currency transactions - was not commercial, but was governmental.[436]

After the judge distinguished the case from *National American Corporation, Texas Trading* and *Verlinden*, that we all discussed earlier in this study, the court came to the final conclusion:

De Sanchez v. Banco Central de Nicaragua
However, in those cases, the letters of credit were issued as the culmination of a series of commercial transactions involving the purchase of cement by the Nigerian government. Here, by con-

> trast, although the relationship between Sanchez and Banco Nacional was commercial, Banco Central's role in that relationship was no different than the role any government plays in facilitating business transactions between its citizens through regulation or licensing. Just as a corporation may not sell shares of its stock without complying with applicable securities laws and obtaining necessary licenses or permits, Banco Nacional could not redeem Sanchez's certificate of deposit without obtaining Banco Central's approval to exchange Cordobas for dollars. Banco Central's C & S check was a necessary element of the commercial transaction between Sanchez and Banco Nacional, but it was not issued as part of any commercial function performed by Banco Central, and consequently cannot form a basis for suit under §1605(a)(2).[437]

After appreciating all the evidence in the record, the court thus came to the conclusion that the issuing of the cheque was a governmental activity of Banco Central, for its role in the complex suite of transactions was solely the regulation of foreign exchange, which is clearly a governmental activity. As a result, the court had to deny the applicability of the 'commercial activity' exception under §1605(a)(2) FSIA.

The court then applied the exceptions §§1605(a)(3) and 1605(a)(5). The Court of Appeals of the 5th Circuit fully confirmed the district court's reasoning regarding the applicability vel non of the 'commercial activity' exception in §1605(a)(2) FSIA.[438]

De Sanchez v. Banco Central de Nicaragua (5th Circuit)

Here, Banco Central's purpose in selling dollars - namely to regulate Nicaragua's foreign exchange reserves - was not ancillary to its conduct; instead, it defined the conduct's nature. Banco Central was not merely engaging in the same activity as private banks with a different purpose; in a basic sense, it was engaging in a different activity. It was performing one of its intrinsically governmental functions as a Nicaraguan Central Bank. (...) As such, it was wearing its sovereign rather than its commercial hat. If we were to hold that a central bank is subject to suit for its actions in regulating foreign exchange reserves, we would interfere with this basic governmental function and would thereby touch sharply on 'national nerves', contrary to the policies underlying the FSIA.[439]

The *De Sanchez* precedent is of paramount importance as to withholding judicial interference in the budgetary activities of foreign states. It is true that the FSIA contains special provision with regard to foreign central banks, §1611(b)(1) but this provision, as we shall see further down in this study, is only applicable regarding immunity from execution.

With regard to immunity from jurisdiction, the protection of the budgetary domain of foreign states was not explicitly stated in the FSIA, and as such, the *De Sanchez* case serves as an important pillar to interpret the statute in a way that it is in accordance with the basic principles of international law and the conduct of states on the international platform.[440]

The decision is also very elucidative how a judge needs to really peel out the decisive question, before evaluating the evidence and distinguishing the case from precedents. Wrong judicial acts are often the result of wrong questions asked.

Here, the ambiguous character of the evidence regarding the facts at issue shows with quite some rigor that the evidence problems in foreign sovereign immunity litigation are not to underestimate. It is for that reason so important that the facts are clearly identified, before even thinking of an appreciation of the evidence.

It was notably tempting in this case to look at the relation between Mrs. Sanchez and *Banco Nacional* and derive conclusions therefrom. But it would have been the wrong question because the cheque was issued by *Banco Central*, while Mrs. Sanchez had no commercial relation with that bank at all. Hence, the decisive action holder here was the central bank of Nicaragua, and once this was clearly identified, the court only had to see if the exercise of that function was private and commercial, or public and governmental, and to that purpose, the witness evidence was clear-cut and unequivocal.

It also has to be seen that, as actions under the FSIA are ruled without jury, §1441(d) FSIA, the judge exercises two different functions as the functions of *judge* and *jury* are united in his or her person. With regard to the problems of evaluating the evidence in foreign sovereign immunity litigation, the handling of these functions by the judge can at times be extremely difficult. This present case is the best proof to demonstrate that and to show how meticulous judges have to proceed in order to rule those cases in a way that is both efficient and farsighted enough to not step on the feet of foreign states' internal powers, thereby creating undesired diplomatic strain and interference.[441]

National Defense

The last category in our catalog of foreign states' sensibly political domains will also be exemplified by one single, but important, precedent; it is *Castro v. Saudi Arabia*.[442]

A relative of the Castro family was killed in a car accident in the United States, whereupon they sued Saudi Arabia for damages because the driver of the car that caused the accident was a Saudi soldier stationed in the United States under a bilateral military treaty between the two countries. It is important to note that the treaty did not contain any compensation clause for the Saudi services rendered to the United States, and was thus a non-profit agreement.[443] Evaluating the nature of the treaty, the court found the fact irrelevant that the military services as such had a government character; only the nature of the activity was the decisive criterion for the court to consider under the FSIA.[444] It is interesting to observe the development of the restrictive immunity doctrine in these cases. Already back in 1923, André Weiss proposed in his course *Compétence ou incompétence des tribunaux à l'égard des états étrangers (1923)*[445] to consider the nature of the activity in question as the exclusive criterion for deciding about immunity *vel non*.

André Weiss

If he [the judge] has to examine the question [of sovereign immunity], there is only one thing to ask: is the action that the litigation is about, by its *nature*, such that only a state can do it and that it's done in the name of the state, which would mean it's an act of public power, a political action, which couldn't be revised by a tribunal without infringing upon the sovereignty of the foreign state. *In this case, the court has no jurisdiction.* By contrast, is the nature of the action such as any private person can do it, such as a contract or a loan, this action, whatever is the purpose or motivation behind it, is by its very nature *private*, and the foreign court would have jurisdiction over it. (…) It is of little importance that normally people don't do such large transactions [except when they conclude with foreign states], and or that the objectives are different. It's a contract, an acquisition, a loan. That is enough. The *nature of the contract*, not its objective, is what is to consider here.[446]

This manner of distinguishing between acts 'de iure imperii' and those 'de iure gestionis', while it sounds clear and straight, was however often misunderstood and criticized when it's about contracts that were concluded with specific military purposes. Hersch Lauterpacht writes in *The Problem of Jurisdictional Immunities of Foreign States (1951)*:

Hersch Lauterpacht

However, upon analysis, that test merely postpones the difficulty. To what extent is it true to say that contracts made by the state for the purchase of shoes for the army or a warship, or of munitions, or of foodstuff necessary for the maintenance of the national economy, are not immune from the jurisdiction for the reason that they were *contracts* and that an individual can make a contract? For can it not be said that these particular contracts can be made by a state only, and not by individuals? Individuals do not purchase shoes for their armies; they do not buy warships for the use of the state; they are not, as such, responsible for the management of the national economy.[447]

Jean-Flavien Lalive cites Lauterpacht in his article *Contrats entre États ou entreprises étatiques et personnes privées (1983)* and adds:

Jean-Flavien Lalive

This reaction is typical for a private lawyer … for who is today the person that would need to buy for himself the luxury to buy a tank or a torpedo defense system?[448]

I cannot see Lalive's criticism justified. There is not a doubt that a private person can buy army boots or a warship. For example, there are drug barons in quite a few countries in South America who have such things, maintain private armies and militias, and while the number of such military personnel may be much smaller than the army of a nation state, it's basically the same. These private militia need their boots, they need their guns, and ammunition, they need uniforms, food and clothing. And as weaponry can be bought, even against national regulations, in black markets, it is not excluded, but rather the rule, that such people also buy heavy weaponry or torpedo boats, to just name these.

Lauterpacht has misunderstood what really means *nature* of an act or action. The nature of a purchasing contract does not change in any way according to the motivations or goals that are connected to it, that is to say, the whole of the human intentional factor. Lalive fell in the same trap and asks the silly question if it was a luxury or whatever, or how a private person would need to buy a warship or other military equipment? *This is simply not the question.* When we look at the nature of a transaction, we do not need to know who can possibly engage in it, how big or small the business volume is, or if people have the necessary financial means to afford such a purchase! *All this is strictly irrelevant.* What counts is the *nature* of the transaction; a contract is a contract, it's a private, commercial activity. Period.

The FSIA embodies, under the definition of §1603(d), and the legislative materials, exactly the doctrine that Weiss has proposed so many years earlier in his brilliant article. The *House Report* expressly underlines that 'a contract by a foreign government to buy provisions or equipment for its armed forces ... constitutes a commercial activity.'[449] This was confirmed in *National American Corporation v. Federal Republic of Nigeria*.[450] This case is particularly interesting. Judge Goettel remarked that, already in 1976, when the case was being dealt with by judge Weinfeld[451], Nigeria argued that the cement 'was intended for the use in governmental works and military installations.'[452] Judge Weinfeld, who had to know this case *before* the entering into force of the Act, referred to *Victory Transport*[453] where immunity was granted 'for the acts concerned the armed forces'. Judge Weinfeld admitted that the military objective of the purchasing contract was a pertinent fact at issue; however he concluded that '[t]here was almost a total failure of proof at trial as to the purpose for which the cement was ordered and, certainly, there was no convincing proof that the majority or a substantial portion was secured with a governmental purpose in mind.'[454] Judge Goettel, however, who had to try the case under the FSIA, wrote:

Victory Transport (Judge Goettel)

Even had this been demonstrated, it would not have materially aided defendants, since the Immunity Act has changed the grounds on which the defense of sovereign immunity rests.[455]

After citing §1603(d) FSIA and the legal materials, the judge continued:

Victory Transport (Judge Goettel)

This definition eliminates the significance attached by Nigeria to its purported intent to use the cement for military purposes.[456]

The judge thus confirmed that it's only the nature of the action or act in question that has to be taken into account, not its purpose or objective. The latter will not be a relevant fact at issue, while it may have been, before the enactment of the FSIA. Despite criticism, we can thus conclude that the old theory established by André Weiss has merit, so much merit in fact that it can be said to be the reigning doctrine right now, not only the United States, in sovereign immunity litigation, but also, as we shall see further down, in other jurisdictions that have enacted sovereign immunity statutes. This is particularly true for the United Kingdom's *State Immunity Act 1978*, and the precedent *Trendtex Trading*, and the interesting opinion of Lord Denning in this judgment.[457]

Contrary of this line of reasoning and the precedents discussed, in *Castro v. Saudi Arabia*, as we saw it already in the OPEC case, the judge performed a rather construed interpretation of the criterion 'commercial activity' that obviously tries to restrict the scope and applicability of this exception:

Castro v. Saudi Arabia

The transaction at issue here could be broadly defined as the 'sale of services' and so be deemed 'commercial'. The activity could also be narrowly viewed as a non-profit agreement between two governments for the training of military personnel. So viewed, the transaction would be public or governmental, and protected by sovereign immunity. In this case, as in the OPEC case, 'commercial activity' is best defined narrowly; Saudi Arabia has the sole power to control its armed forces, and proper training of those forces is an essential ingredient of that control. In addition the fact that the contract is expressly 'non-profit' convinces the court that the arrangement between the two sovereigns is not commercial in nature.[458]

Consequently, the judge rejected the action, after also denying the applicability of §1605(a)(5), concluding that 'defendant has demonstrated that none of the exceptions in FSIA operate to deprive Saudi Arabia of its immunity from this court's jurisdiction.'[459]

This sentence reveals the repartition of the burden of proof. Apart from the evidence submitted by Saudi Arabia as to the exception 1605(a)(5), the court did not need to evaluate the evidence for qualifying the action in question because, at that point, the facts were not contested.

We can see three lines of reasoning in this judgment:

▸ Fact at issue was not the nature of the Saudi soldier participating in public traffic in the United States, but the bilateral treaty that stationed the soldier in the forum state;

▸ The treaty was governmental because of the exclusive control of Saudi Arabia over its troupes stationed in the United States, and over their training;

▸ The treaty had a governmental character also because the military services rendered by Saudi Arabia to the United States were not remunerated because it was a non-profit agreement.

By these reflections, the court has traced a certain demarcation line that marks certain limits under the Act, and this for protecting the sensible area of *internal affairs* of a foreign state, which is undeniably governmental activity of that foreign state. In fact, the military treaty discussed in this judgment can be seen as a sort of inter-governmental cooperation. This expression, while the judge did not use it, can relate us back to the precedent *Yessenin-Volpin*[460], discussed earlier in this study and where the judge had qualified the activities of TASS and NOVOSTI as intra-governmental cooperation with the Soviet government.

With the regard to the first line of reasoning, if the judge had focused not upon the treaty, but upon the mere participation of the soldier in the road circulation in the United States, this participation would have had to be considered *commercial*. However, in focusing exclusively upon the *statute* of the soldier being stationed in the United States, the judge has predetermined the outcome in that, incontestably, such a treaty is public and governmental in character.

Conclusion

With regard to the repartition of the burden of proof, this judg-ment thus follows the schema that we have already established to be valid under *Matter of Sedco, De Sanchez* and other precedents, that is, the facts at issue which determine subject matter jurisdiction and per-sonal jurisdiction are to be proven by the plaintiff, and here the proof is particularly severe in case the latter motions a default judgment against the foreign state under §1608(d) FSIA. The precedents dis-cussed here show that vital interests, foreign affairs and internal affairs of a foreign state are sensible areas that American federal courts tend to protect, thereby preserving something like a hard core of foreign sovereignty that federal jurisdiction doesn't touch upon. To summa-rize, these areas are the following:

Foreign Affairs

Some kind of intra-governmental cooperation between foreign press agencies and the foreign state *(Yessenin-Volpin)* or a nationaliza-tion, that is effected by the foreign state in such a way that it appears to be a weapon of foreign policy *(Carey)*.

Internal Affairs

Police actions undertaken for protecting fishery laws *(Perez)* and immigration laws *(Arango)*. Activities of the foreign state that were un-dertaken for the protection of 'natural resources', for example for crude oil *(OPEC, Matter of Sedco)* or the national wildlife *(Mol)*.

Budgetary Activity

Activities undertaken by foreign central banks in their function as facilitators of foreign exchange and for regulating foreign exchange *(De Sanchez)*.

National Defense

An inter-governmental collaboration for training military troupes under a bilateral treaty between the foreign state and the forum state (Castro).

An all the precedents we thus examined, the judges affirmed that the specific activity for qualifying it as governmental or private, needs to be *clearly identified*. Here, there is sometimes harsh difficulty to see the relevancy versus irrelevancy of certain facts at issue, and all the art is to really peel the onion, so as to speak, to see what in fact the *particular activity is that is the subject of the litigation*. Often, as we have seen, this initial work of the judge in looking at the facts, before appreciating the evidence, leads to a quite clear-cut legal conclusion at the end, and if things had been seen in a slightly different manner, the legal result would have swapped to its opposite. This is quite intriguing to observe in all those cases!

Generally speaking, and with regard to the specific criterion 'commercial activity', all these cases let us see that courts are careful not to infringe upon the political affairs of foreign states, in cases where there is initially a certain temptation to 'help' the plaintiff succeed when the situation is such that it all looks like blunt injustice to grant immunity. However, this cannot and must not entice us to derive from the legally correct path, as the sovereignty of foreign states needs to be respected, when the foreign state has really acted within its public, governmental function.

Regarding the *means of proof*, American federal courts have been quite open to accept a range of possible evidence, such as testimony *(De Sanchez)*, affidavit *(Mol)*, expert evidence *(Yessenin-Volpin, OPEC)* and even a *simple statement by an ambassador of the foreign state (Yessenin-Volpin)*.

CHAPTER SEVEN

The Burden of Proof for Immunity for Execution

Types of Execution Measures

We have to distinguish basically three types of executional measures:

▸ The enforcement of a judgment arising from a lawsuit;

▸ The post-judgment attachment, or attachment in aid of execution;

▸ The pre-judgment attachment.

A forth type of execution, called 'arrest' is mentioned, to be true, in the text of §1609 FSIA, but is not to be found in any of the exceptions from this general rule from immunity from execution contained in §1610 FSIA. The question logically comes up if that means that for arrests, foreign states enjoy an absolute kind of immunity from execution? As the legal materials are silent with regard to this question, we could ponder what 'arrest' actually means, because in American law, there are basically two different definitions of this term. There is the arrest of a person[461], and the arrest of a ship, in an 'in rem' action.[462]

Sompong Sucharitkul asked this question in his course *Immunities of Foreign States Before National Authorities (1976)* and concluded as follows.

Sompong Sucharitkul
It is difficult to imagine how a State qua an international legal entity could be subject to arrest or detention. In actual realities, however, the State often acts through its various organs, agencies, instrumentalities or individual representatives. The representatives as individuals, as well as the properties and assets belonging to a foreign State can be the target of arrest or detention.

By a stretch of imagination, the cloak of State immunities may be said to extent to cover many types of State representatives and agencies as well as their properties from the power of local authorities to effect arrest and detention.[463]

However, the text of section 1609, '... *the property ... of a foreign state ... ',* doesn't really give room for doubting that only measures of execution against foreign property are meant to fall under this rule. However, the arrest of a ship is no longer possible under the FSIA. Against such an action 'in rem', the foreign state enjoys *absolute immunity from execution.* On the other hand, an action 'in personam' is still possible under the conditions of §1605(b) FSIA.

H. R. Report No. 94-1487

In view of section 1609 of the bill, section 1605(b) is designed to avoid arrests of vessels or cargo of a foreign state to commence a suit.[464]

The elimination of attachment as a vehicle for commencing a lawsuit will ease the conduct of foreign relations by the United States and help eliminate the necessity for determinations of claims of sovereign immunity by the State Department.[465]

Sections 1610(a) to (c) of the Act concern the post-judgment attachment. As to the pre-judgment attachment, section 1610(d) provides a peculiar solution. This distinction is justified by the fact that we are facing here different juridical notions; in addition, it was Congress' intention to prohibit the pre-judgment attachment for vessels or cargo for commencing a lawsuit against a foreign state.[466]

28 U.S.C. §1610(d)

The property of a foreign state, ... , shall be immune from attachment prior to the entry of judgment ... , if the purpose of the attachment is to secure satisfaction of a judgment that has been or may ultimately be entered against the foreign state, and not to obtain jurisdiction.

The Allocation of the Burden of Proof

As for jurisdictional immunities of foreign states, the FSIA provides for immunity from execution a rule-and-exception principle. The rule is stated in section 1609.

> **28 U.S.C. §1609**
>
> Subject to existing international agreements to which the United States is a party at the time of enactment of this Act the property of a foreign state shall be immune from attachment, arrest and execution except as provided in sections 1610 and 1611 of this chapter.

The exceptions are stated in section 1610. The formulation of section 1609 is not very clear in this respect, as section 1611 doesn't contain exceptions to the rule, but exceptions to the exceptions ('... notwithstanding the provisions of section 1610 of this chapter ... ').[467]

Astonishingly enough, there is no remark to be found in the legal materials as to the burden of proof regarding sections 1609, 1610, as this was the case for jurisdictional immunity.[468] However, it would not be correct to simply apply the burden of proof rules that apply for immunity from jurisdiction, to immunity from execution.

Neither the text of the legislative history regarding sections 1604, 1605-1607, nor its systematic placement within the section by section analysis of the *House Report*, allow to draw any analogous conclusions for immunity from execution. Furthermore, it has to be seen that the two immunity rules have had different historical developments, and have a different legal character. This was already stated in the *Harvard Draft Convention (1932)*[469], was repeated in the legal materials[470] and is general opinion in the literature.[471]

This means that we have to engage a novel scrutiny as to the burden of proof in matters of immunity from execution, under the FSIA. Interestingly enough, in the International Law Association's *Draft Convention*, the burden of proof is handled differently for each type of immunity. Here are the rules:

Art. II (Immunity from jurisdiction)

In general, a foreign State shall be immune from the adjudicatory jurisdiction of a forum State for acts performed by it in the exercise of its sovereign authority i.e. iure imperii. It shall not be immune in the circumstances provided in Article III.

Article III (Exceptions)

Sovereign immunity shall not be granted when the case in question involved a commercial activity of the foreign state.

Art. VII (Immunity from execution)

A foreign State's property in the forum State shall be immune from attachment arrest and execution except as provided in Article VIII.

In the ILA Report of the Belgrade Conference (1980), it is written that Art. II is considered as a 'somewhat flexible rule',[472] while Art. VII is held to be stricter, in a way that 'there should be an absolute rule of immunity unless a particular exception applied.'[473] It is interesting to note that the two immunity rules are drafted in a different manner. As for jurisdictional immunity, the foreign state is granted immunity only if the activity in question can be demonstrated to have been *iure imperii*. This is exactly how the FSIA handles it in sections 1604, 1605-1607. This is why we can conclude that the ILA Draft Convention appears to handle the burden of proof for jurisdictional immunities in the same manner as the FSIA. In other words, when this can be seen, then the other analogy may also be true.

When we can say that under the ILA Draft, the rule of immunity from execution is principally absolute, and is pierced only in very particular exceptional circumstances, then we might also conclude that under the FSIA, this might also be the case. Fortunately, we do not need to engage in such a shaky argument, while logically it makes sense; we got some precedents that are explicit and that we shall carefully examine under our particular focus on the allocation of the burden of proof.

The Waiver Exception

§§1610(a)(1), 1610(b)(1), 1610(d)

Contrary to the drafting technique regarding immunity from juris-diction, under §§1604, 1605-1607 FSIA, valid for both foreign states and *agencies and instrumentalities of foreign states*, section 1610 clearly distinguishes the case where the property belongs to the foreign state, §1610(a), or to one of its organisms, §1610(b). As to the execution of a judgment or a *post-judgment attachment*, §§ 1610(a)(1) and 1610 (b)(1) state:

> **§1610. Exceptions to the immunity from attachment or execution**
>
> (a) The property in the United States of a foreign state, as defined in section 1603(a) of this chapter, used for a commercial activity in the United States, shall not be immune from attachment in aid of execution, or from execution, upon a judgment entered by a court of the United States or of a State after the effective date of this Act, if –
>
> (1) the foreign state has waived its immunity from attachment in aid of execution or from execution either explicitly or by implication, notwithstanding any withdrawal of the waiver the foreign state may purport to effect except in accordance with the terms of the waiver, (...)
>
> (b) In addition to subsection (a), any property in the United States of an agency or instrumentality of the foreign state en-gaged in commercial activity in the United States shall not be immune from attachment in aid of execution, or from execution, upon a judgment entered by a court of the United States or of a

State after the effective date of this Act, if –

(1) the agency or instrumentality has waived its immunity from attachment in aid of execution or from execution either explicitly or implicitly, notwithstanding any withdrawal of the waiver the agency or instrumentality may purport to effect except in accordance with the terms of the waiver, (…)

(d) The property of a foreign state, as defined in section 1603(a) of this chapter, used for commercial activities in the United States, shall be immune from attachment prior to the entry of judgment in any action brought in a court in the United States or of a State, … , if –

(1) the foreign state has explicitly waived its immunity from attachment prior to judgment, notwithstanding any withdrawal of the waiver the foreign state may purport to effect except in accordance with the terms of the waiver, (…).

A particular handling of the *pre-judgment attachment* is thus provided by §1610(d)(1). Contrary to sections 1610(a)(1), (b)(1) where an *implicit* waiver is admitted, this provision obviously only admits an *explicit* immunity waiver; thus, conditions are stricter for pre-judgment attachments of foreign property, for obvious reasons.

There is case law dealing with defining what an 'explicit immunity waiver' is under these terms. In *Libra Bank v. Banco Nacional de Costa Rica*[474], the Court of Appeals of the 2nd Circuit reversed the district court judgment, holding a waiver for 'explicit' that was formulated as follows:

Explicit Immunity Waiver

The Borrower hereby irrevocably and unconditionally waives any right of immunity from legal proceedings including suit judgment and execution on grounds of sovereignty which it or its property may now or hereafter enjoy.[475]

The immunity waiver was contained in promissory notes that Banco Nacional had given out to Libra Bank, but the defendant argued that the terms of the waiver did not cover the pre-judgment attachment as this form of execution was not expressly mentioned in the waiver. The Court of Appeals however rejected this argument, holding that the wording of section 1610(d)(1) 'does not require recitation of the words 'prejudgment attachment' as an operative formula.'[476] Then the court further explained:

Libra Bank v. Banco Nacional de Costa Rica (2nd Cir.)

This enumeration clearly is not intended to be exhaustive. If anything, it suggests that prejudgment attachment is a form of 'legal proceedings'. The waiver is explicit in the sense that it is clear and unambiguous. Banco Nacional certainly intended to reserve no rights of immunity in any legal proceedings.[477]

The same Court of Appeals confirmed another interesting case, *Sperry International Trade v. Government of Israel*[478], that we mentioned earlier on in this study, and where the district court had to deal with an arbitration sentence against the Israeli government. While the court denied the applicability of the FSIA, it stated in an obiter dictum about the opinion forwarded by the Israeli government that sees the arbitration sentence as a 'prejudgment attachment', and wished the court to apply §1610(d)(1). The judge argued that even if he applied the Act, he had to rule that the waiver contained in the contract with the plaintiff was 'explicit' in the sense of §1610(d)(1).[479]

In *S & S Machinery*[480], a precedent we discussed already, the Court of Appeals of the 2nd Circuit had to decide the question if a clause in the *Agreement on Trade Relations of April 2, 1975* between the United States and Romania was to be considered as an explicit waiver of immunity from prejudgment attachment.[481] This clause reads as follows:

Business Facilitation Clause

Nationals, firms, companies and economic organizations of either Party shall be afforded access to all courts, and, when applicable, to administrative bodies as plaintiffs and defendants, or otherwise, in accordance with the laws in force in the territory of such other Party. They shall not claim or enjoy immunities from suit or execution of judgment or other liability in the territory of the other Party with respect to commercial or financial transactions, except as may be provided in other bilateral agreements.[482]

The court subsumed the prejudgment attachment under the term 'other liability in the territory of the other Party'. As there were not yet any precedents interpreting this clause, the court looked at a similar passage (... 'other liability' ...) in the *Friendship Treaty between the United States and Iran, of August 8, 1955*. As we have seen already earlier in this study, this term was interpreted by case law as to *not* encompass the prejudgment attachment.[483] The *House Report* explains under section 1610:

H. R. Report No. 94-1487

However, the traditional view in the United States concerning execution has been that the property of foreign states is absolutely immune from execution. (...) Even after the 'Tate Letter' of 1952, this continued to be the position of the Department of State and of the courts. (...) Sections 1610(a) and (b) are intended to modify this rule by partially lowering the barrier of immunity from execution, so as to make this immunity conform more closely with the provisions on jurisdictional immunity in the bill.[484]

Indeed, international practice is far from the 'ideal' situation to treat immunity from jurisdiction and immunity from execution in the same manner. Rather the contrary tendency can be made out, and this is so since a considerable period of time. The 'partially lowering of the barrier of immunity from execution' cannot be compared with the situation under sections 1604, 1605-1607, for jurisdictional immunity, where we have a restrictive immunity doctrine that more or less reversed rule and exception, while the Act stated it in the old terms, putting the immunity rule and then the exceptions, while in practice, this drafting technique is rather misleading, as the rule of immunity is, to quote Lord Denning, but a 'residual concept'.

However, for immunity from execution, such a reversal of rule and exception has never taken place, and even the quite liberal statement in the legislative materials starts with saying that 'the property of foreign states is absolutely immune from execution'. In reality, this rule is still absolute in the sense that the exceptions are pointed, and few, while for jurisdictional immunities the exceptions are, so to speak, all over the place, so that there is not much left of that 'rule of immunity' in section 1604. This is not my personal opinion but quite general tenor in the international law literature. To quote only Georges R. Delaume, an eminent expert on the matter.

George R. Delaume

Ideally the rules applicable to immunity from suit and immunity from execution should be coterminous in the sense that there should be no immunity from execution when there is no immunity from suit. In practice, however, this ideal is not always achieved.[485]

In my view, which is the result of careful study of Anglo-American statutory construction and the law of evidence, we can apply, for immunity from execution, the common law standard of statutory interpretation that sees the general rule as a *presumption*. It follows that the burden of proof is upon the party that relies on an exception from the general rule.[486]

The burden of proof is thus upon the plaintiff for demonstrating that one of the tight exceptions to the general rule of immunity from execution is applicable in the case. If the plaintiff fails to prove the exception he relies upon satisfactorily to the court, the general rule acts like a presumption and the court is compelled to dismiss the action because of sovereign immunity from execution.

This is the general schema, and so far, it was principally confirmed by precedents. For example *Behring International v. Imperial Iranian Air*

Force (Behring I)[487], which we discussed already earlier on, the court concluded:

> **Behring International v. Imperial Iranian Air Force (Behring I)**
>
> Summarizing my conclusions with respect to the Immunities Act: First, only section 1610(d) curtails the immunity from prejudgment attachment enjoyed by the property of a foreign state under section 1609. Second, Behring has not shown that section 1610(d) is applicable here because it cannot point to any explicit waiver of immunity from such attachments.[488]

The burden of proof for an implicit or explicit immunity waiver under the terms of §§1610(a)(1), 1610(b)(1), 1610(d) FSIA is thus entirely upon the plaintiff.

Usibus Destinata

§§1610(a)(2), 1610(b)(2), 1611

Already under the absolute immunity doctrine in the United Kingdom, there are precedents to be found where, regarding measures of execution, courts were looking at what was the usage of the property in question.[489] When the property had been destined for public, governmental purposes, *usibus publicis destinata*, then it was immune from execution.[490] This was also the traditional legal situation in France[491], Switzerland[492], and Egypt.[493]

However, in the United States, the protection of property belonging to foreign states was even stricter compared to that standard, which created an anomalous situation as courts affirmed their jurisdiction for a lawsuit, but then declared the property immune from execution - and the plaintiffs had a judgment that was serving them practically nothing.[494]

Such divergence has intently been avoided under the FSIA, and the law giver intended to assimilate the requirements of section 1605(a)(4) FSIA, that we have discussed already, with the standard for the execution of a judgment under §§1610(a)(2), 1610(b)(2). The difference is obvious between the pertinent facts under §1610(a)(2)[495], on one hand, and those for agencies or instrumentalities, under §1610(b)(2)[496], on the other. Only for property belonging to foreign states themselves, the usage of the property is a relevant fact at issue.

Generally speaking, under international law, the usage, or destination for usage, is a well-known criterion in the law of foreign sovereign immunity regarding the property of foreign states. Here, the repartition of the burden of proof is of particular interest.

The literature is not particularly rich to discuss this problem, or ask the question. One of the rare remarks I found on the subject was uttered by George R. Delaume, in *Transnational Contracts*.[497] He compared §1610(a)(2) FSIA with section 13(5) State Immunity Act 1978 of the United Kingdom[498], concluding that to determine if the property was used for commercial or noncommercial purposes 'is a delicate one and left open by the Foreign Sovereign Immunities Act.[499] In a side note, Delaume concludes:

George R. Delaume

In order to anticipate the possible switching of assets and other manipulations §1610(a)(2) subjects to execution property which 'is or was used' by the relevant entity in connection with its commercial activity. The intent of this provision is clear. Its implementation, however, may not be free from difficulty since nothing is said about who should bear the burden of proof.[500]

In fact, there is no provision in the Act nor in the legislative materials that would indicate the allocation of the burden of proof under this section.

Notwithstanding this difficulty, it is possible to draw some conclusions from the mere drafting of the provisions in the Act, namely the relationship of sections 1609/1610, on one hand, and the relationship between 1610/1611, on the other. In other words, we can exhibit here the following hypothesis:

(1) Relationship between §1609 and §1610

If it is true that the exceptions provided in §1610 did only *partially lower* the rule of immunity contained in §1609, which is *otherwise absolute*, then the burden of proof for an exception to this rule, that is, that the property was destined for commercial usage, is upon the plaintiff.

(2) Relationship between §1610 and §1611

If it is true that, with regard to §1611, the exception to an exception, the burden of proof is upon the foreign state, the burden of proof for the exception (to the general rule in §1609) is upon the plaintiff.

Relationship between §1609 and §1610

The solution of this problem depends on answering the question if immunity from execution, under the FSIA, is equally construed as an *affirmative defense*, for which the foreign state bears the burden of proof? We have largely discussed the *House Report* statement to this effect, for jurisdictional immunities, and we have seen to what extent that original legislative intention was later on modified by federal jurisprudence. We concluded that, after all, the legislative materials were lacking precision to this effect, or even appeared to be ambiguous.

We have discussed already that for immunity from execution, this same statement cannot be taken into account because of its systematic placement in the legislative history. It was clearly to be found within the legal provisions valid only for jurisdictional immunity of foreign states, §§1604, 1605-1607, and can for that reason not be applied to immunity from execution. Thus, we have to examine the burden of proof for immunity from execution separately. However, in federal jurisprudence, the problem has not yet been identified to a point that clarity was established with regard to the burden of proof. In *De Letelier v. Republic of Chile (Letelier III)*[501], that we discussed earlier on, the district court asked if §1610(a)(2) could also be applied for the execution of a judgment under §1605(a)(5) FSIA.

The court concluded that §1610(a)(2) and §1610(a)(5) are not mutually exclusive[502] and stated with regard to the burden of proof:

De Letelier v. Republic of Chile (Letelier III)

One would be hard pressed to exaggerate the difficulty of interpreting the Foreign Sovereign Immunities Act. As Judge Kaufmann recently explained, the statute was deliberately left vague, so as to provide only 'very modest guidance' on issues of pre-eminent importance. For answers to these most difficult questions, the authors of the law 'decided to put [their] faith in the U.S. courts. (…) One point that does emerge clearly from the legislative history, however, is that the burden of establishing FSIA immunity lies with the party claiming it. H.R. Rep. No. 94-1487, 94th Cong. 2d Sess., reprinted in [1976] U.S. Code Cong. & Adm. News 6604.[503]

The judge thus applied without hesitation the *House Report* rule of the burden of proof, that was stated for immunity from jurisdiction, to immunity from execution. However, it has to be seen that the court made that statement as an *obiter dictum*, because there was no litigation about facts, and the judge only ruled about legal questions.[504]

The apparent divergence of opinions regarding the repartition of the burden of proof shows that we cannot find the solution by only focusing on the relationship between §1609 and §1610 FSIA, but have to consider the relationship between §1610 and §1611 as well. And there is an additional argument that can be drawn from the drafting technique of §1610(a)(2); in my view this leads to imparting the burden of proof upon the plaintiff. We have to carefully look how this section is drafted; it is namely *not* drafted in a way that the usage of the property is to be considered in an abstract manner. The formulation of that section is quite precise, in that it positively states that when the property 'is or was used for the commercial activity', immunity from execution is to be denied.

Now let us look how its drafted in the *Brussels Convention*, Art. 3, that I mentioned before in the notes. Interestingly enough, we find precisely the opposite solution. The pertinent fact in this article is the governmental usage of the vessel or its cargo, while the rule, contained in Art. 1, states the equality of state ships and private ships.

To come back to the FSIA, when we thus consider that the rule stated in §1609 is not just a residual concept but an inflexible, absolute principle, we are compelled to impart the burden of proof on the plaintiff because he must 'unblock the judicial pathway', so to speak, in *overcoming the presumption* of the property to being immune under the rule. This is a classical case where in the law of evidence, the one is charged with the burden of proof, who has to overcome the presumption.

To repeat it, this argument could *not* be forwarded for jurisdictional immunities, under §§1604, 1605-1607 FSIA, because here we have only a residual, restrictive immunity concept put up as the rule, and thus *not* a presumption. In addition, it is to be seen that statutes usually only fixate already existing legal principles, and when they create new legal principles, such must be clearly follow from the wording of the statute, or its legislative history. This old principle in Anglo-American law was restated in *Broadbent v. Organization of American States (OAS)*[505], where the court quoted *Sutherland Statutory Construction (1975)*.

Sutherland Statutory Construction (1975)

A statute which refers to the law of a subject generally adopts the law on the subject as of the time the law was invoked … including all the amendments and modifications of the law subsequent to the time the reference statute was enacted.[506]

We have already seen that this was precisely the case with the FSIA, which was an enactment of an already existing legal situation that granted only restrictive immunity to foreign states with regard to immunity from jurisdiction. Thus the Act codified, in the terms of the court 'what, in the period between 1946 and 1976, had come to be the immunity enjoyed by sovereign states - *restrictive* - immunity.[507]

However, with regard to immunity from execution, the Act expressly modified the prior juridical practice, thereby giving an excellent example how in one statute, the two methods of statutory construction may be used. *Maxwell on the Interpretation of Statutes (1969)* states that '... [the judge] may also consider whether a statute has intended to alter the law or to leave it exactly where it stood before.'[508]

Relationship between §1610 and §1611

To arrive at a more convincing argumentation, we need to have a closer look at the relationship between sections 1610 and 1611, but also 1609 of the Act.

28 U.S.C. §1611

§1611. Certain types of property immune from execution

(a) Notwithstanding the provisions of section 1610 of this chapter, the property of those organizations designated by the President as being entitled to enjoy the privileges, exemptions, and immunities provided by the International Organizations Immunities Act shall not be subject to attachment or any other judicial process impending the disbursement of funds to, or on the order of, a foreign state as the result of an action brought in the courts of the United States or of the States.

(b) Notwithstanding the provisions of section 1610 of this chapter, the property of a foreign state shall be immune from attachment and from execution, if –

(1) the property is that of a foreign central bank or monetary authority held for its own account, unless such bank or authority, or its parent foreign government, has explicitly waived its immunity from attachment in aid or execution, or from execution, notwithstanding any withdrawal of the waiver which the bank, authority or government may purport to effect except in accordance with the terms of the waiver; or

(2) the property is, or is intended to be, used in connection with a military activity and

(A) is of a military character, or

(B) is under the control of a military authority or defense agency.

It is interesting to note that this section excludes without exception the disbursement of funds held by foreign governments with any international organization or monetary fund. This is to protect the functioning of international organizations situated in the United States, and is thereby an important add-on to the *International Organizations Immunities Act* of the United States, 22 U.S.C., §§288 ff.[509]

22 U.S.C. 288a(b) IOIA

International Organizations, their property and their assets, wherever located and by whomsoever held, shall enjoy the same immunity from suit and every form of judicial process as is enjoyed by foreign governments, except to the extent that such organizations may expressly waive their immunity fro the purpose of any proceedings or by the terms of any contract.

In *Broadbent v. OAS*[510], that we already mentioned, the Court of Appeals stated on the appeal of former employees of the OAS Secretary General who claimed damages for breach of contract. They invoked §288a(b) IOIA, ' … shall enjoy the same immunity from suit … as enjoyed by foreign governments.' Referring to the FSIA, they argued that jurisdictional immunity was restricted under that statute, which is why, they concluded the immunity of international organizations is equally restricted. The Court of Appeals rejected this argument, considering the role and the function of international organizations:

Broadbent v. OAS (D.C.Cir)

An attempt by the courts of one nation to adjudicate the personal claims of international civil servants would entangle those courts in the internal administration of those organizations. Denial of immunity opens the door to divided decisions of the courts of different member states passing judgments on the rules, regulations, and decisions of the international bodies. Undercutting uniformity in the application of staff rules or regulations would undermine the ability of the organization to function effectively.[511]

Within the system of the three sections, 1609, 1610, 1611, the last one is the exception from section 1610 or, in other words, the *exception from the exception.* This conclusion is inevitable when looking at the drafting technique and the wording[512], and it is confirmed by the *House Report.*[513] The question who bears the burden of proof under section 1611 was already asked in federal jurisprudence, and it was answered conclusively; it is the foreign states who has the burden of demonstrating with evidence to the court that an exception from the exception applies in the case, thereby granting immunity to the foreign property. The first precedent was *Behring International v. I.R.I.A.F. (Behring I)*[514], which I discussed already, where the question was answered in an *obiter dictum.* The plaintiff was seeking to attach property of the Iranian Air Force situated in the United States. The defendant invoked section 1611(b)(2)(B) in support of their immunity claim, and the judge stated:

Behring I

As was previously stated ... , I have not felt it necessary to address all other arguments raised by I.R.I.A.F. in its moving papers. Most importantly, this opinion leaves unresolved the applicability of I.R.I.A.F.'s third argument, regarding 28 U.S.C. §1611(b)(2)(B) ...

Although this argument raises serious questions about whether section 1611 governs in spite of prior international agreements, or is merely a codification of prior law, I need not resolve them now because there has been an utter failure of proof on the issue of who controls the property restrained by I.R.I.A.F. in support of this motion. The Verified Complaint alleges that all of the property now restrained in its warehouse is under Behring's control and that Behring is neither a military authority nor a defense agency ...

I.R.I.A.F., which has the burden of proving a defense of immunity, see n. 16, supra, has offered no testimony of any other form of proof that contradicts these verified allegations.[515]

Then, in *Behring II*[516], regarding the attachment of this property, the court again stated on the question of the burden of proof, and concluded:

Behring II

Although I.R.I.A.F. raised its contentions with respect to section 1611(b) of the Act, I refrained from deciding that issue because the record was barren of any facts supporting its claim. In spite of the continued barrenness of the record, which again causes me to conclude that I.R.I.A.F. has not carried its burden of showing that its property is immune, I will address this argument in more detail at this time.[517]

The judge, inter alia[518], looked at the relationship between sections 1610 and 1611 and reasoned in the manner I have shown it above, concluding that 'section 1611 applies notwithstanding only the exception to immunity set out within the act in section 1610.'

Then, the judge added this important argument which makes sense as to the logic of statutory construction:

Behring II

Section 1611 standing alone has no effect on those exception from without the Act virtue of the savings clause of section 1609.[519]

As to the evidence problems under section 1611(b)(2), the court concluded:

Behring II

I.R.I.A.F. has not shown that either of these exceptions apply. There is no proof in the record of this case regarding whether the property sought to be attached is of a military character. It is therefore not immune from attachment under section 1611(b)(2)(A). Likewise, there is no evidence contradicting the allegations of Behring's Verified Complaint and supporting affidavits that the property is in the control of Behring, which is neither a military authority nor a defense agency. The property therefore is not immune from attachment under section 1611(b)(2)(B). The only proof submitted by the defendant which addresses this issue is the affidavit of Colonel Khatami, filed May 4, 1979, at p. 2, to the effect that the materials were purchased for use in connection with I.R.I.A.F. military activities. At most, I.R.I.A.F. has raised an issue of fact with respect to only this last element.

I must conclude that I.R.I.A.F. has not sustained its burden of showing immunity from attachment.[520]

It is interesting to see that a district court, also in the present case, quoted the House Report's statement which is to be found in the section regarding jurisdictional immunity, thereby implicating that that statement could possibly be, or is possibly valid, also for immunity from execution. To repeat it, my view is that such an analogy cannot be drawn, neither from a point of view of statutory construction, nor under the existing principles of international law because of the different character and development of the two immunity rules.

In a more recent precedent, *Banque Compafina v. Banco de Guatemala, Desarrollo de Autopistas y Carreteras de Guatemala S.Al, Estoril Associated, Inc. and Devco Development Co., Inc.*[521], this attribution of the burden of proof was confirmed with regard to §1611(b)(1) FSIA. Compafina, a Swiss bank, sought confirmation of an order of attachment rendered by the New York Supreme Court. Banco de Guatemala, the central bank of that country[522], had the action removed to the competent district court, under §1441(d) FSIA. The property in question was Banco de Guatemala's, situated in the United States. The action was based upon a letter of credit issued by Banco de Guatemala for securing certain promissory notes of defendant Desarrollo de Autopistas y Carreteras de Guatemala, S.A.

With respect to the relationship between sections 1609, 1610, 1611 FSIA, the district court explained:

Banque Compafina v. Banco de Guatemala, et al.

Under the FSIA, a foreign state's property in the United States is generally immune from attachment. §1609. Section 1610 provides some exceptions to this general rule, but §1611(b)(1) overrides these exceptions ... [523]

The court thus confirmed my hypothesis that §1611 contains exceptions from the exceptions in §1610 FSIA. As to the allocation of the burden of proof, the judge held:

Banque Compafina v. Banco de Guatemala, et al.

To come within §1611(b)(1), Banco de Guatemala must show that the attached funds were 'held for its own account', since Compafina does not dispute that Banco de Guatemala is a central bank within the meaning of §1611(b)(1).[524]

The burden of proof for the fact that the funds were 'held for its own account' was thus upon the foreign state, or his agency or instrumentality, respectively. This corresponds to the ruling in *Behring II*, where the same allocation of the burden of proof was held to exist under §1611(b)(2) FSIA.

It is interesting to observe in which way Banco de Guatemala proceeded to produce this evidence, particularly when you think, to anticipate here a bit, at the analogous provision, §13(5) State Immunity Act 1978, of the United Kingdom. The court took reference to the legal materials[525] and explained regarding the criterion 'held for its own account':

Banque Compafina v. Banco de Guatemala, et al.

According to the relevant legislative history, funds held for a central bank's 'own account' are 'funds used or held in connection with central bank activities, as distinguished from funds used solely to finance the commercial transactions of other entities or of foreign states.[526]

In order to prove that the funds were used or detained in connection with central bank activities, Banco de Guatemala provided an affidavit of his vice president, Oscar Alvarez that stated under oath:

Affidavit Oscar Alvarez

In connection with the central banking activities, Banco de Guatemala maintains certain assets in the United States, including gold reserves deposited with the Federal Reserve Bank of New York and funds on deposit with commercial banks in New York City.[527]

The president of the Federal Reserve Bank in New York produced another affidavit, confirming that Banco de Guatemala was the owner of the funds held with the Federal Reserve and that it did not use those reserves in connection with a commercial banking function, or any other commercial activity. In addition, the president provided an important policy argument by stating that 'if foreign central banks such as Banco de Guatemala become concerned that their United States assets are subject to attachment by private litigants, they might withdraw their dollar assets from this country, thereby destabilizing the dollar and the international monetary system.[528] In addition, the affidavit stated under oath that '[t]he assets the Reserve Bank holds for the account of Banco de Guatemala are held solely for the account of Banco de Guatemala and are not held directly or indirectly for any other party ... '.[529] However, Compafina contested this evidence, referring to Alvarez' affidavit and arguing that Banco de Guatemala regularly negotiated loans for import-export banks of various countries and that for this reason the funds were not held exclusively for the central bank's own account.[530] The court carefully examined this argument and concluded:

Banque Compafina v. Banco de Guatemala, et al.

However, the fact that Banco de Guatemala may receive these loans does not contradict Alvarez' statement that Banco de Guatemala's funds in the United States are held '[i]n connection with its central banking activities', ... nor does it tend to show that the funds in the United States are used for commercial activities. At his preliminary stage, Banco de Guatemala has established by a preponderance of evidence before the court that the attached funds are held for its own account.[531]

While the court rejected Compafina's argument, but from a point of view of civil procedure under the FSIA, it was important to see that the plaintiff can contradict the evidence of the central bank and that the court has to use the ordinary evaluation procedure for the evidence in the record. In this respect, §1611 makes no exception, in other words, central banks do not enjoy a higher level of credibility than any other defendant, and the evidence produced by a central bank for claiming sovereign immunity can be contested by the plaintiff, who then of course bears the evidential burden, while the legal burden here is upon the foreign state or its central bank for the criteria contained in §1611. Now, it is interesting to have a look at the analogous solution contained in §13(5) of the UK's *State Immunity Act 1978*, which stipulates:

U.K. State Immunity Act 1978

(5) The head of a State's diplomatic mission in the United Kingdom, or the person for the time being performing his functions, shall be deemed to have authority to give on behalf of the State ... his certificate to the effect that any property is not in use or intended for use by or on behalf of the State for commercial purposes shall be accepted as sufficient evidence of that fact unless the contrary is proved.

This provision contains thus a *proof facilitation* in favor of the foreign state; a simple certificate of the chief of a diplomatic mission, or his representative, suffices for establishing a presumption that the property of the foreign state serves governmental functions. Hence, the burden of proof is upon the plaintiff for rebutting this presumption ('unless the contrary is proved') if he is to succeed with attaching those assets.[532]

Analogous provisions are contained in §15(5) of Singapore's *State Immunity Act 1979* and §14(4) of Pakistan's *State Immunity Ordinance 1981*, while Canada's *State Immunity Act 1982* provides in §11(4) a solution that is almost identical with the one of the FSIA. However, South Africa's *Foreign States Immunities Act 87, 1981*, §§15(3), 14(1),(2) does not allow any attachment of central bank assets, except the bank has explicitly waived its immunity from execution, and that the waiver has been issued in a written document.

Under the FSIA, the formulation used by the court, that the central bank was able to prove, by a preponderance of the evidence, that the assets were held for its own account, shows that the ordinary evidence rules are applicable also for §1611 FSIA, in that a presumption always indicates that the party that must overcome it, bears the burden of proof; this burden is namely not attenuated as in some of the other immunity statutes, under the American Act. The pleadings show this very illustratively in the present case record. There were no simple certificates around here, as in many precedents that regard immunity from jurisdiction; all that was produced were sworn affidavits from high or top officials of the foreign state or its central bank. This is important to note because it shows a cleavage between the American and the Canadian immunity statutes, and the others, in this important matter regarding the problems of proof for immunity from execution. This also confirms my hypothesis that the burden of proof question for immunity from execution needs to be carefully distinguished from the analogous question regarding immunity from jurisdiction, which means the question has to be seen within the legal framework of immunity from execution. The levels of immunity here simply are different and therefore, the two domains need to be carefully distinguished.

To conclude, American federal jurisprudence has clearly unveiled that for immunity from execution, within the framework of sections 1609, 1610, 1611 FSIA, the burden of proof for the exception from the exception, that is, §1611, is upon the foreign state for demonstrating by evidence satisfactorily to the court that the conditions of that section are fulfilled.

As a result, in the whole of the framework of these three sections, regarding to the relationship between the rule, §1609, and the exceptions, §1610, the burden of proof is upon the plaintiff that one of the exceptions to immunity from execution applies. This is the inevitable result, simply as a matter of statutory logic. But there is another logical consequence, it is that the rule of sovereign immunity from execution, §1609, is a real presumption *pro immunitatem*, and not like §1604, a mere residual immunity concept.

We can thus conclude that the burden of proof for the commercial usage of the property in question *(usibus destinata)*, as a criterion contained in §§1610(a)(2),(b)(2) FSIA, is upon the plaintiff.

Conclusion

The burden of proof for the facts pertinent to the applicability of an exception to immunity from execution, §§ 1609, 1610 FSIA, is principally upon the plaintiff. The general rule of foreign sovereign immunity regarding the execution into property belonging to foreign states, or their agencies and instrumentalities, §1609, is *absolute* in the sense that it is only partially lowered through the exceptions contained in §1610. This result is confirmed by the fact that for the exceptions from the exceptions, §1611, the burden of proof is upon the foreign state.

When a private merchant, plaintiff in an action against a foreign state, wishes to execute a judgment against the foreign state by seizing any property of that state situated in the United States, and is to succeed, he must show by a preponderance of the evidence to the court that one of the exceptions contained in section 1610 is applicable. If the plaintiff fails to produce this evidence, the property of the foreign state is immune from execution, without the foreign state needing to plead any further motion, for the presumption of immunity will do its effect, §1610. That means that the rule is, *in dubio pro immunitatem*, as it was once suggested by Professor Dr. Georg Ress, an eminent German legal scholar and expert in matters of foreign sovereign immunity.[533]

CONCLUSION

General Conclusion

Immunity from Jurisdiction

Under the *Sovereign Immunities Act 1976*, the burden of proof is principally upon the foreign state, or its agency or instrumentality, to produce evidence in support of their immunity claim. This means that the foreign state has the right to begin with producing evidence and thus bears the evidential burden, and the legal or persuasive burden for demonstrating that despite the exceptions stipulated in the FSIA, immunity should apply.

However, this burden of proving the facts that are at issue for the immunity claim, is not such that the foreign state had to disprove all and every immunity exceptions, but only those the plaintiff invoked in his complaint. Only on these elements in the record, the foreign state needs to make a *prima facie case*, to demonstrate that the action that is at the basis of the lawsuit before the court was one of a public, governmental character.

The foreign state needs to produce this prima evidence on two elements, that it is:

(i) that it is a foreign state, or an agency or instrumentality of a foreign state, §§1603(a),(b) FSIA;

(ii) that the action under scrutiny, that gave rise to the lawsuit, was of a public, governmental character.

As to the second element, the foreign state or its organism do not need to refute all the exceptions from immunity, but only those that the plaintiff has invoked as a basis of its claim against the foreign state. Once the foreign state has produced such prima face evidence, the evidential burden shifts to the plaintiff in order to demonstrate that the particular exception, or exceptions, that he invoked, really are applicable, and this proof has then to overcome the *prima facie evidence*, which means the proof must be 'more probably than not', or in other words, the facts at issue regarding the applicability of an exception to immunity need to be proven by a *preponderance of the evidence*, satisfactorily to the court.

For all the other elements of the claim, especially *personal jurisdiction* and *minimal contacts, service of process* and *default judgment*, the burden of proof is entirely upon the plaintiff.

Immunity from Execution

The burden of proof in matters of immunity from execution is principally with the plaintiff. He can seize the property of a foreign state or one of its organisms only if he can prove, by a preponderance of the evidence, that an exception to the general rule applies.

Contrary to the situation that governs immunity from jurisdiction under the FSIA, here it's the plaintiff who has the right to begin producing evidence, which means he is charged with the evidential burden, in order to demonstrate that an exception to the general rule of immunity applies. Here it is thus the plaintiff who needs to establish a prima facie case, which the foreign state or its organism may overcome by invoking one of the exceptions from the exception, under §1611 FSIA. In this case, the burden of proof is upon the foreign state to demonstrate that such an exception from the exception applies.

In all cases of *non liquet*, that is, when the court doesn't have enough evidence in the record or the evidence is contradictory to a point that no decision can be made upon it, the ultimate or legal burden, also called persuasive burden, is upon the plaintiff. In other words, for immunity from execution, the immunity rule is still absolute in the sense that in a *non liquet* situation, the rule *in dubio pro immuni-tatem* is to be applied by the court.

ABBREVIATIONS

For Periodicals and Digests

A.B.A.J.
American Bar Association Journal (Chicago, USA)

A 1964 SC 72
The All India Reporter, 1964, Supreme Court,

A.C.
Law Reports Appeal Cases, 1891 -

A.I.R.
The All India Reporter, Bombay, India

A.I.R. Manual
The A. I. R. Manual, Unrepealed Central Acts, Bombay, India

AJIL
American Journal of International Law

A.L.I.
American Law Institute

3 All E R 441 (1957)
All England Law Reports, Vol. 3, 1957, pp. 441 ff.

[1874-80] All E.R. Rep. 104
All England Law Reports, Volume 1874-1880, pp. 104 ff.

[1948] Ann.Dig. 137 (No.42)
Annual Digest, 1948, pp. 137 ff. (Case No. 42)

BDGVR
Berichte der deutschen Gesellschaft für Völkerrecht

C.P.C.
Civil Procedure Code

CPD
Law Reports Common Pleas Division, 1875-1880

D. L. R.
Dominion Law Reports 1912 - date (Canada)

441 F.Supp. 827
Federal Supplement, Vol. 441, pp. 827 ff.

706 F.2d 411
Federal Reporter, Second Series, Vol. 706, pp. 411 ff.

ICLQ
International and Comparative Law Quarterly

ILM
International Legal Materials

ILR
International Law Reports (Lauterpacht)

J.M.C.L.
Journal of Malaysian Comparative Law

K.B.

Law Reports: King's Bench Division, 1901-1952

Laws of Kenya

Laws of Kenya, Revised Edition, Government Printer, Nairobi

L.Ed.

United States Supreme Court Reports, Lawyer's Edition

Lloyd's Rep.

Lloyd's List Law Reports, 1919 - date

Model Code

Model Code of Evidence, American Law Institute, Chestnut, 1942

P.

Law Reports Probate, Divorce and Admiralty, 1981-1971

P.D.

Law Reports Probate Division, 1875-1890

PLD SC

The All Pakistan Legal Decisions, Church Road, Lahore, Pakistan

Public Law

Public Law of the United States

Q.B.

Law Reports: Queen's Bench Division, 1891-1901, 1952 - date

Que.P.R.

Quebec Practice Reports (Canada)

Que.R.P.

Quebec Rapports Pratiques (Canada)

Que.SC

Quebec Official Reports, Superior Court (Quebec), Canada

Rapport C.R.D.C.

Rapport de la Commission de Réforme du Droit de Canada

RCADI

International Law Academy, Collected Cases, Boston, The Hague

R.C.D.I.P.

Revue Critique de Droit International Privé

R.C.S.

Rapports de la Cour Suprême du Canada

1980 (2) SA 709 (E)

South African Law Reports, Vol.2, 1980, pp. 709 ff. (Eastern Cape D.)

1980 (2) SA 111 (T)

South African Law Reports, Vol.2, 1980, pp. 111 ff. (Transvaal Division)

S.C.R.

Supreme Court Reports (Canada)

S.Ct.

Supreme Court Reporter (USA)

STAT

United States Statutes at Large

The Pakistan Code

The Pakistan Code, Government of Pakistan, 1966, Vol. I-XVII

TIAS

Treaties and Other International Act Series, Department of State

13 U.L.A. Civil Proc.

Uniform Laws Annotated, Vol. 13, Civil Procedural and Remedial Law

U.L.C.C. Report
Uniform Law Commission of Canada, Report of the Task Force on Uniform Rules of Evidence, Toronto (Carswell), 1982

UN-Mat.
Materials on Jurisdictional Immunities of States and their Property, Doc. ST/LEG/SER.B./20, New York (United Nations), 1982

U.S.
United States Reports (U.S. Supreme Court)

U.S.C.
United States Code

U.S.C.A.
United States Code Annotated

28 U.S.C.A. §1611
United States Code Annotated, Title 28, Section 1611

UST
United States Treaties and other International Agreements, 1950- date

West's Ann.Evid.Code, §110
West's Annotated California Codes, Evidence Code, Vol. 29 B, St. Paul (West), 1977, Section 110

W.L.R.
Weekly Law Reports

ZaöRV
Zeitschrift für ausländisches öffentliches Recht und Völkerrecht (Max-Planck-Institut für ausländisches öffentliches Recht und Völkerrecht)

ZZP
Zeitschrift für Zivilprozess

BIBLIOGRAPHY

Alphabetical, by Author Last Name

A

American Law Institute

Model Code on Evidence
Chestnut, Philadelphia, 1942

Asencio, Diego C. & Dry, Robert W.

An Assessment of the Service Provisions of the Foreign Sovereign Immunities Act of 1976
8 JOURNAL OF LEGISLATION (Notre Dame Law School) 230-249 (1981)

Ashman, Allan

People's Republic Told to Pay $42.1 Million Debt From 1911
Jackson v. People's Republic of China
69 A.B.A.J. 512(2) (1983)

B

Badr, Gamal Moursi

State Immunity
An Analytical and Prognostic View

The Hague: Martinus Nijhoff, 1984

Bankas, Ernest K.

The State Immunity Controversy in International Law
Private Suits Against Sovereign States
New York: Springer, 2005

Bennion, Francis

Statutory Interpretation
London: Butterworths, 1984

Block, Mark A.

De Sanchez v. Banco Central de Nicaragua:
An Extension of the Restrictive Theory of Sovereign Immunity
7 N.C.J.INT'L L. & COMM.REG. 419-431 (1982)

Brownlie, Ian

Principles of Public International Law
Oxford: Clarendon Press, 1966

Bodin, Jean

On Sovereignty (1576)
Six Books of the Commonwealth
Edited by Professor Julian Franklin
New York: Seven Treasures Publications, 2009

Bowman & Harris

Multilateral Treaties
Index and Current Status
London: Butterworths, 1984

Bradley, A.G.

Service of Process under the Foreign Sovereign Immunities Act of 1976:
The Arguments For Exclusivity
14 CORNELL INT'L L.J. 357-368 (1981)

Brittenham, David L.

Foreign Sovereign Immunity and Commercial Activity: A Conflicts Approach
83 COLUM.L.REV. 1440-1512 (1983)

Brooke, Julia

The International Law Association Draft Convention on Foreign Sovereign Immunity: A Comparative Approach
23 VA.J.INT'L L. 635 (1983)

Brower/Bistline/Loomis

The Foreign Sovereign Immunities Act of 1976 in Practice
73 AJIL 200 (1979)

Brownlie, Jan

Principles of Public International Law
Oxford: Clarendon Press, 1976

Butler, W. E.

International Law in Comparative Perspective
Ed. By William Elliott Butler
Alphen an den Rijn: Sijthoff en Noordhoff, 1980

Comparative Approaches to International Law
190 RCADI (1985-I), 9-90

C

Cairns, G.

Jurisdiction: Foreign Sovereign Immunities Act
TEX.INT'L L.J. 277-289 (1981)

Canada

Uniform Evidence Act, Livre II
Règles Générales de Preuve, Titre I, Fardeau de la Preuve

Commission de Réforme du Droit du Canada
Rapport sur la Preuve (Premier Rapport)
Ottawa: Ministre des Approvisionnements et Services, 1977

Report of the Federal/Provincial Task Force on Uniform Rules of Evidence
Prepared for the Uniform Law Conference of Canada
Toronto: The Carswell Company Ltd., 1982 [U.L.C.C. Report]

Cappelletti, Mauro & Perillo, Joseph M.

Civil Procedure in Italy
The Hague: Martinus Nijhoff, 1965

Carl, B.M.

Suing Foreign Governments in American Courts:
The United States Foreign Sovereign Immunities Act in Practice
33 SOUTHWESTERN L.J. 1009-1077 (1979)

Castel, Jean-Gabriel

Droit International Privé Québécois
Toronto: Butterworths, 1980

Canadian Conflict of Laws
2nd Edition
Toronto: Butterworths, 1986

Coad, Brian Douglas

The Canadian State Immunity Act
XIV LAW & POL'Y INT'L BUS. 1197-1220 (1982-83)

Crocker, Lawrence

Sovereign Immunity in the United States
29 I.C.L.Q. 580-510 (1980)

Coyne, Thomas A.

Rules of Civil Procedure for the United States District Courts
Practice Comments
New York: Clark Boardman Company Ltd., 1983

Cross, Sir Rupert

Cross on Evidence
5th ed.
London: Butterworths, 1979

Cross on Evidence
2nd Australian Edition
By J.A. Gobbo, David Byrne, J.D. Heydon
Sidney: Butterworths, 1980

Introduction to Criminal Law

10th Edition
London: Butterworths, 1984

Cross, Sir Rupert & Wilkins, Nancy

An Outline of the Law of Evidence
5th Edition
London: Butterworths, 1980

Curzon, L.B.

Law of Evidence
Plymouth: McDonald & Evans Ltd., 1978

D

D. Carl IV

The Foreign Sovereign Immunities Act of 1976
N.C.J.INT'L L. & COMM.REG. 206-233 (1978)

Delaume, Georges R.

Transnational Contracts
Applicable Law and Settlement of Disputes (A Study in Conflict Avoidance)
New York, Oceana

E

Eggleston, Sir Richard

Evidence, Proof and Probability
2nd Edition
London: Weidenfels & Nicholson, 1983

F

Fox, Hazel

The Law of State Immunity
Oxford: Oxford Library of International Law, 2004

G

Glasbeek, Harry J.

Evidence Cases and Materials
Toronto: Butterworths, 1977

Cases and Materials on Evidence
Australian Edition
Sydney: Butterworths, 1974

Graham, Michael H.

Evidence
Text, Rules, Illustrations and Problems
The Commentary Method
St. Paul (Minn.): National Institute for Trial Advocacy, 1983

Federal Rules of Evidence in a Nutshell
St. Paul (Minn.): American Textbook Series, 1981

Grzybowsky, Kazimierz

Soviet Public International Law, Doctrines - Diplomatic Practice
Leyden: A.W. Sijthoff, 1970

H

Halsbury's Laws of England

4th Edition, Vol. 17, 'Evidence'
London: Butterworths

Harvard Draft Convention

Competence of Courts in Regard to Foreign States
Rep. by Philip C. Jessup
26 AJIL 452 (1932 Suppl.)

Harvard University

A Uniform System of Citation
13th Edition
Cambridge, Mass.: Harvard Law Review Association, 1982

Hearing before the Subcommittee on Administrative Practice and Procedure

Committee of the Judiciary, United States Senate, 91st Cong., 2nd Session, June 3, 1970
Washington, D.C., 1970

Henkin/Pugh/Schachter/Smit

International Law
Cases and Materials
St. Paul (West): American Casebook Series, 1980

Higgins, Rosalyn

Certain Unresolved Aspects of the Law of State Immunity
XXIX NETH.INT'L L.REV. 265 (1982)

House Report

H.R. Report 94-1487
15 ILM 1398 (1976), U.S.Code & Adm. News 6604 (1976)

Hunt Holmes, Patricia

Establishing Jurisdiction under the Commercial-Activities Exception to the Foreign Sovereign Immunities Act of 1976
19 HOUS.L.REV. 1003-1023 (1982)

I

Inter-American Draft Convention on Jurisdictional Immunity of States

22 ILM 292 (1983)

International Law Association (ILA)

Report of the Fifty-Ninth Conference Held at Belgrade, 1980

International Law Commission (ILC)

United Nations Convention on Jurisdictional Immunities of States and Their Property
Adopted by the General Assembly of the United Nations on 2 December 2004
Not yet in force. See General Assembly resolution 59/38, annex, Official
Records of the General Assembly, Fifty-ninth Session, Supplement No. 49
(A/59/49)

J

James, Fleming & Hazard, Geoffrey

Civil Procedure
2nd Edition
Toronto: Little, Brown & Company, 1977

Johnson, Eric & Worthington, Chr.

Minimum Contacts Jurisdiction under the Foreign Sovereign Immunities Act
12 GA.J.INT'L & COMP.L. 209-230 (1982)

Jurisdiction of U.S. Courts in Suits Against Foreign States

U.S. Congress, House of Representatives
Subcommittee on Administrative Law and Governmental Relations
of the Committee on the Judiciary
Hearing, June 4, 1976
Washington, D.C., 1976

K

Kahale III, G. & Vega, M. A.

Immunity and Jurisdiction
Toward a Uniform Body of Law in Actions Against Foreign States
19 COLUM.J.TRANSNAT'L L. 211-258 (1979)

Kane

Suing Foreign Governments: A Procedural Compass
34 STAN.L.REV. 385 (1982)

L

Lalive, Jean-Flavien

Contrats entre États ou entreprises étatiques et personnes privées
181 RCADI (1983-III), pp. 13 ff.

L'immunité de juridiction des états et des organisations internationales
84 RCADI (1953-III), pp. 209 ff.

Lauterpacht, E., Q.C.

International Law Reports
Cambridge: Grotius Publishers

Lauterpacht, Hersch

International Law
Ed. By E. Lauterpacht, Q.C.
Vol. 3
London: Cambridge University Press, 1977

The Problem of Jurisdictional Immunities of Foreign States
28 BRIT.Y.B.INT'L L. 220-272 (1951)

Leigh, Monroe

Alberti v. Empresa Nicaraguense de la Carne (Case Note)
77 AJIL 888 (1983)

Jackson v. People's Republic of China (Case Note)
Foreign Sovereign Immunities Act - Liability of People's Republic of China
for defaulted 1911 bonds - state succession
77 AJIL 146-148 (1983)

Matter of Sedco, Inc. (Case Note)
Sovereign Immunity - Foreign Sovereign Immunities Act
Commercial Activity and Tortious Conduct Exception not Applicable
to Support Jurisdiction over Defendant in Oil Spill Disaster
77 AJIL 149-151 (1983)

Lilly, Graham C.

An Introduction to the Law of Evidence
St. Paul (West), 1978

M

Machiavelli, Niccolo

The Prince
New York: Soho Books, 2009
Written in 1513
First posthumous publishing 1531

Mann, Francis A.

A New Aspect of the Restrictive Theory of Sovereign Immunity
31 I.C.L.Q. 573-575 (1982)

The State Immunity Act 1978
50 BRIT.Y.B.INT'L L. 43 (1979)

Materials on Jurisdictional Immunities of States and their Property

UN-Doc. ST/LEG- /SER.B./20
New York: United Nations, 1982

Maxwell on the Interpretation of Statutes

12th ed., by P. St. J. Langan
London: Sweet & Maxwell, 1969

McCormick

McCormick on Evidence
by Edward W. Cleary, 3d ed.
Lawyers Edition (Homebook Series)
St. Paul: West, 1984

McDougal/Reisman

International Law in Contemporary Perspective
The Public Order of the World Comity
Cases and Materials
New York: Foundation Press, 1981

Moore, James W.

Moore's Federal Practice
2nd Edition, 1979

N

Nash, Gerard

Civil Procedure
Cases and Text
Sydney: The Law Book Company Ltd., 1976

Nash, Marian Lloyd

Digest of United States Practice in International Law
Vol. 1978
Washington, D.C.: Depart of State Publications 9162, 1980

Ninth Decennial Digest

American Digest System
Part I, 1976-1981

O

Oppenheim, Lassa

International Law
8th Edition, by Hersch Lauterpacht
New York, 1955
Originally published in 1905/1906

Organization of American States (OAS)

Inter-American Draft Convention on Jurisdictional Immunity of States
22 ILM 292 (1983)

P

Patrikis, Ernest T.

Foreign Central Bank Property
Immunity from Attachment in the United States
1982 U.ILL.L.REV. 265-287

Pell, Terence J.

The Foreign Sovereign Immunities Act of 1976: Direct Effects and Minimal Contacts
14 CORNELL INT'L.L.J. 97-115 (1981)

Phipson

Phipson on Evidence
13th ed., by John Huxley Buzzard
Richard May and M. N. Howard
London: Sweet & Maxwell, 1982

Phipson and Elliott

Manual of the Law of Evidence
11th Edition
by D. W. Elliott
London: Sweet & Maxwell, 1980

Pope, Russell J.

Maritime Arrest Under the Foreign Sovereign Immunities Act: An Anachronism
62 TEX.L.REV. 511-535 (1983)

R

Ress, Georg

Entwicklungstendenzen der Immunität ausländischer Staaten
40 ZaöRV 217 (1980)

Les tendances de l'évolution de l'immunité de l'État étranger
in: Droit international et droit interne
Édité par Michael Bothe et Raul E. Vinesa
Colloque argentino-allemand de droit constitutionnel, Buenos Aires, 1979
Berlin: Duncker & Humblot, 1982 (Schriften zum Völkerrecht, Bd. 73)

Rothstein, Paul F.

Evidence in a Nutshell: State and Federal Rules
2nd Edition
St. Paul (West), 1981

Rules of Civil Procedure for the United States District Courts

Practice Comments by Thomas A. Coyne
New York: Clark Boardman Company Ltd., 1983

S

Schmitthoff, C. M. & Wooldridge, F.

*The nineteenth century doctrine of sovereign immunity
and the importance of the growth of state trading*
2 DEN.J.INT'L L. & POL'Y 199 (1972)

Schubert, M. H.

Federal Question Jurisdiction Over Actions Brought by Aliens against Foreign States
CORNELL INT'L L.J. 463-488 (1982)

Schwarzenberger, Georg

The Inductive Approach to International Law
London, 1965

Schwering, Walter

System der Beweislast im englisch-amerikanischen Zivilprozess
Karlsruhe: C. F. Müller, 1969 (Berkeley-Kölner Rechtsstudien, Bd. 11)

Sgro, Jill A.

*China's stance on sovereign immunity: a critical perspective on
Jackson v. People's Republic of China*
22 COLUM.J.TRANSNAT'L L. 101-133 (1983)

Siewert, Clark C.

*Reciprocal Influence of British and United States Law:
Foreign Sovereign Immunity Law from the Schooner Exchange
to the State Immunity Act 1978*
13 VAND.J.TRANSNAT'L L. 761-794 (1980)

Simmons, Kevin P.

*The Foreign Sovereign Immunities Act of 1976:
Giving the Plaintiff His Day in Court*
64 FORDHAM L.REV. 543 (1977)

Sinclair, Ian

The Law of Sovereign Immunity. Recent Developments.
167 RCADI (1980-II) 117

Smallwood, J. M.

Recent Developments in the Anglo-American Doctrine of Foreign Sovereign Immunity
5 INT'L TRADE L.J. 296-318 (1980)

Smit, Hans

The Terms Jurisdiction and Competence in Comparative Law
10 AM.J.COMP.L. 164-169 (1961)

Smith, P. F. / Bailey, S.

The Modern English Legal System
London: Sweet & Maxwell, 1984

Steiner/Vagts

Transnational Legal Problems
Materials and Text
2nd Ed.
Minneola, N.Y.: Foundation Press, 1976

1982 Case and Documentary Supplement
Minneola, N.Y.: Foundation Press, 1982

Stern

Foreign Law in the Courts
Judicial Notice and Proof
54 Calif.L.Rev., 23 (1957)

Stone's Justices Manual

113th Edition
Ed. by John Richman and A. T. Draycott
London: Butterworths, 1981

Sucharitkul, Sompong

Developments and Prospects of the Doctrine of State Immunity
Some Aspects of Codification and Progressive Development
XXIX NETH.INT'L L.REV. 252 (1982)

Immunités Juridictionnelles des États et de leurs Biens
Rapports du rapporteur spécial
Annuaire de la Commission du Droit International, 1986, Volume II, 2e Partie,
New York: Nations Unies, 1988
Annuaire de la Commission du Droit International, 1984, Volume II, 2e Partie,
New York: Nations Unies, 1986

Immunities of Foreign States Before National Authorities
149 RCADI (1976-I) 86

State Immunities and Trading Activities in International Law
London: Steven & Sons, 1959

Sutherland

Statutory Construction
Ed. By Sands
4th Edition
London, 1975

Sutherland, P.

Recent Statutory Developments in the Law of Foreign Sovereign Immunity
7 AUSTRALIAN Y.B.INT'L L. 27-71 (1981)

Sweeny/Oliver/Leech

The International Legal System
Cases and Materials
2nd Edition
Minneola, N.Y.: Foundation Press, 1981

T

Tayer, James Bradley

A Preliminary Treatise on Evidence
1898

Tesón, Fernando A.

The Relations Between International Law and Municipal Law:
The Monism/Dualism Controversy
in: *International Law and Municipal Law*, ed. by Michael Bothe and Raul E. Vinesa
Colloque argentino-allemand de droit constitutionnel
Buenos Aires, 1979
Berlin: Duncker & Humblot, 1982
(Schriften zum Völkerrecht, Bd. 73)

The English and Empire Digest

Vol. 22, 'Evidence'
London: Butterworths, 1974

The Statesman Yearbook

119th Edition, 1982-83
Ed. by John Paxton
London, 1982

Troya Cevallos, José Alfonso

Elementos de Derecho Procesal Civil, Tomo 1
Quito: Centro de Publicaciones Pontificia Universidad Católica del Ecuador, 1978

U

United Nations

Materials on Jurisdictional Immunities of States and their Property
UN-DOC. ST/LEG/SER.B./20
New York: United Nations, 1982 (UN-MAT.)

United Nations Convention on Jurisdictional Immunities of States and Their Property
Adopted by the General Assembly of the United Nations on 2 December 2004
Not yet in force. See General Assembly resolution 59/38, annex,
Official Records of the General Assembly
Fifty-ninth Session, Supplement No. 49 (A/59/49)

Urteaga, Pedro S.

Derecho Procesal Civil
Tomo II
Secunda Edición
Lima, 1982

V

Vallée, Charles

A propos de la convention européenne sur l'immunité des États
9 REV.TRIM.DR.EUR. 205 (1973)

Varela/Bezerra/Sampio e Nova

Manual de Processo Civil
Coimbra: Coimbra Editora Limitada, 1984

Von Mehren, R. B.

The Foreign Sovereign Immunities Act of 1976
17 COLUM.J.TRANSNAT'L L. 33-66 (1978)

W

Walder-Bohner, Hans Ulrich

Zivilprozessrecht
3. Auflage
Zürich: Schulthess, 1983

Walker & Walker

The English Legal System
6th Edition, by R.J. Walker
London: Butterworths, 1985

Walter, Peter-Fritz

Gibt es eine Beweislastverteilung bei der Immunität von Staaten?
30 RECHT DER INTERNATIONALEN WIRTSCHAFT (RIW/AWD) 9-14 (1984)

Weber

The Foreign Sovereign Immunities Act of 1976: Its Origin, Meaning and Effect
3 YALE STUD.WORLD PUB.ORD. 1 (1976)

Weiss, André

Compétence ou incompétence des tribunaux à l'égard des états étrangers
1 RCADI (1923) 525

West's Encyclopedia of American Law

Second Edition
New York: Gale Group, 2008

Wharton

Wharton's Criminal Law
14th ed. by Charles E. Torcia
Vol. II, §§99-282
Rochester, New York: The Lawyers Cooperative
Publishing Co., 1979

White, Robin C. A.

The State Immunity Act 1978
42 MODERN L.REV. 72-79 (1979)

Whiteman

Digest of International Law
Vol. 6
Washington, D.C.: Department of State Publication 8350, 1968

Wigmore, John Henry

A Treatise on the Anglo-American System of Evidence in Trials at Common Law
10 Volumes, Vol. 9 'Evidence in Trials at Common Law'
Rev. by James H. Chadburn
Boston, Toronto: Little, Brown & Company, 1981

Words and Phrases Legally Defined

Ed. by John B. Saunders
2nd Edition
London: Butterworths, 1969

Wright, Miller & Cooper

Federal Practice and Procedure, 1975

Y

Yaffe, Robert H.

Direct Financial Effects under the Foreign Sovereign Immunities Act
14 LAW.AMERICAS 361-365 (1982)

Yannopoulos, A. N.

*Foreign sovereign immunity and the arrest of state-owned ships:
the need for an admiralty foreign sovereign immunities act*
57 TUL.L.REV. 1274-1342 (1983)

STATUTES

The FSIA 1976

The Foreign Sovereign Immunities Act, 1976

See also Wikipedia on the Foreign Sovereign Immunities Act

See also U.S. Code Collection

Public Law 94-583 (H.R. 11315), 90 STAT 2891-2898, 28 U.S.C.1330, 1391, 1602-1611, 71 AJIL 595 (1977), 15 ILM 1388 (1976).

Literature

Kane, *Suing Foreign Sovereigns: A Procedural Compass,* 34 STAN. L. REV. 385 (1982).

Robert B. von Mehren, *The Foreign Sovereign Immunities Act of 1976,* 17 COLUM. J. TRANSNAT'L L. 33-66 (1978).

G. Kahale/M.A. Vega, *Immunity and Jurisdiction: toward a uniform body of law in actions against foreign states,* 18 COLUM. J. TRANSNAT'L L. 211-258 (1979).

N. H. Schubert, *Federal question jurisdiction over actions brought by aliens against foreign states,* CORNELL INT'L L. J. 463-488 (1982)

J. M. Smallwood, *Recent Developments in the Anglo-American Doctrine of Foreign Sovereign Immunity,* 5 INT'L TRADE L. J. 296-318 (1980).

B. M. Carl, *Suing Foreign Governments in American Courts: the United States Foreign Sovereign Immunities Act in Practice*, 33 SOUTHWESTERN L. J. 1009-1077 (1979).

D. Clark IV, *The Foreign Sovereign Immunities Act of 1976*, N. C. J. INT'L L. & COMM. REG. 206-233 (1978).

K. P. Simmons, *The Foreign Sovereign Immunities Act of 1976, Giving the Plaintiff His Day in Court*, 46 FORDHAM L. REV. 543 (1977).

Weber, *The Foreign Sovereign Immunities Act of 1976: Its Origin, Meaning and Effect*, 3 YALE STUD. WORLD PUB. ORD. 1 (1976).

Gamal Moursi Badr, *State Immunity*, The Hague, Boston, Lancaster: Martinus Nijhoff, 1984.

Ian Sinclair, *The Law of Sovereign Immunity, Recent Developments*, RCADI (1980-II), pp. 121-128 and 161-170.

§ 1330. Actions against foreign states

(a) The district courts shall have original jurisdiction without regard to amount in controversy of any nonjury civil action against a foreign state as defined in section 1603(a) of this title as to any claim for relief in personam with respect to which the foreign state is not entitled to immunity either under sections 1605-1607 of this title or under any applicable international agreement.

(b) Personal jurisdiction over a foreign state shall exist as to every claim for relief over which the district courts have jurisdiction under subsection (a) where service has been made under section 1608 of this title.

(c) For purposes of subsection (b), an appearance by a foreign state does not confer personal jurisdiction with respect to any claim for relief not arising out of any transaction or occurrence enumerated in sections 1605-1607 of this title.

§ 1602. Findings and declaration of purpose

The Congress finds that the determination by United States courts of the claims of foreign states to immunity from the jurisdiction of such courts would serve the interests of justice and would protect the rights of both foreign states and litigants in United States courts. Under international law, states are not immune from the jurisdiction of foreign courts insofar as their commercial activities are concerned, and their commercial property may be levied upon for the satisfaction of judgments rendered against them in connection with their commercial activities. Claims of foreign states to immunity should henceforth be decided by courts of the United States and of the States in conformity with the principles set forth in this chapter.

§ 1603. Definitions

For purposes of this chapter—

(a) A 'foreign state', except as used in section 1608 of this title, includes a political subdivision of a foreign state or an agency or instrumentality of a foreign state as defined in subsection (b).

(b) An 'agency or instrumentality of a foreign state means any entity—

(1) which is a separate legal person, corporate or otherwise, and

(2) which is an organ of a foreign state or political subdivision thereof, or a majority of whose shares or other ownership interest is owned by a foreign state or political subdivision thereof, and

(3) which is neither a citizen of a State of the United States as defined in section 1332 (c) and (d) of this title, nor created under the laws of any third country.

(c) The 'United States' includes all territory and waters, continental or insular, subject to the jurisdiction of the United States.

(d) A 'commercial activity' means either a regular course of commercial conduct or a particular commercial transaction or act. The commercial character of an activity shall be determined by reference to the nature of the course of conduct or particular transaction or act, rather than by reference to its purpose.

(e) A 'commercial activity carried on in the United States by a foreign state' means commercial activity carried on by such state and having substantial contact with the United States.

§ 1604. Immunity of a foreign state from jurisdiction

Subject to existing international agreements to which the United States is a party at the time of enactment of this Act a foreign state shall be immune from the jurisdiction of the courts of the United States and of the States except as provided in sections 1605 to 1607 of this chapter.

§ 1605. General exceptions to the jurisdictional immunity of a foreign state

(a) A foreign state shall not be immune from the jurisdiction of courts of the United States or of the States in any case—

(1) in which the foreign state has waived its immunity either explicitly or by implication, notwithstanding any withdrawal of the waiver which the foreign state may purport to effect except in accordance with the terms of the waiver;

(2) in which the action is based upon a commercial activity carried on in the United States by the foreign state; or upon an act performed in the United States in connection with a commercial activity of the foreign state elsewhere; or upon an act outside the territory of the United States in connection with a commercial activity of the foreign state elsewhere and that act causes a direct effect in the United States;

(3) in which rights in property taken in violation of international law are in issue and that property or any property exchanged for such property is present in the United States in connection with a commercial activity carried on in the United States by the foreign state; or that property or any property exchanged for such property is owned or operated by an agency or instrumentality of the foreign state and that agency or instrumentality is engaged in a commercial activity in the United States;

(4) in which rights in property in the United States acquired by succession or gift or rights in immovable property situated in the United States are in issue;

(5) not otherwise encompassed in paragraph (2) above, in which money damages are sought against a foreign state for personal injury or death, or damage to or loss of property, occurring in the United States and caused by the tortious act or omission of that foreign state or of any official or employee of that foreign state while acting within the scope of his office or employment; except this paragraph shall not apply to—

(A) any claim based upon the exercise or performance or the failure to exercise or perform a discretionary function regardless of whether the discretion be abused, or

(B) any claim arising out of malicious prosecution, abuse of process, libel, slander, misrepresentation, deceit, or interference with contract rights;

(6) in which the action is brought, either to enforce an agreement made by the foreign state with or for the benefit of a private party to submit to arbitration all or any differences which have arisen or which may arise between the parties with respect to a defined legal relationship, whether contractual or not, concerning a subject matter capable of settlement by arbitration under the laws of the United States, or to confirm an award made pursuant to such an agreement to arbitrate, if

(A) the arbitration takes place or is intended to take place in the United States,

(B) the agreement or award is or may be governed by a treaty or other international agreement in force for the United States calling for the recognition and enforcement of arbitral awards,

(C) the underlying claim, save for the agreement to arbitrate, could have been brought in a United States court under this section or section 1607, or (D) paragraph (1) of this subsection is otherwise applicable; or

(7) not otherwise covered by paragraph (2), in which money damages are sought against a foreign state for personal injury or death that was caused by an act of torture, extrajudicial killing, aircraft sabotage, hostage taking, or the provision of material support or resources (as defined in section 2339A of title 18) for such an act if such act or provision of material support is engaged in by an official, employee, or agent of such foreign state while acting within the scope of his or her office, employment, or agency, except that the court shall decline to hear a claim under this paragraph—

(A) if the foreign state was not designated as a state sponsor of terrorism under section 6(j) of the Export Administration Act of 1979 (50 App. U.S.C. 2405 (j)) or section 620A of the Foreign Assistance Act of 1961 (22 U.S.C. 2371) at the time the act occurred, unless later so designated as a result of such act or the act is related to Case Number 1:00CV03110(EGS) in the United States District Court for the District of Columbia; and

(B) even if the foreign state is or was so designated, if—

(i) the act occurred in the foreign state against which the claim has been brought and the claimant has not afforded the foreign state a reasonable opportunity to arbitrate the claim in accordance with accepted international rules of arbitration; or

(ii) neither the claimant nor the victim was a national of the United States (as that term is defined in section 101(a)(22) of the Immigration and Nationality Act) when the act upon which the claim is based occurred.

(b) A foreign state shall not be immune from the jurisdiction of the courts of the United States in any case in which a suit in admiralty is brought to enforce a maritime lien against a vessel or cargo of the foreign state, which maritime lien is based upon a commercial activity of the foreign state: Provided, That—

(1) notice of the suit is given by delivery of a copy of the summons and of the complaint to the person, or his agent, having possession of the vessel or cargo against which the maritime lien is asserted; and if the vessel or cargo is arrested pursuant to process obtained on behalf of the party bringing the suit, the service of process of arrest shall be deemed to constitute valid delivery of such notice, but the party bringing the suit shall be liable for any damages sustained by the foreign state as a result of the arrest if the party bringing the suit had actual or constructive knowledge that the vessel or cargo of a foreign state was involved; and

(2) notice to the foreign state of the commencement of suit as provided in section 1608 of this title is initiated within ten days either of the delivery of notice as provided in paragraph (1) of this subsection or, in the case of a party who was unaware that the vessel or cargo of a foreign state was involved, of the date such party determined the existence of the foreign state's interest.

(c) Whenever notice is delivered under subsection (b)(1), the suit to enforce a maritime lien shall thereafter proceed and shall be heard and determined according to the principles of law and rules of practice of suits in rem whenever it appears that, had the vessel been privately owned and possessed, a suit in rem might have been maintained. A decree against the foreign state may include costs of the suit and, if the decree is for a money judgment, interest as ordered by the court, except that the court may not award judgment against the foreign state in an amount greater than the value of the vessel or cargo upon which the maritime lien arose. Such value shall be determined as of the time notice is served under subsection (b)(1). Decrees shall be subject to appeal and revision as provided in other cases of admiralty and maritime jurisdiction. Nothing shall preclude the plaintiff in any proper case from seeking relief in personam in the same action brought to enforce a maritime lien as provided in this section.

(d) A foreign state shall not be immune from the jurisdiction of the courts of the United States in any action brought to foreclose a preferred mortgage, as defined in the Ship Mortgage Act, 1920 (46 U.S.C. 911 and following). Such action shall be brought, heard, and determined in accordance with the provisions of that Act and in accordance with the principles of law and rules of practice of suits in rem, whenever it appears that had the vessel been privately owned and possessed a suit in rem might have been maintained.

(e) For purposes of paragraph (7) of subsection (a)—

(1) the terms 'torture' and 'extrajudicial killing' have the meaning given those terms in section 3 of the Torture Victim Protection Act of 1991;

(2) the term 'hostage taking' has the meaning given that term in Article 1 of the International Convention Against the Taking of Hostages; and

(3) the term 'aircraft sabotage' has the meaning given that term in Article 1 of the Convention for the Suppression of Unlawful Acts Against the Safety of Civil Aviation.

(f) No action shall be maintained under subsection (a)(7) unless the action is commenced not later than 10 years after the date on which the cause of action arose. All principles of equitable tolling, including the period during which the foreign state was immune from suit, shall apply in calculating this limitation period.

(g) Limitation on Discovery.—

(1) In general.—

(A) Subject to paragraph (2), if an action is filed that would otherwise be barred by section 1604, but for subsection (a)(7), the court, upon request of the Attorney General, shall stay any request, demand, or order for discovery on the United States that the Attorney General certifies would significantly interfere with a criminal investigation or prosecution, or a national security operation, related to the incident that gave rise to the cause of action, until such time as the Attorney General advises the court that such request, demand, or order will no longer so interfere.

(B) A stay under this paragraph shall be in effect during the 12-month period beginning on the date on which the court issues the order to stay discovery. The court shall renew the order to stay discovery for additional 12-month periods upon motion by the United States if the Attorney General certifies that discovery would significantly interfere with a criminal investigation or prosecution, or a national security operation, related to the incident that gave rise to the cause of action.

(2) Sunset.—

(A) Subject to subparagraph (B), no stay shall be granted

or continued in effect under paragraph (1) after the date that is 10 years after the date on which the incident that gave rise to the cause of action occurred.

(B) After the period referred to in subparagraph (A), the court, upon request of the Attorney General, may stay any request, demand, or order for discovery on the United States that the court finds a substantial likelihood would—

(i) create a serious threat of death or serious bodily injury to any person;

(ii) adversely affect the ability of the United States to work in cooperation with foreign and international law enforcement agencies in investigating violations of United States law; or

(iii) obstruct the criminal case related to the incident that gave rise to the cause of action or undermine the potential for a conviction in such case.

(3) Evaluation of evidence.— The court's evaluation of any request for a stay under this subsection filed by the Attorney General shall be conducted ex parte and in camera.

(4) Bar on motions to dismiss.— A stay of discovery under this subsection shall constitute a bar to the granting of a motion to dismiss under rules 12(b)(6) and 56 of the Federal Rules of Civil Procedure.

(5) Construction.— Nothing in this subsection shall prevent the United States from seeking protective orders or asserting privileges ordinarily available to the United States.

§ 1606. Extent of liability

As to any claim for relief with respect to which a foreign state is not entitled to immunity under section 1605 or 1607 of this chapter, the foreign state shall be liable in the same manner and to the same extent as a private individual under like circumstances; but a foreign state except for an agency or instrumentality thereof shall not be liable for punitive damages; if, however, in any case wherein death was caused, the law of the place where the action or omission occurred provides, or has been construed to provide, for damages only punitive in nature, the foreign state shall be liable for actual or compensatory damages measured by the pecuniary injuries resulting from such death which were incurred by the persons for whose benefit the action was brought.

§ 1607. Counterclaims

In any action brought by a foreign state, or in which a foreign state intervenes, in a court of the United States or of a State, the foreign state shall not be accorded immunity with respect to any counterclaim—

(a) for which a foreign state would not be entitled to immunity under section 1605 of this chapter had such claim been brought in a separate action against the foreign state; or

(b) arising out of the transaction or occurrence that is the subject matter of the claim of the foreign state; or

(c) to the extent that the counterclaim does not seek relief exceeding in amount or differing in kind from that sought by the foreign state.

§ 1608. Service; time to answer; default

(a) Service in the courts of the United States and of the States shall be made upon a foreign state or political subdivision of a foreign state:

(1) by delivery of a copy of the summons and complaint in accordance with any special arrangement for service between the plaintiff and the foreign state or political subdivision; or

(2) if no special arrangement exists, by delivery of a copy of the summons and complaint in accordance with an applicable international convention on service of judicial documents; or

(3) if service cannot be made under paragraphs (1) or (2), by sending a copy of the summons and complaint and a notice of suit, together with a translation of each into the official language of the foreign state, by any form of mail requiring a signed receipt, to be addressed and dispatched by the clerk of the court to the head of the ministry of foreign affairs of the foreign state concerned, or

(4) if service cannot be made within 30 days under paragraph (3), by sending two copies of the summons and complaint and a notice of suit, together with a translation of each into the official language of the foreign state, by any form of mail requiring a signed receipt, to be addressed and dispatched by the clerk of the court to the Secretary of State in Washington, District of Columbia, to the attention of the Director of Special Consular Services—and the Secretary shall transmit one copy of the papers through diplomatic channels to the foreign state and shall send to the clerk of the court a certified copy of the diplomatic note indicating when the papers were transmitted.

As used in this subsection, a 'notice of suit' shall mean a notice addressed to a foreign state and in a form prescribed by the Secretary of State by regulation.

(b) Service in the courts of the United States and of the States shall be made upon an agency or instrumentality of a foreign state:

(1) by delivery of a copy of the summons and complaint in accordance with any special arrangement for service between the plaintiff and the agency or instrumentality; or

(2) if no special arrangement exists, by delivery of a copy of the summons and complaint either to an officer, a managing or general agent, or to any other agent authorized by appointment or by law to receive service of process in the United States; or in accordance with an applicable international convention on service of judicial documents; or

(3) if service cannot be made under paragraphs (1) or (2), and if reasonably calculated to give actual notice, by delivery of a copy of the summons and complaint, together with a translation of each into the

official language of the foreign state—

  (A) as directed by an authority of the foreign state or political subdivision in response to a letter rogatory or request or

  (B) by any form of mail requiring a signed receipt, to be addressed and dispatched by the clerk of the court to the agency or instrumentality to be served, or

  (C) as directed by order of the court consistent with the law of the place where service is to be made.

(c) Service shall be deemed to have been made—

(1) in the case of service under subsection (a)(4), as of the date of transmittal indicated in the certified copy of the diplomatic note; and

(2) in any other case under this section, as of the date of receipt indicated in the certification, signed and returned postal receipt, or other proof of service applicable to the method of service employed.

(d) In any action brought in a court of the United States or of a State, a foreign state, a political subdivision thereof, or an agency or instrumentality of a foreign state shall serve an answer or other responsive pleading to the complaint within sixty days after service has been made under this section.

(e) No judgment by default shall be entered by a court of the United States or of a State against a foreign state, a political subdivision thereof, or an agency or instrumentality of a foreign state, unless the claimant establishes his claim or right to relief by evidence satisfactory to the court. A copy of any such default judgment shall be sent to the foreign state or political subdivision in the manner prescribed for service in this section.

§ 1609. Immunity from attachment and execution of property of a foreign state

Subject to existing international agreements to which the United States is a party at the time of enactment of this Act the property in the United States of a foreign state shall be immune from attachment arrest and execution except as provided in sections 1610 and 1611 of this chapter.

§ 1610. Exceptions to the immunity from attachment or execution

(a) The property in the United States of a foreign state, as defined in section 1603 (a) of this chapter, used for a commercial activity in the United States, shall not be immune from attachment in aid of execution, or from execution, upon a judgment entered by a court of the United States or of a State after the effective date of this Act, if—

(1) the foreign state has waived its immunity from attachment in aid of execution or from execution either explicitly or by implication, notwithstanding any withdrawal of the waiver the foreign state may purport to effect except in accordance with the terms of the waiver, or

(2) the property is or was used for the commercial activity upon which the claim is based, or

(3) the execution relates to a judgment establishing rights in property which has been taken in violation of international law or which has been exchanged for property taken in violation of international law, or

(4) the execution relates to a judgment establishing rights in property—

    (A) which is acquired by succession or gift, or

    (B) which is immovable and situated in the United States:
Provided, That such property is not used for purposes of maintaining a diplomatic or consular mission or the residence of the Chief of such mission, or

(5) the property consists of any contractual obligation or any proceeds from such a contractual obligation to indemnify or hold harmless the foreign state or its employees under a policy of automobile or other liability or casualty insurance covering the claim which merged into the judgment, or

(6) the judgment is based on an order confirming an arbitral award rendered against the foreign state, provided that attachment in aid of execution, or execution, would not be inconsistent with any provision in the arbitral agreement, or

(7) the judgment relates to a claim for which the foreign state is not immune under section 1605 (a)(7), regardless of whether the property is or was involved with the act upon which the claim is based.

(b) In addition to subsection (a), any property in the United States of an agency or instrumentality of a foreign state engaged in commercial activity in the United States shall not be immune from attachment in aid of execution, or from execution, upon a judgment entered by a court of the United States or of a State after the effective date of this Act, if—

(1) the agency or instrumentality has waived its immunity from attachment in aid of execution or from execution either explicitly or implicitly, notwithstanding any withdrawal of the waiver the agency or instrumentality may purport to effect except in accordance with the terms of the waiver, or

(2) the judgment relates to a claim for which the agency or instrumentality is not immune by virtue of section 1605 (a)(2), (3), (5), or (7), or 1605 (b) of this chapter, regardless of whether the property is or was involved in the act upon which the claim is based.

(c) No attachment or execution referred to in subsections (a) and (b) of this section shall be permitted until the court has ordered such attachment and execution after having determined that a reasonable period of time has elapsed following the entry of judgment and the giving of any notice required under section 1608 (e) of this chapter.

(d) The property of a foreign state, as defined in section 1603 (a) of this chapter, used for a commercial activity in the United States, shall not be immune from attachment prior to the entry of judgment in any action brought in a court of the United States or of a State, or prior to the elapse of the period of time provided in subsection (c) of this section, if—

(1) the foreign state has explicitly waived its immunity from attachment prior to judgment, notwithstanding any withdrawal of the waiver the foreign state may purport to effect except in accordance with the terms of the waiver, and

(2) the purpose of the attachment is to secure satisfaction of a judgment that has been or may ultimately be entered against the foreign state, and not to obtain jurisdiction.

(e) The vessels of a foreign state shall not be immune from arrest in rem, interlocutory sale, and execution in actions brought to foreclose a preferred mortgage as provided in section 1605 (d).

(f)

(1)

(A) Notwithstanding any other provision of law, including but not limited to section 208(f) of the Foreign Missions Act (22 U.S.C. 4308 (f)), and except as provided in subparagraph (B), any property with respect to which financial transactions are prohibited or regulated pursuant to section 5(b) of the Trading with the Enemy Act (50 App. U.S.C. 5 (b)), section 620(a) of the Foreign Assistance Act of 1961 (22 U.S.C. 2370 (a)), sections 202 and 203 of the International Emergency Economic Powers Act (50 U.S.C. 1701–1702), or any other proclamation, order, regulation, or license issued pursuant thereto, shall be subject to execution or attachment in aid of execution of any judgment relating to a claim for which a foreign state (including any agency or instrumentality or such state) claiming such property is not immune under section 1605 (a)(7).

(B) Subparagraph (A) shall not apply if, at the time the property is expropriated or seized by the foreign state, the property has been held in title by a natural person or, if held in trust, has been held for the benefit of a natural person or persons.

(2)

(A) At the request of any party in whose favor a judgment has been issued with respect to a claim for which the foreign state is not immune under section 1605 (a)(7), the Secretary of the Treasury and the Secretary of State should make every effort to fully, promptly, and effectively assist any judgment creditor or any court that has issued any such judgment in identifying, locating, and executing against the property of that foreign state or any agency or instrumentality of such state.

(B) In providing such assistance, the Secretaries—

(i) may provide such information to the court under seal; and

(ii) should make every effort to provide the information in a manner sufficient to allow the court to direct the United States Marshall's office to promptly and effectively execute against that property.

(3) Waiver.— The President may waive any provision of paragraph (1) in the interest of national security.

§ 1611. Certain types of property immune from execution

(a) Notwithstanding the provisions of section 1610 of this chapter, the property of those organizations designated by the President as being entitled to enjoy the privileges, exemptions, and immunities provided by the International Organizations Immunities Act shall not be subject to attachment or any other judicial process impeding the disbursement of funds to, or on the order of, a foreign state as the result of an action brought in the courts of the United States or of the States.

(b) Notwithstanding the provisions of section 1610 of this chapter, the property of a foreign state shall be immune from attachment and from execution, if—

(1) the property is that of a foreign central bank or monetary authority held for its own account, unless such bank or authority, or its parent foreign government, has explicitly waived its immunity from attachment in aid of execution, or from execution, notwithstanding any withdrawal of the waiver which the bank, authority or government may purport to effect except in accordance with the terms of the waiver; or

(2) the property is, or is intended to be, used in connection with a military activity and

        (A) is of a military character, or

        (B) is under the control of a military authority or defense agency.

(c) Notwithstanding the provisions of section 1610 of this chapter, the property of a foreign state shall be immune from attachment and from execution in an action brought under section 302 of the Cuban Liberty and Democratic Solidarity (LIBERTAD) Act of 1996 to the extent that the property is a facility or installation used by an accredited diplomatic mission for official purposes.

TABLE OF PRECEDENTS

Listed Alphabetically

A

Ali Akbar v. U.A.R.

A 1966 SC 230

Allan Construction Ltd. v. Government of Venezuela

[1968] Que.P.R. 145, Que.S.C. 523

Amanat Khan v. Fredson Travel Inc.

[1982] 36 O.R.17 (Ont.H.C.), 64 ILR 733 (1983)

Arango v. Guzman Travel Advisors Corp.

621 F.2d 1371 (5th Cir. 1980)

B

Banco Nacional de Cuba v. Chase Manhattan Bank

505 F.Supp. 412 (S.D.N.Y. 1981)

Banque Compafina v. Banco de Guatemala et. al.

583 F.Supp. 320 (S.D.N.Y. 1984), 23 ILM 782 (1984)

Beacon Enterprises v. Menzies

715 F.2d 757 (2d Cir. 1983)

Behring International Inc. v. Imperial Iranian Air Force (Behring I)

475 F.Supp. 383 (D.N.J. 1979), UN-Mat. 479, 63 ILR 261 (1982)

Behring International Inc. v. Imperial Iranian Air Force (Behring II)

475 F.Supp. 396 (D.N.J. 1979), UN-Mat. 492

Berizzi Brothers Co. v. Steamship Pesaro

271 U.S. 562, 46 S.Ct. 611 (1926)

Beschluss des Bundesverfassungsgerichts zu Fragen der Staatenimmunität

vom 13 Dezember 1977
BVerfGE 46, 342, ZaöRV 1978, 245
RECHT DER INTERNATIONALEN WIRTSCHAFT (RIW/AWD), 1978, 122

Comment by Prof. Dr. Seidl-Hohenveldern
UN-Mat. 297, 65 IRL 146 (1984)

Booth Newspapers Inc. v. Regents of University of Michigan

280 N.W.2d 883, 90 Mich.App. 99 (Mich.App. 1979)

Boyce v. United States

93 F.Supp. 866 (D.C.Iowa 1950)

Braka v. Bancomer S.N.C.

762 F.2d 222 (2d Cir. 1985), 24 ILM 1047 (1985)

Broadbent v. Organization of American States (OAS)

19 ILM 208 (1980) (D.C.Cir. 1980)

Brown v. Rolls Royce Ltd.

[1960] 1 W.L.R. 210 (H.L.)

C

Callajo v. Bancomer S.A.

764 F.2d 1101 (5th Cir. 1985), 24 ILM 1050 (1985)

Carey et. al. v. National Oil Corporation and Libyan Arab Republic

453 F.Supp. 1097 (S.D.N.Y. 1978), 17 ILM 1180 (1978), UN-Mat. 477, 63 ILR 164
Confirmed 592 F.2d 673 (2d Cir. 1979)

Carlson v. Nelson

285 N.W.2d 505, 204 Neb. 765 (Neb. 1979)

Castro v. Saudi Arabia

510 F.Supp. 309 (W.D.Tex. 1980), 63 ILR 419

Chapman v. Oakleigh Animal Products Ltd.

[1970] 8 KIR 1063

Chicago Bridge & Iron Comp. v. The Islamic Republic of Iran

19 ILM 1436 (N.D.Ill. 1980)

Civil Aeronautics v. Alitalia-Linee Aeree Italiane

328 F.Supp. 759 (E.D.N.Y. 1971)

Coast Pump Associates v. Stephen Tyler Corporation

133 Cal.Rptr. 88, 62 C.A.3d (Cal.App. 1976)

Commercial Ins. of Newark v. Pacific-Peru Construction Co.

558 F.2d 948 (9th Cir. 1977)

Compania Española v. Navemar

303 U.S. 68, 58 S.Ct. 432, 82 L.Ed. 667.

Congo v. Venne

[1971] R.C.S. 997, [1971] 22 D.L.R.2d 669, 64 ILR 24 (1983)

Corporación Venezolana de Fomento v. Vintero Sales

629 F.2d 786 (2d Cir. 1980)

D

Delahite v. United States

346 U.S. 15 (1953)

Dames & More v. Regan

453 U.S. 654, 101 S.Ct. 2972, 69 L.Ed.2d 218 (1981)
Online Publication

De Howorth v. The SS 'India'

1921 CPD 451

Democratic Republic of the Congo v. Jean Venne

[1971] R.C.S. 997, [1971] 22 D.L.R.2d 669, 64 ILR 24 (1983)

De Sanchez v. Banco Central de Nicaragua

515 F.Supp. 900 (E.D.La. 1981)

Desikacharyulu v. S.

A 1964 SC 807

Dessaules v. Republic of Poland

[1944] 4 D.L.R. 1, [1944] S.C.R. 275

Dickinson v. Minister of Pensions

[1953] 1 Q.B. 228, [1952] 2 All E R 1031

Discroll v. United States

525 F.2d 136 (9th Cir. 1975)

Duff Development Co. v. The Government of Kelantan

[1924] A.C. 797

E

Edlow International Co. v. Nuklearna Elektrikarna Krsko

414 F.Supp. 827 (D.D.C. 1977), 63 ILR 100 (1982)

Ex Parte Muir

254 U.S. 522, 41 S.Ct. 185, 65 L.Ed. 383

Ex Parte Peru

318 U.S. 578

F

First National City Bank v. Banco Para el Comercio Exterior de Cuba (BANCEC)

103 S.Ct. 2591 (1983)

Flota Maritima Browning de Cuba v. Motor Vessel Ciudad

335 F.2d 619 (4th Cir. 1964)

Flota Maritima Browning de Cuba v. 'Canadian Conqueror' and Republic of China

[1962] 34 D.L.R.2d 628, [1962] S.C.R. 598

Frovola v. Union of Soviet Socialist Republics

761 F.2d 370 (7th Cir. 1985)

G

Giampaoli v. Califano

628 F.2d 1190 (9th Cir. 1980)

Gilson v. Republic of Ireland

682 F.2d 1022 (D.C. Cir. 1982)

Gittler v. German Information Center

408 N.Y.S.2d 600 (Sup.Ct.N.Y. 1978), Digest United States Practice, 1978, 879-883

Gray v. Permanent Mission of the Congo to the United Nations

443 F.Supp. 816 (S.D.N.Y. 1978), 63 ILR 121 (1982)

Gurdwara & Co. v. Rattan

A 1955 SC 576

H

Harris Corporation v. National Iranian Radio and Television

691 F.2d 1344 (11th Cir. 1982), 22 ILM 434 (1983)

Harris v. VAO Intourist, Moscow

481 F.Supp. 1056 (E.D.N.Y. 1979), 63 ILR 318 (1982)

Hispano Americana Mercantil S.A. v. Central Bank of Nigeria

[1979] 2 Lloyd's Rep. 277 (C.A.)

Hochgurtel v. San Felipo

253 N.W. 2d 526, 78 Wis.2d 70 (Wis.1977)

Home v. Guy

[1877] 5 Ch.D. 901

Hunt v. Mobil Oil Corporation

550 F.2d 68 (2d Cir. 1977), cert. den., 434 U.S. 984, 98 S.Ct. 608, 57 L.Ed.2d 477

Hurst v. Evans

[1917] 1 K.B. 351

I

I Congreso del Partido

[1981] 2 All E R 1064 (H.L.), [1981] 2 Lloyd's Rep. 367, [1983] 1 A.C. 244, 64 ILR 307 (1983)

International Association of Machinists and Aerospace Workers (IAM) v. Opec

477 F.Supp. 553 (C.D. Cal. 1979)

International Shoe Co. v. Washington

326 U.S. 310 (1945)

Inter-Science Research and Development Services (PTY) Ltd. v. Republica Popular de Moçambique

1980 2 SA 111 (T), 64 ILR 689 (1983)

Intro Properties (U.K.) Ltd. v. Sauvel

[1983] 1 Q.B. 1019 (1983), 2 W.L.R. 1

Ipitrade International S.A. v. Federal Republic of Nigeria

465 F.Supp. 824 (D.D.C. 1978), 17 ILM 1395 (1978), 63 ILR 196 (1982)

J

Jafari v. Islamic Republic of Iran

539 F.Supp. 209 (N.D.Ill. 1982), 21 ILM 767 (1982)

Jackson v. People's Republic of China

550 F.Supp. 869 (N.D.Ala. 1982)

Jet Line Services Inc. v. M/V Marsa El Hariga

462 F.Supp. 1165 (D.Md. 1978)

Joseph Constantine Steamship Line Ltd. v. Imperial Smelting

[1942] A.C. 154, [1941] 2 All E R 165 (H.L.)

Juan Ismael & Co. v. Indonesian Government

[1954] 3 All E R 236, [1955] A.C. 72, [1954] 3 W.L.R. 531, [1954] 2 Lloyd's Rep. 175

K

Kaffraria Property v. The Government of Zambia

1980 (2) SA 709 (E), 64 ILR 708 (1983)

Kalamazoo Spice Extraction Co. v. The Provisional Military Government of Socialist Ethiopia

24 ILM 1278 (W.D.Mich. 1985)

Kashani v. United Arab Republics

A.I.R. 1966 SC 230, 60 AJIL 861 (1966), 64 ILR 489 (1983)

Krajina v. Tass Agency

[1949] 2 All E R 274 (C.A.)

L

Le Gouvernement de la République Démocratique du Congo v. Jean Venne

[1971] R.C.S. 997, [1971] 22 D.L.R.2d 669, 64 ILR 24 (1983)

Letelier v. Republic of Chile (Letelier I)

488 F.Supp. 665 (D.D.C. 1980), 19 ILM 409 (1980)

Letelier v. Republic of Chile (Letelier II)

502 F.Supp. 259 (D.D.C. 1980), 19 ILM 1418 (1980)

Letelier v. Republic of Chile (Letelier III)

567 F.Supp. 1490 (S.D.N.Y. 1983)

Libra Bank Ltd. v. Banco Nacional de Costa Rica

676 F2d 47 (2d Cir. 1982), 21 ILM 618 (1982)

Libyan American Oil Company (LIAMCO) v. Socialist People's Libyan Arab Jamahiriya

482 F.Supp. 1175 (D.D.C. 1980)

Lindgren v. United States

665 F2d 978 (9th Cir. 1982)

M

Marine Steel Ltd. v. The Government of the Marshall Islands

NEW ZEALAND L.J. 506 (1981), High Court of Auckland, 29 July 1981 (A 533/81)

Maritime International Nominees Establishment (MINE) v. The Republic of Guinea

21 ILM 1355 (D.C.Cir. 1982)

Matter of Rio Grande Transport Inc.

516 F.Supp. 1155 (S.D.N.Y. 1981), 63 ILR 604 (1982)

Matter of Sedco Inc.

543 F.Supp. 561, 21 ILM 318 (S.D.Tex. 1982)

McDonnell Douglas Corp. v. The Islamic Republic of Iran

758 F.2d 341 (8th Cir. 1985)

McGee v. International Life Insurance Co.

355 U.S. 220 (1957)

McKeel v. The Islamic Republic of Iran

722 F.2d 582 (9th Cir. 1983)

Mighell v. Sultan of Johore

[1894] 1 Q.B. 149

Miller v. Minister of Pensions

[1947] 2 All E R 372

Mol Inc. v. People's Republic of Bangladesh

572 F.Supp. 79 (D.Or. 1983)

N

National American Corporation v. Federal Republic of Nigeria

448 F.Supp. 622 (S.D.N.Y. 1978), 17 ILM 1407 (1978), 63 ILR 63 (1982)
Confirmed 597 F.2d 314 (2d Cir. 1979), 63 ILR 137

O

O'Connell Machinery Company Inc. v. M/V 'Americana'

566 F.Supp. 1381 (S.D.N.Y. 1983)

Ohntrup v. Firearms Center Inc.

516 F.Supp. 1281 (Ed.D.Pa. 1981)

Olsen by Sheldon v. Government of Mexico

729 F.2d 641 (9th Cir. 1984)

Outbound Maritime Corporation v. P.T. Indonesian Consortium of Construction Industries(ICCI)

Outbound I

575 F.Supp. 1222 (S.D.N.Y. 1983)

Outbound II

582 F.Supp. 1136 (D.Md. 1984)

P

Pan American Tankers Corp. v. Republic of Vietnam

291 F.Supp. 49 (S.D.N.Y. 1968)

Penthouse Studios Inc. v. Government of Venezuela

[1969] 8 D.L.R.3d 686 (C.A.), 64 ILR 20 (1983)

Perez v. The Bahamas

482 F.Supp. 1208 (D.D.C. 1980), 63 ILR, 350 (1982)

Planmount Ltd. v. The Republic of Zaire

[1980] 2 Lloyd's Rep. 393

Prejean v. Sonatrach Inc.

652 F.2d 1260 (5th Cir. 1981)

Puente v. Spanish National State

116 F.2d 43 (2d Cir. 1940), cert. den., 314 U.S. 627, 62 S.Ct. 57, 86 L.Ed. 501 (1941)

Q

Qureshi v. Union of Soviet Socialist Republics

PLD 1981, 1, Supreme Court, 377, 20 ILM 1060 (1981), 64 ILR 585 (1983)

R

Rahimtoola v. Nizam of Hyderabad

[1957] 3 All E.R. 441, [1957] 3 W.L.R. 884, [1958] A.C. 379

Republic of Mexico v. Hoffmann

324 U.S. 30 (1945)

République Démocratique du Congo v. Jean Venne

[1971] R.C.S. 997, [1971] 22 D.L.R.2d 669, 64 ILR 24 (1983)

Re Royal Bank of Canada and Corriveau et al.

[1980] 103 D.L.R.3d 520 (Ont.H.C.), 64 ILR 69 (1983)

S

Sherman Inc. v. United States

199 F.2d 504 (8th Cir. 1952)

Skeen v. Federative Republic of Brazil

566 F.Supp. 1414 (D.D.C. 1983)

Smith v. Canadian Javelin Ltd.

[1976] 68 D.L.R.3d 428 (Ont.H.C.), 64 ILR 47 (1983)

Sperry International Trade v. Government of Israel

532 F.Supp. 901 (S.D.N.Y. 1982), 21 ILM 1073 (1982)
Confirmed 21 ILM 1066 (2d Cir. 1982)

S & S Machinery Co. v. Masinexportimport (MASIN)

706 F.2d 411 (2d Cir. 1983)

Sugerman v. Aeromexico

626 F.2d 270 (3d Cir. 1980)

T

Texas Trading Corp. v. Federal Republic of Nigeria and Central Bank of Nigeria

647 F.2d 300 (2d Cir. 1981)

Thai-Europe Tapioca Service Ltd. v. Government of Pakistan

[1975] 3 All E R 961, [1975] 1 W.L.R. 1485 (C.A.), 64 ILR 81 (1983)

The Bremen v. Zapata-Off-Shore Co.

407 U.S. 1, 92 S.Ct. 1907, 32 L.Ed.2d 513 (1972)

The Christina

[1938] A.C. 484

The Glendarroch

[1894] P. 226, 63 L.J. Adm. 89, 6 R. 686, 70 L.T. 344

The Parlement Belge

[1880] 5 P.D. 197, [1874-80] All E R 104

The Pesaro

255 U.S. 216 (1921), 41 S.Ct. 308, 65 L.Ed. 592

The Philippine Admiral

[1977] A.C. 373

The Porto Alexandre

[1920] P. 30, [1918-19] All E R 615, [1920] A.C. 30

The Schooner Exchange v. McFaddon et al.

11 U.S. [7 Cranch] 116 (1812)

The Uganda Holding Co. (Holdings) Ltd. v. The Government of Uganda

[1979] 1 Lloyd's Rep. 481

Thompson v. United States

592 F.2d 1104 (9th Cir. 1979)

Tigchon v. Island of Jamaica

591 F.Supp. 765 (W.D.Mich. 1984)

Transamerican S.S. Corp. v. Somali Democratic Republic

767 F.2d 998 (D.D.C. 1985)

Trendtex Trading Co. v. Central Bank of Nigeria

[1977] 1 Lloyd's Rep. 581

U

U Kyaw Din v. His Britannic Majesty's Government of the United Kingdom and the Union of Burma

23 ILR 214 (1956), [1948] Ann.Dig. 137 (No. 42)

United Arab Republic v. Kashani

64 ILR 394 (1983)

United Euram v. U.S.S.R.

461 F.Supp. 609 (S.D.N.Y. 1978), 63 ILR 228 (1982)

United States v. Lee

106 U.S. 196 (1882)

United States v. Sampol

636 F.2d 621 (D.C. Cir., 1980)

Upton v. Empire of Iran

459 F.Supp. 264 (D.D.C. 1978), 63 ILR 211 (1982)

V

Velidor v. C/P/G Benghazi

653 F.2d 812 (3d Cir. 1981), 21 ILM 621 (1982), 63 ILR 622 (1982)

Verlinden B.V. v. Central Bank of Nigeria (Supreme Court)

461 U.S. 480, 103 S.Ct. 1962, 76 L.Ed.2d 81, 51 U.S.L.W. 4567, 22 ILM 647 (1983)

Verlinden B.V. v. Central Bank of Nigeria (District Court)

647 F.2d 320 (2d Cir. 1981)

Venne v. République Démocratique du Congo

[1968] Que.R.P. (2) 6 (C.S.), [1969] 5 D.L.R.3d, 128, 64 ILR 1 (1983)

Victory Transport Inc. v. Comisaria General de Abasticimientos y Transportes

336 F.2d 354 (2d Cir. 1964)

W

Williams v. United States

350 U.S. 857, 76 S.Ct. 100, 100 L.Ed. 761 (1955)

Wolf v. Banco Nacional de Mexico S.A.

739 F.2d 1458 (9th Cir. 1984)

Wood v. Schwartz

88 F.Supp. 385 (W.D.Pa. 1950)

Wyle v. Bank Melli of Teheran, Iran

577 F.Supp. 1148

Y

Yessenin-Volpin v. Novosti Press Agency (Tass)

443 F.Supp. 849 (S.D.N.Y. 1978)

Youssef M. Nada Establishment v. Central Bank of Nigeria

16 ILM 501 (1977), Landgericht Frankfurt (Germany)

Z

Zodiak v. Polish People's Republic

[1977] 81 D.L.R.3d 656 (C.A.Que.), 64 ILR 51 (1983)

NOTES

Annotations

[1] 461 U.S. 480, 103 S.Ct. 1962, 76 L.Ed.2d 81, 51 U.S.L.W. 4567, 22 ILM 647 (1983).

[2] The question was initially raised by Georg Ress, *Les tendances de l'évolution de l'immunité de l'État étranger (1979)*, and he refers to it also in his later article *Entwicklungstendenzen der Immunität ausländischer Staaten*, 40 ZaöRV 217 (1980), at 257 ff.

[3] See *Maritime International Nominees Establishment (MINE) v. The Republic of Guinea*, 21 ILM 1355, 1360 (D.C.Cir.1982): 'The Act thereby connects the issue of subject matter jurisdiction to the issue of sovereign immunity: the absence of immunity is a condition to the presence of subject matter jurisdiction.'

[4] The House Report, p. 13, 15 ILM 1398, 1405 (1976) notes: '... section 1330(b) also satisfies the due process requirement of adequate notice by prescribing that proper service is made under section 1608 of the bill.'

[5] H. R. Report No. 94-1487, p. 14, 15 ILM 1398, 1405 (1976) and *Maritime International Nominees Establishment (MINE) v. The Republic of Guinea*, 21 ILM 1355, 1360 (D.C.Cir.1982). See also *Upton v. Empire of Iran*, 459 F.Supp. 264, 265 (D.D.C.1978), *Velidor v. L/P/G Benghazi*, 653 F.2d 812, 817 (3d Cir.1981), *Texas Trading & Milling Corp. v. Federal Public of Nigeria and Central Bank of Nigeria*, 647 F.2d 300, 307-308 (2d Cir.1981), *Ohntrup v. Firearms Center, Inc.*, 516 F.Supp. 1281, 1283 (E.D.Pa.1981).

[6] *Upton v. Empire of Iran*, 459 F.Supp. 264, 265 (D.D.C.1978).

[7] Id. See also *Letelier v. Chile*, 488 F.Supp. 665, 671 (D.D.C.1980).

[8] James Bradley Tayer, A Preliminary Treatise on Evidence (1898), I, 1.

[9] John Henry Wigmore, Evidence in Trials at Common Law (1981), §1, p. 11.

[10] Mauro Cappelletti & Joseph M. Perillo, *Civil Procedure in Italy (1965)*, p. 80.

[11] John Henry Wigmore, *Evidence in Trials at Common Law (1981)*, Vol. I, §§1, 2.

[12] The (direct) proof of a legal right must be distinguished from the (indirect) proof of a fact that a legal right is based upon. In the first case, it's for the court a legal question to decide, while in the second case, it's a question about facts. In Anglo-American law, foreign law is considered to be *a fact* and thus the usual rules of evidence are applicable. See Hersch Lauterpacht, *International Law (1979)*, §58, p. 158.

[13] See Halsbury's Laws of England, Vol. 17 'Evidence', §32: relevant facts are called 'facts probative to an issue'.

[14] Phipson and Elliott, *Manual of the Law of Evidence (1980)*, p. 15.

[15] I have italicized all the potential facts in issue. The plaintiff may invoke either of them in his pleadings.

[16] See the similar provisions in §5(2)(a) of Singapore STIA 1979, §5(3)(a) of Pakistan STIO 1981, and §4(3)(a) of South Africa FSIA 1981. Under the United States FSIA 1976, such contracts fall under §1603(d) and Canada STIA 1982 defines them in §5.

[17] See in general for French civil procedure, Ghestin & Goubeaux, *Traité de Droit Civil (1982)*, Vol. I, pp. 485 ff., Dalloz, *Encyclopédie Juridique*, 'Preuve', Chap. 2, Sect. 2, Mazeaud, Leçons de Droit Civil (1983), Tome I, Vol. 1, pp. 429 ff. ('La charge de la preuve').

[18] See in general for German civil procedure, Hans Prütting, *Gegenwartsprobleme der Beweislast (1965)*, pp. 5-43, Hans-Joachim Musielak, *Die Grundfragen der Beweislast im Zivilprozess (1984)*, pp. 1-57, Musielak/Stadler, *Grundfragen des Beweisrechts (1984)*, pp. 102 ff., Rosenberg-Schwab, *Zivilprozessrecht (1981)*, §118, pp. 680-692.

[19] See in general for **Spanish Civil Procedure**, art. 1214 of the Código Civil Español: 'Incumbe la prueba de las obligaciones al que reclama su cumplimiento, y la de su extinción al que la opone'. This provision corresponds to art, 1315 of the French Code Napoléon, as cited above in the text. See the comment on the adoption of this article in the Spanish Civil Code from the French Civil Code Brocá/Majada, *Práctica Procesal Civil (1979)*, Tome I, pp. 936 ff. The countries of Middle and South America are equally part of the continental law system. See René David, *Les Grands Systèmes de Droit Contemporains (1974)*, pp. 72-72 and Phanor J. Eder, *A Comparative Survey of Anglo-American and Latin-American Law, New York (1950)*. **For Ecuador**: See José Alfonso Troya Cevallos, *Elementaros de Derecho Procesal Civil (1978)*, Tomo I, pp. 245-246. **For Mexico**: Art. 281 of the Código de Procedimientos Civiles corresponds to art. 1214 of the Código Civil of Spain, see Carlos Arellano García, *Derecho Procesal Civil (1981)*, pp. 153-155. **For Peru**: See Pedro Sagastegui, Urteaga, *Derecho Procesal Civil (1982)*, Tomo II, pp. 84-91. **For Chile**: Emilio Rioseco Enriquez, *La Prueba ante la Jurisprudencia (1982)*, pp. 59-80. **For Argentina**: Art. 377 of the Código Civil y Comercial de la Nación is drafted after the model of art. 1214 of the Código Civil of Spain, but stipulates more details. **For Uruguay**: Eduardo J. Couture, *Fundamentos del Derecho Procesal Civil (1981)*, pp. 240-248. **For Colombia**: Hernando Davis Echandia, *Teoría General de la Prueba Judicial (1981)*, Tomo I, pp. 393 ff. It is interesting to note that the German treatise of Rosenberg is quoted here, which has been translated to Spanish, see p. 450, note 132, which is just another puzzle stone that witnesses for the supranational coherence of evidence laws, also in the continental legal system. See also Gustavo Humberto Rodriguez, *Curso de Derecho Probatorio (1983)*, pp. 70 ff. **For Bolivia**: Art. 375 of the Código de Procedimiento Civil which also is a recapitulation of art. 1214 of the Código Civil of Spain.

[20] See for **Portugal**, Varela/Bezerra/Sampio e Nova, *Manual de Processo Civil (1984)*, pp. 430-451, with many references from French, Italian and German evidence law textbooks.

[21] Augenti, *L'onere della prova (1932)*, Micheli, *L'onere della prova (1942)*, Aurelio Scardaccione, *Le Prove (1971)*, Parte Prima, pp. 3-84, Crisanto Mandrioli, *Corso di Diritto Processuale Civile (1978)*, Tome II, pp. 113-120, Andrea Lugo, *Manuale di Diritto Processuale Civile (1983)*, pp. 131-132, Cappelletti & Perillo, *Civil Procedure in Italy (1965)*, pp. 185 ff. with many references from Italian law textbooks and a short comparison of Italian evidence law with Anglo-American evidence law (pp. 82 and 185)

[22] See Dagmar Coester-Waltjen, *Internationales Beweisrecht (1983)*, pp. 254-303.

[23] See, for example for Austria Hans W. Fasching, *Lehrbuch des österreichischen Zivilprozessrechts (1984)*, pp. 417-426, and for Switzerland Max Guldener, *Schweizerisches Zivilprozessrecht (1979)*, pp. 325-327. It has to be noted that procedural law is in Switzerland regionally bound, and every Canton has its own civil procedure code.

[24] See Guldener, *Schweizerisches Zivilprozessrecht (1979)*, p. 325. See also Walder-Bohner, *Zivilprozessrecht (1983)*, pp. 327-334, Walther J. Habscheid, *Droit Judiciaire Privé Suisse (1981)*, pp. 423-426, Max Kummer, *Grundriss des Zivilprozessrechts (1978)*, pp. 136-140.

25 See Hans Prütting, *Gegenwartsprobleme der Beweislast (1965)*, §4, pp. 23 ff., Dagmar Coester-Waltjen, *Internationales Beweisrecht (1983)*, pp. 274, 296.

26 See Raynaud/Vanel, *Répertoire de Procédure Civile (1984)*, 'Preuve', Section 2 'Charge de la Preuve', §1 'Ordre de la Preuve'.

27 See *Prieto-Castro, Tratado de Derecho Procesal Civil (1982)*, pp. 624 ff.

28 Aurelio Scardaccione, *Le Prove (1971)*, Parte Prima, pp. 4 ff., Cappelletti & Perillo, *Civil Procedure in Italy (1965)*, pp. 185 ff.

29 See Hans Prütting, *Gegenwartsprobleme der Beweislast (1965)*, §3, pp. 20 ff., Dagmar Coester-Waltjen, *Internationales Beweisrecht (1983)*, pp. 281 ff.

30 See Raynaud/Vanel, *Répertoire de Procédure Civile (1984)*, 'Charge de la Preuve', §2 'Risque de la Preuve'.

31 See Prieto-Castro, *Tratado de Derecho Procesal Civil (1982)*, pp. 626 ff.

32 Aurelio Scardaccione, *Le Prove (1971)*, Parte Prima, pp. 4 ff., Cappelletti & Perillo, *Civil Procedure in Italy (1965)*, pp. 185 ff.

33 Id., p. 185.

34 Id., note 82.

35 James & Hazard, *Civil Procedure (1977)*, §1.2, p. 4. [45].

36 See in general Schwering, *System der Beweislast (1969)*, pp. 41 ff. and *Cross on Evidence (1979)*, pp. 58 ff.

37 Reproduced in *Stone's Justices' Manual (1981)*, Vol. 1, pp. 506 ff, 521 ff.

38 Reproduced in *Statutes of the Republic of South Africa*, Vol. 11, pp. 51 ff.

39 Worked out by the Federal/Provincial Task Force on *Uniform Rules of Evidence* and reproduced in the *U.L.C.C. Report (1982)*.

40 Id., Appendix 4, pp. 541 ff.

41 *Phipson on Evidence (1982)*, p. 15, n. 1-24.

42 See for the United Kingdom Walker & Walker, *The English Legal System (1985)*, pp. 244-245.

43 Phipson & Elliott, *Manual of the Law of Evidence (1980)*, p. 37.

44 *Cross on Evidence (1979)*, p. 92 and Lilly, *Introduction to the Law of Evidence (1978)*, p. 47, note 13.

45 Phipson and Elliot, *Manual of the Law of Evidence (1980)*, p. 51. See also Schwering, *System der Beweislast im englisch-amerikanischen Zivilprozess (1969)*, pp. 60 ff.

[46] James & Hazard, *Civil Procedure (1977)*, §7.5, pp. 240-241.

[47] See *Cross on Evidence (1979)*, p. 85, *Cross on Evidence, Australian Edition (1980)*, §§4.2 ff., Hoffmann/Zeffert, *South African Law of Evidence (1983)*, pp. 385-386.

[48] Cross on Evidence (1979), p. 86.

[49] Id., p. 92.

[50] Id., p. 93.

[51] Graham, *Federal Rules of Evidence in a Nutshell (1981)*, §301.3, p. 42.

[52] *Phipson on Evidence (1982)*, p. 44, n. 4-03.

[53] See, for example, Nash, *Civil Procedure (1976)*, p. 328 and Rothstein, *State and Federal Rules (1981)*, Ch. II, p. 99.

[54] Anglo-American law professionals have not lacked fantasy to coin synonyms to these terms; however their fantasy did not necessarily lead to more clarity; and what is needed in matters of terminology is *precision*. The term 'risk of non-persuasion of the jury' is employed by Wigmore, Vol. 9, §2485, Cross on Evidence, p. 27, Lilly, p. 41, Phipson & Elliott, p. 51, Glasbeek, p. 633 and Curzon, §5, p. 48. The term 'legal burden' is to be found in Halsbury's Laws of England, §13, Cross on Evidence, p. 86, Glasbeek, p. 633. The term 'burden of persuasion' is used by Lilly, p. 40, Graham, Rules of Evidence, §310.5, p. 45 and Graham, Evidence, p. 755. In addition, you can find the terms 'persuasion burden' with Cross on Evidence, p. 93 and Rothstein, Ch. 2, p. 107 as well as 'fixed burden of proof' with Cross on Evidence, p. 87. That is not yet all there is. I also found the term 'general burden of proof' with Walker and Walker, p. 613 and Aguda, n. 21-12, the term 'burden of establishing the case' with Sarkar on Evidence, §102, p. 911, 'onus of proof' with Cross on Evidence, p. 97, 'onus' with Hoffmann & Zeffert, p. 386, 'burden of proof on the pleadings' with Sarkar's Law of Evidence, 'persuasive burden' with Phipson on Evidence, n. 4-04, 'ultimate burden' with Cross on Evidence, p. 93 and Lilly, p. 44 or simply 'burden of proof' with Cross on Evidence, p. 86 or 'burden of proof simpliciter' with Woodroffe & Amer Ali's Law of Evidence, Sect. 104, n. 2, p. 2107.

55 The term 'duty of producing evidence to the judge' is to be found with Wigmore, Vol. 9, §2486; the term 'evidential burden' is employed by Halsbury's Laws of England, §13; the term 'burden of adducing evidence' is used by Lilly, p. 44 and by Phipson on Evidence, n. 4-04. In addition, the expression 'onus of proof' is used for this burden by Sarkar's Law of Evidence, §102, p. 912 and §103, p. 913 and by Woodroffe & Amer Ali's Law of Evidence, Sect. 104, n. 2, p. 2107. This is not yet all there is in terminological fantasy. 'Burden of producing evidence' as well as 'burden of production' are used by Lilly, p. 44 and Phipson on Evidence, n. 4-04, the expression 'burden of going forward with evidence' can be found in the Federal Rules of Evidence, Rule 301, the term 'production-of-evidence burden' is to be found with Rothstein, Ch. 2, p. 99 as well as 'production burden' with the same author on p. 100, 'evidentiary burden' can be found with Hoffmann & Zeffert, p. 386, 'risk of not-adducing evidence' is coined by Glasbeek, p. 638, and 'burden of introducing evidence' is a term Aguda comes up with on n. 21-16. For avoiding the danger of confusion between the two burdens, Cross on Evidence, pp. 27-28, suggests to not use the expression 'evidential burden of proof'.

56 See, for example, *Phipson and Elliott (1980)*, p. 52.

57 The formulation used in two U.S. district court decisions shows the nature of both burdens very well: 'Burden of proof has two elements, the burden of producing evidence and the burden of persuading the fact finder', *Abilene Sheet Metal Inc. v. N.L.R.B.*, 619 F.2d 332 (3d Cir. 1980) and *Hochgurtel v. San Felippo*, 253 N.W.2d 526, 78 Wis.2d 70 (Wis. 1977).

58 See *Cross on Evidence (1979)*, p. 29, *Hoffmann & Zeffert (1983)*, pp. 390-391, *Phipson & Elliott (1980)*, p. 63. If, exceptionally, the legal burden is on the defendant, it's the defendant who has the right to begin. The right to begin also has been called 'onus probandi', see *The English and Empire Digest (1974)*, §131, *Sarkar's Law of Evidence (1981)*, §102, p. 911, *Phipson on Evidence (1982)*, n. 4-07, pp. 47-48.

59 *Halsbury's Laws of England*, §17.

60 This is not a particularity of Anglo-American civil procedure, but a general principle. Every proof must relate to a specific fact in issue, otherwise it would be off-track and irrelevant. As a result, a burden of proof 'in general' is inconceivable. For every fact in issue, there is a burden of proof that one of the parties is charged with. *Cross on Evidence (1979)*, p. 29, expresses it this way: 'In the context of the law of evidence, the expression 'burden of proof' is meaningless unless it is used with reference to a particular issue'.

61 *Standard of proof* is a measure for the adequateness of the proof presented. All evidence must meet a certain standard to be adequate, to be sufficient; as a result, all evidence has to be evaluated by the judge for meeting the standard of proof applicable in the particular litigation. The term *prima facie case* or *prima facie evidence* in Anglo-American civil procedure has nothing in common with the notion of *Prima-Facie Beweis* in German civil procedure law, while literally translated it seems to be equivalent, see Frédéric W. Eisner, *Beweislastfragen und Beweiswürdigung im deutschen und amerikanischen Zivilprozess*, ZZP, Bd. 89, 78-90, pp. 86 ff.

[62] See in general *Cross on Evidence (1979)*, p. 87, *Cross on Evidence, Australian Edition (1980)*, §4.4, Cross & Wilkins, *An Outline of the Law of Evidence (1980)*, p. 29, Lilly, *An Introduction in the Law of Evidence (1978)*, p. 44, *Phipson on Evidence (1982)*, n. 4-07, John Henry Wigmore, *Evidence in Trials at Common Law (1981)*, Vol. 9, §2488, Rothstein, *Evidence in a Nutshell (1981)*, Ch. 2, p. 100, Curzon, *Law of Evidence (1978)*, p. 49, Graham, *Evidence (1983)*, pp. 754-755, Graham, *Federal Rules of Evidence in a Nutshell (1981)*, §303.3, p. 42, Glasbeek, *Evidence, Cases and Materials (1977)*, p. 638, *Glasbeek Australian Edition (1974)*, §11.40 ff., Hoffmann & Zeffert, *South African Law of Evidence (1983)*, pp. 386 ff.

[63] *Cross on Evidence (1979)*, p. 91.

[64] American Law Institute, *Model Code on Evidence (1942)*.

[65] *Cross on Evidence (1979)*, p. 91.

[66] See Phipson and Elliott, *Manual of the Law of Evidence (1980)*, p. 37, who state: 'Although the two parts of the tribunal are separate in function, the English system of trial has always been marked by a high degree of control by the judge of the jury. The judge is in control to a much greater extent than in, say, the United States'.

[67] For example the instruction regarding the allocation of the burden of proof, see Phipson and Elliott, *Manual of the Law of Evidence (1980)*, p. 62, Model Code on Evidence, Rule 1, comment on §§(2) and (3), pp. 73-74: 'In a jury case this means that the party has to satisfy this burden in order to escape an adverse peremptory instruction as to that fact'.

[68] See *Model Code on Evidence (1942)*, p. 74 and Curzon, *Law of Evidence (1978)*, p. 49 under (b): 'A failure by a party to discharge the evidential burden brings the risk … of that party's failing on the issue, wholly or in part'.

[69] Cross & Wilkins, *An Outline of the Law of Evidence (1980)*, p. 27. See also *Model Code on Evidence (1942)*, p. 74: 'Neither the rules nor the decisions require that the evidence discharging either burden shall have been introduced by the party having the burden'.

[70] *Cross on Evidence (1979)*, pp. 119-120 remarks that 'no precise formulae have been laid down with regard to the standard of proof required for the discharge of the evidential burden and, as this is not a matter upon which it can ever be necessary for a judge to direct a jury, there is no reason why it should ever become a subject of formulae'.

[71] Cross & Wilkins, *An Outline of the Law of Evidence (1980)*, p. 20. See also Graham, *Federal Rules of Evidence in a Nutshell (1981)*, §301.4, p. 43, and Phipson and Elliott, *Manual of the Law of Evidence (1980)*, p. 60: ' … if the evidence is believed, any reasonable man could infer that the fact exists'.

[72] See Phipson and Elliott, *Manual of the Law of Evidence (1980)*, p. 62: 'It has been seen that the discharge of the evidential burden by one side puts the other side under a similar burden, or, as it is often put, 'passes' the burden upon him'.

[73] Regarding the notion of a *shifting* burden, see Schwering, *System der Beweislast im englisch-amerikanischen Zivilprozess (1969)*, pp. 75-79 and *Cross on Evidence, Australian Edition (1980)*, §§4.9 ff. Curzon, *Law of Evidence (1978)*, p. 50, remarks: 'This phrase indicates the moving, during the trial, of the burden of proof from one side to another, when one party has discharged his obligation of proof.' This explanation is not correct as it suggests that also the persuasive burden shifts.

[74] Sir Richard Eggleston, *Evidence, Proof and Probability (1983)*, p. 27.

[75] While normally the expression 'rebutting' is used only for presumptions, I have found it in the literature in one instance. Hoffmann & Zeffert, *South African Law of Evidence (1983)*, p. 404 ff. speak of 'rebutting a prima facie case'. In some sense, a *prima facie case* works like a presumption, while it's technically speaking not the same.

[76] See *Cross on Evidence (1979)*, p. 28.

[77] Cross on Evidence (1979), p. 27, Graham, *Federal Rules of Evidence in a Nutshell (1981)*, §301.4, p. 43.

[78] 550(b) of the *California Evidence Code* stipulates: 'The burden of producing evidence as to a particular fact is initially on the party with the burden of proof as to this fact'. (West's Ann.Cal.Evid.Code §550, Vol. 29B, p. 508).

[79] *Cross on Evidence (1979)*, p. 95. See also Cross & Wilkins, *An Outline of the Law of Evidence (1980)*, p. 29

[80] [1960] 1 W.L.R. 210, 215 (H.L.).

[81] West's Ann.Cal.Evid.Code §550, Vol. 29B, p. 508.

[82] Reproduced in Akinola Aguda, *Law and Practice Relating to Evidence in Nigeria (1980)*, n. 21-03.

[83] See in general Walker & Walker, *The English Legal System (1985)*, p. 617, Curzon, *Law of Evidence (1978)*, p. 60, *Cross on Evidence (1979)*, p. 110, Cross & Wilkins, *An Outline of the Law of Evidence (1980)*, p. 36, *Phipson on Evidence (1982)*, n. 4-35, Eggleston, *Evidence, Proof and Probability (1983)*, p. 129, Glasbeek, *Evidence Cases and Materials (1977)*, p. 594, Schwering, *System der Beweislast (1969)*, pp. 79-85.

[84] See §281, 1, ZPO and Prütting, *Gegenwartsprobleme der Beweislast (1965)*, pp. 58 ff. and Rosenberg-Schwab, *Zivilprozessrecht (1981)* p. 253.

[85] See for example, Glasbeek, *Evidence Cases and Materials (1977)*, p. 594, Hoffmann & Zeffert, *South African Law of Evidence (1983)*, pp. 409 ff., *Glasbeek Australian Edition (1974)*, §§11.02 ff.

[86] See James & Hazard, *Civil Procedure (1977)*, §7.6, p. 243: 'The usual formulation of the test in civil cases is that there must be a preponderance of evidence in favour of the party having the persuasion burden (the proponent) before he is entitled to a verdict'. See also Lilly, *An Introduction to the Law of Evidence (1978)* p. 41: ' … in a typical civil case, a party must prove the elements of his claim by a preponderance of the evidence (sometimes expressed by the phrases 'greater weight of the evidence' or 'more probable than not'). The same is stated for Canada in the *U.L.C.C. Report 1982*, §2.3(a), p. 23.

[87] *Cross on Evidence (1979)*, pp. 111 ff., 118.

[88] *Miller v. Minister of Pensions*, [1947] 2 All E R 372, 373-374.

[89] Id. '… if the probabilities are equal it is not.'

[90] See *Model Code on Evidence (1942)*, Rule 1(5).

[91] [1970] 8 KIR 1063, 1072.

[92] *Model Code on Evidence (1942)*, Rule 701, p. 312.

[93] Walker & Walker, *The English Legal System (1985)*, pp. 606-610, *Halsbury's Laws of England*, §§111 ff., *Cross on Evidence (1979)*, pp. 121 ff., *Phipson on Evidence (1982)*, n. 4-23 ff., Phipson & Elliott, *Manual of the Law of Evidence (1980)*, p. 75, Lilly, *An Introduction to the Law of Evidence (1978)*, p. 47, *Model Code on Evidence (1942)*, pp. 306 ff.

[94] See Wigmore, *Evidence in Trials at Common Law (1981)*, Vol. 9, §2485, Cross & Wilkins, An Outline of the Law of Evidence (1980), p. 27, Lilly, *An Introduction to the Law of Evidence (1978)*, p. 41.

[95] The term 'trier of fact' is defined in the *Model Code on Evidence (1942)*, Rule 1(14), p. 72: 'Trier of fact includes a jury, and a judge when is is trying an issue of fact other than one relating to the admissibility of evidence'.

[96] See, for example, Glasbeek, *Evidence Cases and Materials (1977)*, p. 634, *Halsbury's Laws of England*, §13, *Phipson on Evidence (1982)*, n. 4-07, p. 47, Lilly, *An Introduction to the Law of Evidence (1978)*, p. 45, Graham, Federal Rules in a Nutshell (1981), §301.5, p. 45.

[97] *Cross on Evidence (1979)*, p. 87

[98] *Halsbury's Laws of England*, §13, *Phipson on Evidence (1982)*, n. 4-06. Sometimes, in the literature there is question of a 'burden of pleadings'. The expression however is awkward as the burden of pleadings can't be a valid guideline for finding out about the incidence of the persuasive burden, see Schwering, *System der Beweislast im englisch-amerikanischen Zivilprozess (1969)* , pp. 99-100, and p. 90.

[99] Cross & Wilkins, *An Outline of the Law of Evidence (1980)*, p. 27. See also Curzon, *Law of Evidence (1978)*, §5, p. 48, Phipson and Elliott, *Manual of the Law of Evidence (1980)*, p. 51, Lilly, *An Introduction to the Law of Evidence (1978)*, p. 41.

[100] *Phipson on Evidence (1982)*, n. 4-02, Eggleston, *Evidence, Proof and Probability (1983)*, p. 103. A synonymous expression is *'ei incumbit probatio qui dicit, non qui negat'*, see *Cross on Evidence (1979)*, p. 97, *Sarkar's Law of Evidence (1981)*, §101, p. 908, *Cross on Evidence, Australian Edition (1980)*, §§4.13 ff., Hoffmann & Zeffert, *South African Law of Evidence (1983)*, pp. 396 ff.

[101] It would not be logical to ask for a simple negation to be proven because the latter is the very reason that the initial allegation needs to be proven in the first place. A plaintiff who meets a defendant who fully complies with the demand of the plaintiff, does not need to prove anything. In such a case, not a real litigation takes place but a peaceful settlement. Only facts that are contested need to be proven. This is a general principle valid for all jurisdictions.

[102] See Glasbeek, *Evidence Cases and Materials (1977)*, p. 634: 'Each party will wish to have certain facts found so that the pertinent substantive law will be applied in his favour. Accordingly, it is logical to place the risk of non-persuasion, i.e. the legal burden, in respect of each fact-in-issue on the party who will fail in his claim if the fact-in-issue is not found to exist'.

[103] See Cross & Wilkins, *An Outline of the Law of Evidence (1980)*, p. 28: 'The question is usually not a particularly difficult one, for a fundamental requirement of any judicial system is that the person who desires the court to take action must prove his case to its satisfaction. This means that, as a matter of common sense, the burden of proving of all facts to their claim normally rests upon the plaintiff.' See also *Cross on Evidence (1979)*, p. 96 and *Halsbury's Laws of England*, §14: 'The legal burden of proof normally rests upon the party desiring the court to take action; thus a claimant must satisfy the court or tribunal that the conditions which entitle him to an award have been satisfied', citing *Dickinson v. Minister of Pensions*, [1953] 1 Q.B. 228, 232, [1952] 2 All E R 1031, 1033.

[104] This principle is expressed in the *Indian Evidence Act*, §101, in the following way: 'Whoever desires any Court to give judgment as to any legal right or liability dependent on the existence of facts which he asserts, must prove that those facts exist. When a person is bound to prove the existence of any fact, it is said that the burden of proof lies upon that person.' Regarding Pakistan, which has adopted the Indian Evidence Act, see *The Pakistan Code*, Vol. II, 1, at 46. Kenya equally has literally overtaken the *Indian Evidence Act*, see §107 of the *Evidence Act of Kenya*, Laws of Kenya, Rev. Ed. 1977, Chap. 80, p. 37. For Nigeria, see §134 of the *Evidence Act of Nigeria*, cited by Aguda, *Law and Practice Relating to Evidence in Nigeria (1980)*, p. 237.

[105] Cross and Wilkins, *An Outline of the Law of Evidence (1980)*, p. 28: 'The rule is sometimes expressed in such maxims as 'he who affirms must prove', but this must not be taken to mean that the burden of proof cannot lie upon a party who makes a negative allegation. There are numerous instances in which the plaintiff or prosecutor assumes the burden of proving a negative. (…) In these cases the phrase 'burden of proof' includes the burden of disproof'. See also Wigmore, *Evidence in Trials at Common Law (1981)*, Vol. 9, §2484, p. 288: 'The burden is often on one who has a negative assertion to prove'.

[106] See, for example, Lilly, *An Introduction to the Law of Evidence (1978)*, p. 42 and Cairns, *Australian Civil Procedure (1981)*, p. 130.

[107] Phipson and Elliott, *Manual of the Law of Evidence (1980)*, p. 58, Lilly, *An Introduction to the Law of Evidence (1978)*, p. 40. This is established case law.

[108] The US Supreme Court decided this important question in *Verlinden B.V. v. Central Bank of Nigeria* (461 U.S.480, 103 S.Ct.1962, 76 L.Ed.2d 81, 51 U.S.L.W. 4567, 22ILM 647 (1983); in that case, the foreign state did not enter an appearance to assert an immunity defense. The Supreme Court ruled that in such a case a district court still must determine that immunity is unavailable under the FSIA, as this is a condition for the court's jurisdiction (103 S.Ct.1962, 1971, note 20. Hence, the wording of the House Report that sovereign immunity is to be considered as an affirmative defense cannot be taken literally.

[109] Graham, *Federal Rules of Evidence in a Nutshell (1981)*, §301.2, p. 41 and *Carlson v. Nelson*, 285 N.W.2d 505, 204 Neb.765 (Neb.1979).

[110] *Coast Pump Associates v. Stephen Tyler Corp.*, 133 Cal.Rptr.88, 62 C.A.3d (Cal.App.1976) and *Booth Newspapers Inc., v. Regents of University of Michigan*, 280 N.W.2d 883, 90 Mich.App.99 (Mich.App. 1979)

[111] H.R. Report No. 94-1487, 94th Cong., 2d Session., pp. 1-55, U.S. Code Cong. & Adm. News 6604, 15 ILM 1398 (1976).

[112] JURISDICTION OF U.S. COURTS IN SUITS AGAINST FOREIGN STATES, U.S. Congress, House of Representatives, Subcommittee on Administrative Law and Governmental Relations of the Committee on the Judiciary, Hearing, June 4, 1976, Washington, D.C., 1976 and HEARING before the Subcommittee on Administrative Practice and Procedure of the Committee on the Judiciary, United States Senate, 91st Cong., 2d Session, June 3, 1970, Washington, D.C., 1970.

[113] 621 F.2d 1371, 1378 (5th Cir. 1980).

[114] 647 F.2d 320, 326 (2d Cir. 1981).

[115] 515 F.Supp. 900, 903 (E.D.La. 1981).

[116] 543 F.Supp. 561, 564, 21 ILM 318 (S.D.Tex. 1982).

[117] 767 F.2d 998, 1002 (D.D.C. 1985).

[118] 461 U.S.480, 103 S.Ct.1962, 76 L.Ed.2d 81, 51 U.S.L.W. 4567, 22 ILM 647 (1983).

[119] 103 S.Ct.1962, 1971, note 20.

[120] 761 F.2d 370 (7th Cir. 1985).

[121] Id., pp. 372, 373.

[122] 705 F.2d 250, 22 ILM 835 (7th Cir. 1983).

[123] 705 F.2d 250, 256, 22 ILM 835, 839.

[124] 77 AM.J.INT'L L. 888 (1983).

[125] 23 VA.J.INT'L L. 635, 642 (1983).

[126] 488 U.S. 428, 443, 102 L. Ed. 2d 818, 109 S. Ct. 683 (1989).

[127] *International Shoe Co. v. Washington*, 326 U.S. 310 (1945), *McGee v. International Life Insurance Co.*, 355 U.S. 220, 223 (1957). See also the *House Report*, 15 ILM 1398, 1408 (1976).

[128] 577 F. Supp. 1148, 1157 (N. D. Cal. 1983).

[129] 577 F. Supp. 1148, 1157 (N. D. Cal. 1983).

[130] See, for example, Johnson & Worthington, *Minimum Contacts Jurisdiction under the FSIA*, 12 GA. J. INT'L & COMP. L. 209-230 (1982), Terence J. Pell, *The FSIA of 1976: Direct Effects and Minimal Contacts*, 14 CORNELL INT'L L. J. 97-115 (1981) as well as *Direct Effect Jurisdiction under the FSIA of 1976*, 13 N.Y.U.J. INT'L L. & POL. 571 (1981), *Effects Jurisdiction under the FSIA and the Due Process Clause*, 55 N. Y. U. L. REV. 474 (1980), *The Nikkei Case: Toward a More Uniform Application of the Direct Effect Clause of the FSIA*, 4 FORDHAM INT'L L. J. 109 (1980).

[131] 591 F. Supp. 765, 766 (W. D. Mich. 1984).

[132] *Beacon Enterprises v. Menzies*, 715 F.2d 757, 762 (2d Cir. 1983).

[133] The *House Report* explains under section 1608: 'Provisions in section 1608 are closely interconnected with other parts of the bill - particularly the … section 1330 and sections 1605-1607. If notice is served under section 1608 and if the jurisdictional contacts embodied in sections 1605-1607 are satisfied, personal jurisdiction over a foreign state would exist under section 1330(b).' (H.R. Report, p. 23, 15 ILM 1398, 1410 (1976).

[134] Admiralty actions, §1605(b) FSIA are not within the scope of the present monograph as they have no parallel to continental law. This restriction however only applies with regard to jurisdictional immunities. Regarding immunity from execution, the seizure of vessels belonging to foreign states is a custom common to all jurisdictions. See, in detail, A.N. Yannopoulos, *Foreign Sovereign Immunity and the Arrest of State-Owned Ships: The Need for an Admiralty Sovereign Immunities Act*, 57 TUL.L.REV. 1274-1342 (1983), Kevin P. Simmons, *Admiralty Practice under the FSIA - A Trap for the Unwary*, 12 J.MAR.L. & COMM. 109-121 (1980).

[135] H. R. Report No. 94-1487, p. 22, 15 ILM 1398, 1410 (1976). It suffices thus to prove the commencement of service and the plaintiff doesn't need to demonstrate that service has been effectively accomplished. The House Report explains that this means an attenuation of proof for the specific case of admiralty actions and is different under 'ordinary' procedural law.' (Id.) See also *Federal Rules of Civil Procedure*, Rules 1, 81, 82, 9(h).

[136] See, for example, Thomas A. Coyne, *Rules of Civil Procedure for the United States District Courts (1983)*.

[137] Thomas A. Coyne, *Rules of Civil Procedure for the United States District Courts (1983)*, with comments.

[138] Rule 55(e) Federal Rules of Civil Procedure states: 'Judgment against the United States. No judgment by default shall be entered against the United States or an officer or agency thereof unless the claimant establishes his claim or right to relief by evidence satisfactorily to the court.'

[139] Rule 55(a) Federal Rules of Civil Procedure states: 'Entry. When a party against whom a judgment for affirmative relief is sought has failed to plead or otherwise defend as provided by these rules and that fact is made to appear by affidavit or otherwise, the clerk shall enter his default.'

[140] 628 F.2d 1190, 1195-1196 (9th Cir. 1980).

[141] See, for example, *Gray v. Permanent Mission of People's Republic of the Congo in the United States*, 443 F.Supp. 816, 821-822 (S.D.N.Y. 1978), 63 IRL 121 (1982), *Velidor v. L/P/G Benghazi*, 653 F.2d 812, 821 (3d Cir. 1981), 21 ILM 621, 623-624 (1982), 63 ILR 622, *Harris Corp. V. National Iranian Radio and Television*, 691 F.2d 1344, 1352 (11th Cir. 1982), 22 ILM 434, 439 (1983), *Alberti v. Empresa Nicaraguense de la Carne*, 705 F.2d 250, 253 (7th Cir. 1983), 22 ILM 835, 836 (1983).

[142] See also *Maritime International Nominees Establishment (MINE) v. Republic of Guinea*, 21 ILM 1355, 1360 (D. C. Cir. 1982): 'The Act thereby connects the issue of subject matter jurisdiction to the issue of sovereign immunity: the absence of immunity is a condition to the presence of subject matter jurisdiction'.

[143] See *House Report*, §1604, p. 17, 15 ILM 1398, 1407 (1976): '... the burden will remain on the foreign state to produce evidence in support of its claim of immunity. Thus, evidence must be produced to establish that a foreign state or one of its subdivisions, agencies or instrumentalities is the defendant in the suit ...'.

[144] 462 F.Supp. 1165 (D.Md. 1978).

[145] This is a simplification of the facts; the bill that was not paid only amounted to $91.310, while the value of the vessel was 24 million dollars!

[146] 462 F.Supp. 1165, 1171-1172.

[147] 453 F.Supp. 1097 (S.D.N.Y. 1978), 63 ILR 164, 232 (1982).

[148] 462 F.Supp. 1165, 1172.

[149] Id.

[150] 291 F.Supp. 49 (S.D.N.Y. 1968).

151 116 F.2d 43 (2nd Cir. 1940). This case was ruled even before the *Tate Letter (1952)* and it was an admiralty case where special rules apply.

152 291 F.Supp. 49, 52-53.

153 Id., p. 53.

154 See also *Sugarman v. Aeromexico*, 626 F.2d 270, 272 (3d Cir. 1980) that I already discussed and where the Court of Appeals of the 3rd Circuit stated: 'We agree with the district court that clause two and three of section 1605(a)(2) afford no basis for piercing the immunity which, prima facie, Aeromexico derives from its sovereign parent.'

155 706 F.2d 411 (2d Cir. 1983).

156 Id., p. 414.

157 H.R. Report, p. 15, 15 ILM 1398, 1406 (1976): '… that the entity be a separate legal person, is intended to include a corporation, association, foundation, or any other entity which, under the law of the foreign state where it was created, can sue or be sued in its own name, contract in its own name and hold property in its own name.'

158 706 F.2d 411, 414.

159 Id., referring to the House Report, id., pp. 15-16 and the precedent *Banco Nacional de Cuba v. Chase Manhattan Bank*, 505 F.Supp. 412, 428 (S.D.N.Y. 1981) where the Foreign Trade Bank of Cuba (Banco Para El Comercio Exterior de Cuba) was considered as an organism of the Cuban government.

160 706 F.2d 411, 414. The court stated about the evidence: 'There was additional evidence of the Bank's state-ownership and its position as a state foreign trade organ. The uncontroverted affidavits of Sava, Consul to the Socialist Republic of Romania, and Radu, the managing director of the Bank, and of Hersovici, an expert in Romanian law, corroborated the Bank's assertion that it is owned by the state and that it serves the foreign trade goals of the state. Finally, a report published by the United States Department of Commerce characterizes the Romanian Bank in the same terms.'

161 103 S.Ct. 259 (1983).

162 706 F.2d 411, 415.

163 414 F.Supp. 827 (D.D.C. 1977), 63 IRL 100 (1982). This was an action against a Yugoslav trade union. In this case, there was only the presumption of state property without any additional proof, which is why the district court found the proof inadequate and insufficient.'

164 706 F.Supp. 411, 415.

165 Id., MASIN had provided an affidavit by the Romanian Consul to the effect that MA-SIN 'is a state foreign trade company wholly-owned and controlled by the Romanian Government.' Regarding this affidavit, the court held: 'Although S & S belittles this sworn statement as the catechism of a brainwashed functionary, statements of foreign officials - regardless of their political or ideological orientation - have been accorded great weight in determining whether an entity is entitled to claim the protection of the FSIA. (706 F.2d 411, 415, citing *Yessenin-Volpin v. Novosti Press Agency, Tass*, 443 F. Supp. 849, 854 (S.D.N.Y. 1978), UN-MAT., p. 468, 63 ILR 127.

166 706 F.2d 711, 715: 'MASIN introduced a variety of material detailing the role of the Romanian state in foreign trade.'

167 See Thomas A. Coyne, Thomas A. Coyne, *Rules of Civil Procedure for the United States District Courts (1983)*, Rule 44.1, Practice Comment, p. 543: 'The Rule imposes a notice burden on a party who intends to raise an issue about foreign law', citing *Commercial Ins. Co. of Newark v. Pacific-Peru Construction Corp.*, 558 F.2d 948, 952 (9th Cir. 1977). As to the reason for such a restriction of judicial notice of foreign law, Coyne remarks: 'This would put an extreme burden on the court in many cases; and it avoids use of 'judicial notice' in any form because of the uncertain meaning of that concept as applied to foreign law.' (Id.) See also Stern, *Foreign Law in the Courts: Judicial Notice and Proof*, 45 CALIF.L.REV. 23, 43 (1957) and Schlesinger, *A Recurrent Problem of Transnational Litigation: The Effect of Failure to Invoke or Prove the Applicable Foreign Law*, 59 CORNELL L.REV 1 (1973) as well as the whole issue of STAN. J.INT'L L., Spring 1983, entitled *Pleading and Proof of Foreign Law*, 19 STAN.J.INT'L L., Issue 1, Spring 1983, with further references and bibliography.

168 566 F.Supp. 1381 (S.D.N.Y. 1983).

169 566 F.Supp. 1381, 1384, citing the *House Report*, pp. 15-16.

170 *Outbound I*: 575 F.Supp. 1222 (S.D.N.Y. 1983), *Outbound II*: 582 F.Supp. 1136 (D.Md. 1984). There was still one more defendant, ICCI/AMF Joint Venture (JV).

171 575 F.Supp. 1222, 1224, citing the precedents *Alberti* and *Jet Line* that I discussed above in the text.

172 It is of course very difficult to appreciate the value of the proof that was submitted to the judge. For this reason, I can only refer to the arguments given by the judge in the record, and this information, in the present case, is rather scarce.

173 575 F.Supp. 1222, 1224.

174 Id.

175 336 F.2d 354, 358-359, note 7 (2d Cir. 1964), cert. denied, 381 U.S. 934, 85 S.Ct. 1763, 14 L.Ed.2d 698 (1965).

176 328 F.Supp. 759, 761 (E.D.N.Y. 1971).

177 See *Victory Transport*, 336 F.2d 354, 358.

[178] Id., note 7.

[179] *O'Connell Machinery*, 566 F.Supp. 1381, 1384 (S.D.N.Y. 1983), *S. & S. Machinery*, 706 F.2d 411, 415 (2d Cir. 1983) and *Yessenin-Volpin*, 443 F.Supp. 849, 854 (S.D.N.Y. 1978).

[180] 575 F.Supp. 1222, 1224. This despite the fact that the court had stated that 'a letter from the ambassador of a foreign country claiming immunity for an agency or instrumentality of a foreign state has a persuasive quality. (Id. and 48 C.J.S.2d Intern'l Law, §52, p. 89 (1981), citing the precedents *Harris* and *Yessenin-Volpin*.

[181] Id.

[182] 582 F.Supp. 1136 (D.Md. 1984).

[183] Id., p. 1143.

[184] Id., p. 1144.

[185] Id., p. 1146: 'Both rulings by the New York court are interlocutory and subject to revision. Neither ruling is 'final' within the meaning of 28 U.S.C. §1291 and hence neither ruling has a res judicata effect.'

[186] Id., p. 1147.

[187] Id.

[188] 582 F.Supp. 1136, 1147.

[189] 443 F.Supp. 816 (S.D.N.Y. 1978).

[190] Id., p. 820.

[191] In *Sugarman v. Aeromexico, Inc.*, 626 F.2d 270, 272 (3d Cir. 1980), the court stated: 'Aeromexico, asserting by way of affidavit that it was a Mexican corporation wholly-owned by the Mexican government … Sugarman filed a responsive affidavit asserting that a New York-based public relations officer of Aeromexico had advised Sugarman's attorney that Aeromexico 'was a Mexican corporation and … a New York corporation.' The relevance of this affidavit was that if, in addition to being a Mexican corporation, Aeromexico had been incorporated in New York, it would have fallen outside the sovereign immunity decreed by the Foreign Sovereign Immunities Act. 28 U.S.C. §§1332(a) and (c) and 1603(b)(3). (…) Thereafter, Aeromexico submitted a further affidavit enclosing a letter from New York's Secretary of State certifying that Aeromexico was not to be found on the roster of New York corporations.'

[192] As to the relation between international treaties and the FSIA, the House Report remarks under section 1604: 'All immunity provisions in section 1604 through 1607 are made subject to 'existing' treaties and other international agreements to which the United States is a party. In the event an international agreement expressly conflicts with this bill, the international agreement would control. Thus, the bill would not alter the rights of duties of the United States under the NATO Status of Forces Agreement or similar agreements with other countries; nor would it alter the provisions of commercial contracts or agreements to which the United States is a party, calling for exclusive nonjudicial remedies through arbitration or other procedures for the settlement of disputes. Treaties of friendship, commerce and navigation and bilateral air transport agreements often contain provisions relating to the immunity of foreign states. Many provisions in such agreements are consistent with, but do not go as far as, the current bill. To the extent such international agreements are silent on a question of immunity, the bill would control: the international agreement would control only where a conflict was manifest.' 15 ILM 1398, 1407 (1976)

[193] H.R. Report No. 94-1487, 9th Cong., 2d Session, 1, 17, 15 ILM 1398, 1407 (1976).

[194] *Behring International Inc. v. Imperial Iranian Air Force (IIAF)*, 475 F.Supp.383 (D.N.J.1979), UN-Mat. 479, 63 ILR 261 (1982).

[195] See 475 F.Supp. 383, 385, note 2: 'Defendant claims only that sovereign immunity bars the prejudgment attachment of its property. It does not claim that it is immune from suit in this court'.

[196] 475 F.Supp, 383, 389. In a more recent precedent, *Transamerican S.S. Corp. v. Somali Democratic Republic*, 767 F.2d 998, 1002 (D.D.C.1985), the court stated: 'In accordance with the restrictive view of sovereign immunity reflected in the FSIA, the burden of proof in establishing the inapplicability of these exceptions is upon the party claiming immunity ...'

[197] See, for example, Habscheid & Schaumann, *Die Immunität ausländischer Staaten nach Völkerrecht und deutschem Zivilprozessrecht*, BDGVR, Vol. 8 (1968), p. 7 and pp. 24 ff., Gamal Moursi Badr, *State Immunity (1984)*, p. 138, *Behring v. IIAF*, 475 F.Supp. 383, 389, note 13, *IAM v. OPEC*, 477 F.Supp. 553, 565, note 10, *Letelier v. Republic of Chile*, 488 F.Supp. 665, 667, *Moore's Federal Practice*, §0.60[4], at 624-28, Wright, Miller & Cooper, *Federal Practice and Procedure*, §3522, at 46-48.

[198] See, from the large literature, only Sutherland, *Recent Statutory Developments in the Law of Foreign Sovereign Immunity*, 7 AUSTRALIAN Y. B. INT'L L. 27-71 (1981), at 51, and Georges R. Delaume, *Transnational Contracts*, Vol. 2, XI., Booklet 13 (May 1985), §11.05.

[199] *Verlinden B.V. v. Central Bank of Nigeria*, 461 U.S. 480, 103 S.Ct. 1962, 76 L.Ed.2d 81, 51 U.S.L.W. 4567, 22 ILM 647 (1983).

[200] 103 S.Ct. 1962, 1971, note 20.

[201] *Frovola v. Union of Soviet Socialist Republics*, 761 F.2d 370, 372-373 (7th Cir. 1985).

[202] See also *De Sanchez v. Banco Central de Nicaragua*, 515 F.Supp. 900, 903 (E.D.La.1981): 'This [the incidence of the burden of proof according to the House Report] is in contrast to the usual rule that upon challenge, the plaintiff bears the burden of proving that subject matter jurisdiction exists over its claim'. See e.g. *Save Our Cemeteries, Inc. v. Archdiocese of New Orleans*, 568 F.2d 1074, 1076 (5th Cir. 1978), cert. denied, 439 U.S. 836, 99 S.Ct. 120, 58 L.Ed.2d 13 (1978), *Rosemond Sand and Gravel Co. v. Lambert Sand and Gravel Co.*, 469 F.2d 416, 418 (5th Cir. 1972).

[203] 705 F.2d 250, 22 ILM 835 (7th Cir. 1983).

[204] 705 F.2d 250, 253, 22 ILM 835, 836.

[205] Id., p. 256, 22 ILM 835, 839.

[206] Id.

[207] Id.

[208] Julia B. Brooke, *The International Law Association Draft Convention on Foreign Sovereign Immunity: A Comparative Approach*, 23 VA.J.INT'L L. 635.

[209] Id., p. 642.

[210] 705 F.2d 250, 256, 22 ILM 835, 839.

[211] 77 AJIL 888 (1983).

[212] Id., p. 891.

[213] 705 F.2d 250, 254, 256.

[214] Id., p. 256.

[215] Id.

[216] 481 F.Supp. 1056 (E.D.N.Y. 1979), 63 ILR 318 (1982).

[217] 516 F.Supp. 1155 (S.D.N.Y. 1981), 63 ILR 604 (1982).

[218] Id., p. 1158.

[219] 46 U.S.C. §§183, 185. Section 185 stipulates that within six months from service of process, the owner of a vessel can file a counterclaim for reducing its financial responsibility which, in admiralty matters, can be considerable and is usually limited by maritime counterclaims.

[220] 516 F. Supp. 1155, 1159: 'CNAN did everything possible to preserve substantive rights it reasonably expected it would lose if its sovereign immunity claim was denied; its actions cannot be considered an express or implied waiver of its sovereign immunity defense.'

[221] 407 U.S. 1, 19-20, 92 S.Ct. 1907, 1918, 32 L.Ed.2d 513 (1972).

[222] 516 F.Supp. 1281 (E.D.Pa. 1981), 63 ILR 632 (1982).

[223] 477 F.Supp. 553, 575 (C.D. Cal. 1979), UN-MAT., p. 503, 63 ILR 284 (1982). See also *Castro v. Saudi Arabia*, 510 F.Supp. 309, 312 (W.D.Tex. 1980), 63 ILR 419.

[224] *H. R. Report No. 94-1487*, 15 ILM 1398, 1407-1408. See also *Flota Maritima Browning de Cuba v. Motor Vessel Ciudad*, 335 F.2d 619 (4th Cir. 1964) where the court pronounced the same reasoning.

[225] *H. R. Report No. 94-1487*, p. 13, 15 ILM 1398, 1408 (1976).

[226] See, for example, Johnson & Worthington, *Minimum Contacts Jurisdiction under the FSIA*, 12 GA.J.INT'L & COMP.L. 209-230 (1982), Terence J. Pell, *The FSIA of 1976: Directs Effects and Minimal Contacts*, 14 CORNELL INT'L L.J. 97-115 (1981).

[227] 626 F.2d 270 (3d Cir. 1980).

[228] The court stated, id., p. 272: '… if we felt confined by the recitals of the complaint, standing alone, we would acknowledge that the complaint does not provide very sturdy underpinning for the finding that Sugarman's claim is 'based upon a commercial activity carried on in the United States', as called for by the first clause of section 1605(a)(2).'

[229] 488 F.Supp. 128 (S.D.N.Y. 1980).

[230] Id., p. 1294. The judgment was confirmed by the Court of Appeals of the 2nd circuit, 647 F.2d 320 (2d Cir. 1981), but the appeal was reversed by the Supreme Court, however for other reasons, 103 S.Ct. 1962 (1983), 22 ILM 647 (1983).

[231] 682 F.2d 1022 (D.C. Cir. 1982).

[232] Id., p. 1027, note 20: 'The district court apparently accepted plaintiff's assertion that the acts involved were 'commercial', and our disposition of the case today does not call for review of this issue.'

[233] Appeal courts only revise legal questions. See id., p. 1026 where the court stated: 'Our conclusion that the district court's dismissal for lack of jurisdiction was improper is based on our finding that the facts 'as alleged' - and generously interpreted - make a dismissal at least premature in light of the dearth of fact-finding done by the district court thus far.'

[234] 459 F.Supp. 264 (D.D.C. 1978), 63 ILR 211 (1982).

[235] 577 F.Supp. 1148 (N.D.Cal. 1983).

[236] 459 F.Supp. 264, 266.

[237] 459 F.Supp. 264, 265.

[238] 443 F.Supp. 849, 851, note 1 (S.D.N.Y. 1978).

[239] 629 F.2d 786, 790 (2d Cir. 1980).

[240] Ports and Shipping Organization of Bushire, Iran.

[241] 577 F.Supp. 1148, 1157.

[242] Id.

[243] See, for example, Henkin/Pugh/Schachter/Smit, *International Law (1980),* Chapter 11, pp. 685-803, Steiner/Vagts, *Transnational Legal Problems (1976),* Chapter IV, pp. 357 ff, and the work of the International Law Commission, *Draft Articles on State Responsibility,* [1978] 2 Y.B.I.L.C. 78, reproduced in Henkin et al., *Basic Documents Supplement,* pp. 257 ff. However, in the 2004 final *United Nations Convention on Jurisdictional Immunities of States and Their Property (2004),* a clause to that effect is missing.

[244] H.R. Report, pp. 19, 20, 15 ILM 1398, 1408 (1976).

[245] 705 F.2d 250 (7th Cir. 1983), 22 ILM 835 (1983).

[246] Id., p. 255.

[247] Id.

[248] The court took reference to *Banco Nacional de Cuba v. Chase Manhattan Bank,* 658 F.2d 875, 888 (2n Cir. 1981) and Dawson & Weston, *Prompt, Adequate and Effective: A Universal Standard of Compensation?,* 30 FORDHAM L.REV. 727 (1962).

[249] Id. See also H.R. Rep, pp. 19-20.

[250] Id., p. 256, 22 ILM 835, 839. The quote of the *House Report* refers to U.S.Code Cong. & Adm. News 6604 (1976). It is page 17 in the original text and corresponds to 15 ILM 1398, 1407 (1976).

[251] 482 F.Supp. 1175, 1179 (D.D.C. 1980).

[252] Id.

[253] 24 ILM 1278 (W.D.Mich. 1985).

[254] Id., p. 1284.

[255] 515 F.Supp. 900 (E.D.La. 1981).

[256] Id., p. 910, note 10.

[257] 515 F.Supp. 900, 911-912.

[258] Id.: 'From Incer's testimony, it is clear that Banco Central used the C & S account as part of certain commercial activities conducted in the United States. Checks from the C & S account were used to pay for letters of credit issued through C & S for Nicaragua imports and to pay for principle and interest on credit extended to Banco Central by C & S. Incer at 11-12. The account was also used to collect all other American checks tendered to Banco Central. Id., at 11.'

[259] 647 F.2d 320 (2d Cir. 1981), 461 U.S. 480, 103 S.Ct. 1962, 76 L.Ed.2d 81, 51 U.S.L.W. 4567, 22 ILM 647 (1983).

[260] 515 F. Supp. 900, 911.

[261] Id., note 11.

[262] Id.

[263] 705 F.2d 250 (7th Cir. 1983), 22 ILM 835 (1983).

[264] 577 F.Supp. 1148.

[265] 705 F.2d 250, 256.

[266] 682 F.2d 1022 (D.C. Cir. 1982).

[267] See Hersch Lauterpacht, *International Law (1977)*, pp. 340, 341: 'There is uniform authority in support of the view that there is no immunity from jurisdiction with respect to actions relating to immovable property.' See also Sompong Sucharitkul, *State Immunities and Trading Activities in International Law (1959)*, p. 167.

[268] See, for example the *Harvard Draft Convention*, Art. 9, 26 AJIL 572, 577 (1932 Suppl.), where this is called 'submission to the jurisdiction of the situs.' Regarding immunity waivers in general, under the FSIA, see further down in the text.

[269] H.R. Report 94-1487, p. 20, 15 ILM 1398, 1411 (1976).

[270] This was not contested by Monroe Leigh, in his case note critique of the *Alberti* precedent.

[271] 516 F.Supp. 1155 (S.D.N.Y. 1981).

[272] 516 F. Supp. 1155, 1160.

[273] The expression 'noncommercial tort exception' is to be found in the *House Report* and in the subsequent federal jurisprudence, see for example, *Matter of Sedco, Inc.*, 543 F.Supp. 561, 566 (S.D.Tex. 1982).

[274] H.R. Report, pp. 20-21, 15 ILM 1398, 1409 (1976).

[275] 482 F.Supp. 1208 (D.D.C. 1980), 63 IRL 350, 601 (1982).

[276] Regarding the 'commercial activity exception', §1605(a)(2), the court denied the commercial character of the police action, despite the fact that the patrolling of the police is ultimately founded upon the safeguarding of commercial interests. But the police action itself was of course governmental, not commercial, by nature.

[277] 482 F.Supp. 1208, 1210-1211. The judgment was confirmed by the Court of Appeals of the District of Columbia Circuit, 652 F.2d 186, 189 (D.C.Cir. 1981) who pronounced itself accordingly: 'Appellant has failed to demonstrate how section 1605(a)(5) or any of the statutory exceptions to sovereign immunity, are applicable to The Bahamas in this case.'

[278] 722 F.2d 582 (9th Cir. 1983).

[279] 729 F.2d 641 (9th Cir. 1984).

[280] 722 F.2d 582, 589.

[281] Tijuana airport is very close to the American border, and the faulty piloting of the plane occurred while the plane was still over the American territory.

[282] 729 F.2d 641, 646.

[283] 591 F.Supp. 765 (W.D.Mich. 1984).

[284] Id., p. 766.

[285] Julia B. Brooke, *The International Law Association Draft Convention on Foreign Sovereign Immunity: A Comparative Approach*, 23 VA.J.INT'L L. 635-669, 641-642, notes 18 to 23 (1983).

[286] Id., p. 642, note 23.

[287] See also Robert von Mehren, *The Foreign Sovereign Immunities Act of 1976*, 17 COLUM.J.TRANSNAT'L L. 33 (1978) who made that necessary distinction: 'The plaintiff would still have to show that the commercial act … caused a direct effect in the United States.' (Id., p. 98).

[288] N.Y. SCP. Law §301: 'Jurisdiction over persons, property or status. A court may exercise such jurisdiction over persons, property, or status as might have been exercised heretofore.' According to the *Federal Rules of Civil Procedure*, Rule 4(d)(7) and 4(e), jurisdiction of a federal court against a non-resident defendant is ruled by the long-arm statute of the forum state. See also *Prejean v. Sonatrach, Inc.*, 652 F.2d 1260, 1264, note 2 (5th Cir. 1981), with further references.

[289] 715 F.2d 757 (2d Cir. 1983).

[290] Id., p. 762: 'As plaintiff, Beacon bore the ultimate burden of proving the court's jurisdiction by a preponderance of evidence.' The burden of proof is even more severe in a summary action, as the court points out: 'For a plaintiff to prevail on summary judgment when defendant contests personal jurisdiction, his burden is even greater; he must demonstrate that there is no genuine issue as to any material fact on the jurisdictional question.' (Id.) See, in general, Diego C. Asencio, Robert W. Dry, *An Assessment of the Service Provisions of the Foreign Sovereign Immunities Act of 1976*, 8 JOURNAL OF LEGISLATION (Notre Dame Law School) 230-249 (1981). With regard to the exclusivity of these provisions, see A.G. Bradley, *Services of Process under the FSIA of 1976: The Arguments for Exclusivity*, 14 CORNELL INT'L L.J. 357-368 (1981) and Georges R. Delaume, *Transnational Contracts*, Vol. II, XI (Booklet 13), §11.09 'Service of Process'.

[291] 28 U.S.C. §1606 FSIA (Extent of Liability) states: 'As to any claim for relief with respect to which a foreign state is not entitled to immunity under section 1605 or 1607 of this chapter, the foreign state shall be liable in the same manner and to the same extent as a private individual under like circumstances; (...)'

[292] See, for example, *Phipson on Evidence (1982)*, 4-06, note 33, *Cross on Evidence (1979)*, p. 108. See also *The Glendarroch*, [1894] 226, 63 L.J.Adm. 89, 6 R. 686, 70 L.T. 344 and *Hurst v. Evans*, [1917] 1 K.B. 351.

[293] See Phipson and Elliott, *Manual of the Law of Evidence (1980)*, pp. 15-16: 'Thus in an action in tort, it is the law of the tort which prescribes the elements of the tort; these the plaintiff must prove if he is to win.' While according to Clerk & Lindsell, *On Torts (1982)*, 1-87, 'the law has not followed a uniform course in casting the burden of proof either on the plaintiff or the defendant[.], the proof for 'negligence' or 'malicious prosecution' is upon the plaintiff, see Charlesworth & Percy, *On Negligence (1983)*, 5-16 and Salmand & Heuston, *On the Law of Torts (1981)*, p. 13: '... , in torts such as negligence or malicious prosecution the onus lies on the plaintiff to show that the conduct of the defendant is legally unjustified.'

[294] 28 U.S.C. §1346, §§2671-2680, see also *House Report*, p. 21 and above in the text.

[295] 28. U.S.C. §1346(b) states: '§1346 United States as defendant. (...) (b) Subject to the provisions of chapter 71 of this title, the district courts together with the United States District Court of the District of the Canal Zone and the District of the Virgin Islands, shall have exclusive jurisdiction of civil actions and claims against the United States, for money damages, accruing on and after January 1, 1945, for injury or loss of property, or personal injury or death caused by the negligent or wrongful act or omission of any employee of the Government while acting within the scope of his office or employment, under circumstances where the United States, if a private person, would be liable to the claimant in accordance with the law of the place where the act or omission occurred.'

[296] 28 U.S.C.A. §1346, notes 415, 416 and the respective notes in the Cumulative Annual Pocket Part, For Use in 1984, in volume Title 28, §§1346 to 1390. See also 28 U.S.C.A. §2674 note 146 and the respective note in the Cum.Ann.Pock.Part, For Use in 1984, in volume Title 28, §2501 to End, with references of all precedents.

[297] 510 F.Supp. 309 (W.D.Tex. 1980).

[298] 510 F.Supp. 309, 313: 'At the adversary hearing, Saudi Arabia proved that there were no flight training activities schedules either on the 16th or the 17th September … and that Al-Quassimie [the soldier] was in civilian clothes at the time of the accident. (…) Applying state law principles of respondeat superior, *Williams v. United States,* 350 U.S. 857, 76 S.Ct 100, 100 L.Ed. 761 (1955), the court fails to see how the soldier can be said to have been in the course of his employment even while off duty and pursuing an entirely personal matter.'

[299] Id.: 'In addition, Saudi Arabia put on evidence that Al-Quassimie was subject to the United States Air Force regulations while at Laughlin Air Force Base. Thus, it was the United States government who apparently had the right to control the soldier's behavior in off-duty hours, not the Saudi Arabian government.'

[300] Id.

[301] Id. Instead of contesting the evidence of the defendant foreign state, the plaintiffs argued that Saudi Arabia was responsible for the soldier for another reason; that it had been obliged to better train the soldier for participating in road traffic in the United States, and that it thus had 'negligently entrusted the automobile to the soldier' (Id.). This argument was rejected by the court for the simple reason that Saudi Arabia was not the owner of the car and that the soldier had a valid Texas drivers license.' (Id.)

[302] 566 F.Supp. 1414 (D.D.C. 1983).

[303] Id., p. 1417.

[304] 510 F.Supp. 309 (W.D.Tex. 1980).

[305] 566 F.Supp. 1414, 1417.

[306] Id.

[307] Id., pp. 1418-1420.

[308] 28 U.S.C.A. §2674, notes 143, 155 and the respective notes in the Cum.Ann.Pock.Part, For Use in 1984, in volume T. 28, §2501 to End, and 28. U.S.C.A., §1346, note 416.

[309] 566 F.Supp. 1414, 1417, note 5.

[310] 28 U.S.C. §§2680(a),(h) state that the provisions of this chapter and section 1346(b) of this title shall not apply to '(a) Any claim based upon an act or omission of an employee of the Government, exercising due care, in the execution of a statute or regulation be valid, or based upon the exercise or performance or the failure to exercise or perform a discretionary function or duty on the part of a federal agency or an employee of the Government whether or not the discretion involved be abused. (…) (h) Any claim arising out of assault, battery, false imprisonment, false arrest, malicious prosecution, abuse of process, libel, slander, misrepresentation, deceit, or interference with contract rights.'

[311] *Boyce v. US*, 93 F.Supp. 866 (D.C. Iowa 1950), 28 U.S.C.A. §2680, note 75, with further references.

[312] 346 U.S. 15 (1953).

[313] Please note that the syllabus is merely informative, *not normative*, and doesn't represent the judgment.

[314] 346 U.S. 15, 30-36.

[315] Id., p. 15.

[316] 488 F.Supp. 665 (D.D.C. 1980), 19 ILM 409 (1980), 63 ILR 378 (1982).

[317] The government of Chile seriously opposed the allegation of the plaintiff to have been involved in the murder but that allegation was not only directed toward the government, but also the other defendants, Michael Vernon Towley, Alvin Ross Diaz, Ignacio Novo Sampol and Guillermo Novo Sampol. The original judgment, that I will henceforth term *Letelier I* was a default judgment under §1608(e) FSIA and was affirmed in *Letelier II*, 502 F. Supp. 259 (D.D.C. 1980) and in *Letelier III*, 567 F.Supp. 1490 (S.D.N.Y. 1983), which was a litigation involving foreign property, and immunity from execution. The respective penal action is *United States v. Sampol*, 636 F.2d 621 (D.D. Cir. 1980).

[318] 488 F.Supp 665, 671, 19 ILM 409, 422.

[319] 488 F.Supp. 665, 673, 19 ILM 409, 426-427.

[320] 502 F.Supp. 259 (D.D.C. 1980), 19 ILM 1418 (1980).

[321] 502 F.Supp. 259, 266, 19 ILM 1418, 1431.

[322] 729 F.2d 641 (9th Cir. 1984).

[323] 729 F.2d 641, 646 ff.

[324] Id., p. 646.

[325] Id. Such reference to the FTCA was made by American district courts already in *Letelier I*, 488 F.Supp. 665, 673 and in *Matter of Sedco, Inc.*, 543 F.Supp. 561, 567.

[326] Apart from the leading case *Dalehite v. United States,* 346 U.S. 15 (1953), the Court of Appeals quoted the precedents *Discroll v. United States*, 525 F.2d 136, 138 (9th Cir. 1975), *Thompson v. United States*, 592 F.2d 1104, 1111 (9th Cir. 1979), and *Lindgren v. United States,* 665 F.2d 978, 980 (9th Cir. 1982), noting that '[o]ver the years, the definition of discretion has been refined and qualified somewhat', 729 F.2d 641, 647.

[327] See House Report, p. 16, 15 ILM 1398, 1406-1407 (1976).

[328] See, for example, *National American Corporation v. Federal Republic of Nigeria*, 448 F.Supp. 622, 641-642 (S.D.N.Y. 1978), 17 ILM 1407 (1978), 63 ILR 63 (1982), conf'd, 597 F.2d 314 (2d Cir. 1979), 63 ILR 137, or *Texas Trading & Milling Corporation v. Federal Republic of Nigeria and Central Bank of Nigeria*, 647 F.2d 300, 310 (2d Cir. 1981), 20 ILM 620 (1981) as well as the case note by Georges R. Delaume, 20 ILM 618, UN-MAT., p. 527, 63 ILR 459 (1982), cert. den'd, 454 U.S. 1148, 102 S.Ct. 1012, 71 L.Ed.2d 301 (1982). See also, for example, the affairs litigated in the United Kingdom, such as *Trendtex Trading Corporation v. Central Bank of Nigeria*, [1977] 2 W.L.R. 356, 369, 1 All E.R. 881, 1 Lloyd's Rep. 581, 588 ff. (Lord Denning), and one of the affairs litigated in Germany, *Youssef M. Nada Establishment v. Central Bank of Nigeria*, Landgericht Frankfurt, August 25, 1976, 16 ILM 501 (1977).

[329] Regarding *Texas Trading*, see also the case notes by Robert H. Yaffe, *Direct Financial Effect under the Foreign Sovereign Immunities Act*, 14 LAW.AMERICAS 361-365 (1982) and *Effects Jurisdiction Under the FSIA and the Due Process Clause*, 55 N.Y.U.L.REV. 474 (1980).

[330] 461 F.Supp. 609 (S.D.N.Y. 1978), 63 ILR 228 (1982).

[331] The judge held that the precedent *Gittler v. German Information Center*, 408 N.Y.S.2d 600 (Sup.Ct.N.Y. 1978), Digest of United States Practice in International Law, 1978, 879-883, was overruled by the FSIA.

[332] 550 F.Supp. 869, 873 (N.D.Ala. 1982).

[333] 22 ILM 1077, 1108 (1983). See also the case notes by Allan Ashman, *People's Republic Told to Pay $41.3 Million Debt from 1911*, 69 A.B.A.J. 512(2)(1983), Jill A. Sgro, *China's Stance on Sovereign Immunity: A Critical Perspective on Jackson v. People's Republic of China*, 22 COLUM.J.TRANSNAT'L L. 101-133 (1983), and Monroe Leigh, *Foreign Sovereign Immunities Act - Liability of People's Republic of China for Defaulted 1911 Bonds - State Succession*, 77 AJIL 146-148. As to the interpretation of the term 'commercial activity', more in general, see David L. Brittenham, *Foreign Sovereign Immunity and Commercial Activity: A Conflicts Approach*, 83 COLUM.L.REV. 1440-1512 (1983), Patricia Hunt Holmes, *Establishing Jurisdiction Under the Commercial Activities Exception to the FSIA of 1976*, 19 HOUS.L.REV. 1003-1023 (1982), D. Schloss, *'Commercial Activity' in the FSIA of 1976*, J.INT'L L. & ECON. 163-173 (1979), G. Cairns, *Jurisdiction: FSIA*, TEX.INT'L L.J. 277-289 (1981), J.H. Friend, *Suing A Foreign Government under the United States Antitrust Laws: The Need for Clarification of the Commercial Activity Exception to the FSIA of 1976*, 1 NW.J.INT'L L. & BUS. 657-699 (1979).

[334] On January 19, 1977.

[335] 443 F.Supp. 849 (S.D.N.Y. 1978), 17 ILM 720 (1978), UN-MAT., p. 468, 63 ILR 127 (1982). Another defendant was *Daily World*, a magazine published by the United States' Communist Party.

[336] S.D.N.Y.

337 28 U.S.C. §1441(d) reads as follows: 'Any civil action brought in a State court against a foreign state as defined in section 1603(a) of this title may be removed by the foreign state to the district court of the United States for the district and division embracing the place where such action is pending. Upon removal the action shall be tried by the court without jury …'

338 443 F.Supp. 849, 855.

339 Id.: 'Thus, the plaintiff's argument is based on the unstated premise that an entity which engages in commercial activity is a commercial entity and thus not entitled to claim sovereign immunity. The Immunities Act does not embody such a principle, however. Rather, it clearly contemplates that a given entity may at some time engage in commercial activities, on which it would be immune, and at other times take actions whose essential nature is public or governmental, on which it would be immune.'

340 Id.: 'Thus, the inquiry under subsection (a)(2) must focus on the specific activity at issue and determine whether it may be characterized as 'commercial.'

341 Id., p. 856.

342 Id.

343 Id.: 'The four publications in which the alleged libels appeared are all publications of the U.S.S.R. itself.'

344 Id.

345 Id.

346 Id.

347 Id., citing Novosti's statutes, §I(2)(c).

348 Id.

349 Id.

350 Id.

351 Id.

352 453 F.Supp. 1097 (S.D.N.Y. 1978), 17 ILM 1180 (1978), UN-MAT., p. 477, 63 ILR 232 (1982). On the plaintiff side was also the 'New England Petroleum Corporation' (NEPCO); on the defendant side was in addition the Arab Republic of Libya. The plaintiff CAREY was the trustee of NEPCO's two affiliates, the 'Grand Bahama Petroleum Company' (PETCO) and the 'Antco Shipping Company' (ANTCO), these latter companies founded under the law of the Bahamas.

353 There were in total eight suits, both against NOC and Libya itself; here only the sixth and the seventh law suit, directed against Libya itself, are of interest.

354 The oil was sold by CALASIA to 'Chevron Oil Trading Company' (COT), an affiliate of CALASIA, then to PETCO and finally to NEPCO.

355 See also the extensive arbitrage decisions regarding NEPCO, TEXACO and LIAMCO against Libya, discussed by an eminent expert on the matter, the Geneva-based international lawyer Jean-Flavien Lalive, in his course *Contrats entre Etats ou entreprises éta-tiques et personnes privés,* 181 RCADI (1983-III), 13 ff,, 83 ff. I have discussed at the time with Jean-Flavien Lalive, Esq, matters regarding my doctoral thesis, and my conclusions regarding the burden of proof and the evidence problems in foreign sovereign immunity litigation.

356 453 F.Supp. 1097, 1099, 'Factual Background'.

357 Id.

358 453 F.Supp. 1097, 1102.

359 336 F. Supp. 354 (2d Cir. 1964), cert. den'd, 381 U.S. 934, 85 S.Ct. 1763, 14 L.Ed.2d 698 (1965), Whiteman, *Digest of International Law (1968),* pp. 577 ff., Sweeny/Oliver/Leach, *The International Legal System (1981),* pp. 306 ff, McDougal/Reisman, *International Law in Contemporary Perspective (1981),* pp. 1458 ff., Henkin/Pugh/Schachter/Smit, *International Law (1980),* p. 506, Steiner/Vagts, *Transnational Legal Problems (1976),* p. 649.

360 336 F.2d 354, 360, Whiteman, p. 579, Sweeny, p. 307, McDougal, p. 1461, Henkin, pp. 507-508, Steiner, p. 653.

361 Id.

362 *Contrats entre Etats ou entreprises étatiques et personnes privés,* 181 RCADI (1983-III), pp. 209 ff.

363 28 BRIT.Y.B.INT'L L. 220-272 (1951).

364 550 F.Supp. 869 (N.D.Ala. 1982).

365 482 F.Supp. 1208 (D.D.C. 1980), 63 ILR 350, 601 (1982), conf'd, 652 F.2d 186 (D.C.Cir 1981).

366 482 F.Supp. 1208, 1210.

367 621 F.2d 1371 (5th Cir. 1980), 63 IRL 467 (1982).

368 The fact that DOMINICANA was an agency or instrumentality of the Dominican Republic under §§1603(a),(b) FSIA was not contested by the plaintiff (621 F.2d 1371, 1378).

369 Id.

[370] The court held that 'Dominicana's actions in connection with the 'involuntary re-routing' were not commercial. Dominicana was impressed into service to perform these function, for which it apparently was not compensated by Dominican immigration officials pursuant to that country's laws. Dominicana acted merely as an arm or agent of the Dominican government in carrying out this assigned role, and, as such, is entitled to the same immunity from any liability arising from that governmental function as would inure to that government itself. (Id.)

[371] 477 F.Supp. 553 (D.Cal. 1979), UN-MAT., p. 503, 63 ILR 284 (1982), Henkin et al., p. 511, conf'd for other motives, 649 F.2d 1354 (9th Cir. 1981), cert. den'd, 454 U.S. 1163, 102 S.Ct. 1036, 71 L.Ed.2d 319 (1982).

[372] This case was broadly discussed in the American international law literature, see for example, Don Wallace, Jr., *Extraterritorial Jurisdiction*, XV L.POL.INT'L BUS. 1099, 1131-1132 (1983, Stanley E. Hilton, *The Demise of the Restrictive Theory of Sovereign Immunity and of the Extraterritorial Effect of the Sherman Act Against Foreign Sovereigns (Case Note)*, 41 U.PITT.L.REV. 841-857 (1980), Russell S. Burman, *Restrictive Immunity and the Opec Cartel: A Critical Examination of the Foreign Sovereign Immunities Act and International Association of Machinists v. Organization of Petroleum Exporting Countries (Case Note)*, 8 HOFSTRA L.REV., 771-809 (1980), *Note: Jurisdiction - Act of State Doctrine - Foreign Sovereign Immunities Act*, 3 J.INT'L & COMP. L. 119-120 (1981), Lynn Berat, *Act of State Doctrine - Act of State Doctrine Applied as a Bar to Antitrust Suit Against Foreign Sovereigns (Case Note)*, 17 TEX.INT'L L.J. 82-91 (1982), David Aronofsky, *Private Antitrust Actions Against Foreign States: Problems and Issues After International Association of Machinists and Aerospace Workers v. OPEC*, 17 TEX.INT'L L.J. 82-91 (1982), Michael H. Roffer, *Antitrust Law - International Law - Act of State Doctrine - Foreign Antitrust Violations (Case Note)*, 27 N.Y.L.SCH.L.REV. 1013-1041 (1982), Charles W. Pollard, *The Ninth Circuit Breathes New Life Into the Act of State Doctrine in Commercial Settings (Case Note)*, 16 GEO.WASH.J.INTL'L L. & ECON. 427-449 (1982), Richard Bardos, *Judicial Abstention Through the Act of State Doctrine (Case Note)*, 7 INT'L TRADE L.J. 177-192 (1982), Eric D. Isicott, *An Alternative Justification for Judicial Abstention in Politically Sensitive Disputes Involving Acts of Foreign States (Case Note)*, 14 LAW.AMERICAS 85-90 (1982), John A. Kenward, *Sovereign Immunity - Oil Fixing by Member States of OPEC is a Governmental Act, Not a Commercial Act, and Thus is Exempt from Suit under the Foreign Sovereign Immunities Act: Foreign States Can Sue, But Cannot Be Sued Under American Antitrust Laws (Case Note)*, 9 DEN.J.Int'L L. & POL'Y 141-144 (1980), Lawrence Crocker, *Sovereign Immunity in the United States*, 29 INT'L & COMP. L.Q. 508-510 (1980), H. Smit & al., *Sovereign Immunity. Act of State. Opec*, Am.SOC.INT'L PROC. 49-81 (1980), J.A. Jostad, *Status of Foreign Sovereign in Private Antitrust Actions*, 10 DEN.J.INT'L L. & POL'Y 81-104 (1981), C.A. Corcoran, *IAM v. OPEC: Commercial Activity - One Factor in a Balancing Approach to the Act of State Doctrine*, XIV L.POL.INT'L BUS. 215-243 (1982).

[373] 477. F.Supp. 553, 567.

[374] Id.

[375] Id.

[376] Id.

[377] 477 F.Supp. 553, 566.

[378] 477 F.Supp. 553, 566, note 12: 'The Court, dissatisfied with the apparent expertise and proposed testimony of the plaintiff's experts, Dr. Arnold E. Safer, Dr. James R. Kurth, and Dr. Stanley J. Foster, and after consulting the outstanding academic economic authorities in the United States, appointed as its own experts, Dr. M.A. Adelman, Professor of Economics at Massachusetts Institute of Technology, and Dr. Philip K. Verleger, Jr., Senior Research Scientist, School of Organization and Management, Yale University, who until very recently had been working as Special Assistant to the Assistant Secretary for Economic Policy in the Department of the Treasury. Both of the experts were unanimously acknowledged by their peers as the two most outstanding and erudite experts in the field of both World and domestic petroleum economics.'

[379] The judge has the power to call forth evidence and can nominate sua sponte expert witnesses, see Graham, *Federal Rules of Evidence in a Nutshell (1981)*, p. 194, Wigmore, *Evidence in Trials at Common Law (1981)*, Vol. IX, §2484, p. 276. Rule 614 of the *Federal Rules of Evidence* states: '(a) Calling by Court. The court may, on its own motion or at the suggestion of a party, call witnesses, and all parties are entitled to cross-examine witnesses thus called.'

[380] 477 F.Supp. 553, 566, note 12.

[381] Id., p. 566.

[382] Id.

[383] Id., p. 568.

[384] Id., pp. 568-569, note 14.

[385] Id., pp. 568-569.

[386] Id., p. 567: '1. The right of people and nations to permanent sovereignty over their national wealth and resources must be exercised in the interest of their national development and of the well-being of the people of the State concerned.'

[387] Contrary to, for example, the international arbitration verdict in the *Texaco* affair, 17 ILM 1 (1978), Steiner/Vagts, *Transnational Legal Problems (1982)*, Case and Documents Supplement, pp. 227 ff.

[388] 477 F.Supp. 553, 567.

[389] See for example, the precedents, *Matter of Sedco, Inc, Mol, De Sanchez* or *Castro*, that I discussed earlier on.

[390] 649 F.2d 1354 (9th Cir. 1981).

[391] 649 F.2d 1354, 1359.

[392] Id., p. 1360.

393 See, for example, Marian Lloyd Nash, *Digest of United States Practice in International Law (1980)*, Vol. 1979, §8, pp. 947 ff, Sweeny/Oliver/Leech, *The International Legal System (1981)*, Chapter 6, pp. 365 ff., McDougal/Reisman, *International Law in Contemporary Perspective (1981)*, Chapter 14, pp. 1513 ff., Henkin/Pugh/Schachter/Smit, International Law (1980), p. 516, Steiner/Vagts, *Transnational Legal Problems (1982)*, pp. 672-673, Brian S. Fraser, *Adjudicating Acts of State in Suits Against Foreign Sovereigns: A Political Question Analysis*, 51 FORDHAM L.REV. 722-746, 737 ff. See also particularly on the controversial question how the FSIA relates to the act of state doctrine, Antonia Dolar, *Act of State and Sovereign Immunities Doctrines: The Need to Establish Congruity*, 17 U.S.F.L.REV. 91-116 (1982), Stephen C. Krane, *Rehabilitation and Exoneration of the Act of State Doctrine*, 12 N.Y.U.J.INT'L L. & POL'Y 599-651 (1980), T.H. Hill, *Sovereign Immunity and the Act of State Doctrine*, 14 VAND.J.TRANSNAT'L L. 909-930 (1981), Monroe Leigh & M.D. Sandler, *Dunhill: Toward a Consideration of Sabbatico*, 16 VA.J.INT'L L. 685-718 (1976), J.S. Williams, *The Act of State Doctrine: Alfred Dunhill of London, Inc. v. Republic of Cuba*, 9 VAND.J.TRANSNAT'L L. 735-770 (1976), Jacobs, Stephen et al., The Act of State Doctrine: A History of Judicial Limitation and Exceptions, 18 HARV.INT'L L.J. 677-679 (1979), Hans-Ernst Folz, *Die Geltungskraft fremder Hoheitsäusserungen, Eine Untersuchung über die anglo-amerikanische Act of State Doctrine (1975)*.

394 649 F.2d 1354, 1358.

395 454 U.S. 1163, 102 S.Ct. 1036, 71 L.Ed.2d 319 (1982).

396 543 F.Supp. (S.D.Tex. 1982), 21 ILM 318 (1982). See also the case note by Monroe Leigh, *Sovereign Immunity - Foreign Sovereign Immunities Act - Commercial Activity and Tortious Conduct Exception Not Applicable to Support Jurisdiction Over Defendant in Oil Spill Disaster*, 77 AJIL 149-151 (1983).

397 543 F.Supp. 561, 565: 'Beyond of doubt, Pemex is a 'foreign state' as contemplated by §1603(d) of the FSIA.'

398 543 F.Supp. 561, 564.

399 Id., p. 565.

400 Id.: 'There is little doubt that where a foreign nation enters into the world marketplace to purchase or sell goods, it has engaged in commercial activity for purposes of the FSIA.'

401 Id.

402 The court also considered the precedents *Rio Grande Transport* and *Harris*, already discussed in this study.

403 543 F.Supp. 561, 566: '... integral to the Mexican government's long range planning and policy making process concerning the production and utilization of state-owned minerals.'

404 Id.

405 Id.

406 Id.

407 572 F.Supp. 79 (D.Or. 1983).

408 572 F.Supp. 79, 85-86. The court referred to the IAM v. OPEC precedent.

409 The licensing agreement required from the licensee to build a breeding farm for the animals in 1978 and it contained in addition a clause that the monkeys 'shall be used exclusively for the purpose of medical and other scientific research by highly skilled and competent personnel *for the general benefit of all peoples of the world.*' (572 F.Supp. 79, 81). The plaintiff failed to construe the breeding farm, and in addition, Bangladesh argued the 'humanitarian clause' in the license had been violated when the plaintiff delivered monkeys to the Armed Force Radiobiology Research Institute for Neutron Bomb Radiation Experiments.' (Id., pp. 81-82).

410 Id., p. 82.

411 Even after the enactment of the FSIA, the State Department can still deliver their opinions to the courts, in their role as *amicus curiae*. Such a suggestion does not bind the court, however, and sometimes courts do not follow those suggestions, as we have seen in the spectacular case *Jackson v. People's Republic of China.*

412 572 F.Supp. 79, 84.

413 Id.

414 Id.

415 Id.

416 Id., p. 85.

417 Id., p. 84.

418 515 F.Supp. 900 (E.D.La. 1981), 63 IRL 584 (1982). See also the case note by Mark A. Block, *De Sanchez v. Banco Central de Nicaragua: An Extension of the Restrictive Theory of Foreign Sovereign Immunity*, 7 N.C.J.INT'L L. & COMM.REG. 419-431 (1982).

419 There was no litigation about the fact that *Banco Central* represented an agency or instrumentality of a foreign state under §1603(b) FSIA, see 515 F.Supp. 900, 902, note 3.

420 515 F.Supp. 900, 903.

421 515 F.Supp. 900, 904: '... as both the language of the statute and its legislative history make clear, in determining the existence of immunity, the purpose of the challenged conduct is irrelevant; ... '.

[422] 515 F.Supp. 900, 905: 'In this case, both sides have offered sworn statements by officials of Banco Central and the Nicaraguan Government attesting to the governmental or commercial nature of the bank, and to the nature of the particular transaction giving rise to Sanchez's claim.'

[423] Id., pp. 905-906: 'For example, Gonzalo Meneses-Ocon, chief counsel of Banco Central, stated that the bank was created by the Nicaraguan Congress on August 23, 1960 through Decree N° 525 as the central bank of Nicaragua, with its main objective, as defined in the Decree, 'to create, promote and keep monetary exchange and credit conditions favorable to the orderly development of the national economy.' Accordingly, Meneses-Ocon declared, 'Banco Central is not a commercial bank and does not operate with a mercantile objective.' Affidavit of Gonzalo Meneses-Ocon at pp. 3, 4.'

[424] Id., p. 906.

[425] Id.

[426] Id., p. 907.

[427] Id.: '... I cannot decide this motion under §1605(a)(2) on the basis of Banco Central's general character, for just as a government entity may nevertheless be engaged in a commercial activity and thus be subject to suit, ... so may a commercial entity perform a governmental function and avoid liability for claims arising therefrom.'

[428] 448 F.Supp. 622 (S.D.N.Y. 1978), 17 ILM 1407 (1978), 63 ILR 63 (1982), conf'd 597 F.2d 314 (2d Cir. 1979), 63 ILR 137.

[429] 515 F.Supp. 900, 907.

[430] See Wigmore, *Evidence in Trials at Common Law (1981)*, Vol. IX, §2484, p. 278, Fed.R.EVID. §614(b), Michael H. Graham, *Federal Rules of Evidence in a Nutshell (1981)*, §614.2, p. 194.

[431] See Rule 50(a) Federal Rules of Civil Procedure.

[432] See Rule 50 Federal Rules of Civil Procedure and Thomas A. Coyne, *Federal Rules of Civil Procedure for the United States District Courts (1983)*, Rule 50, Practice Comment, Subdivision (a), p. 577.

[433] 515 F.Supp. 900, 907.

[434] Id.

[435] Id.

[436] Id.

[437] Id., p. 910.

[438] 770 F.2d 1385, 1387 (5th Cir. 1985).

[439] Id., pp. 1393-1394.

[440] In more recent precedents, this interpretation of the FSIA was confirmed and even more fine-tuned, see *Wolf v. Banco Nacional de Mexico, S.A.*, 739 F2d 1458 (9th Cir. 1984), *Braka v. Bancomer, S.N.C.*, 762 F.2d 222 (2d Cir. 1985), 24 ILM 1047 (1985) and *Callajo v. Bancomer, S.A.*, 764 F.2d 1101 (5th Cir. 1985), 24 ILM 1050 (1985).

[441] One could cite here §2(4) United Nations Charta as a supportive argument, the *non-interference* clause.

[442] 510 F.Supp. 309 (W.D.Tex. 1980), 63 ILR 419 (1982).

[443] We have already discussed the question if such a clause could be interpreted as an implicit immunity waiver.

[444] 510 F.Supp. 309, 312.

[445] 1 RCADI (1923) 525.

[446] Id., p. 546 (Translation mine).

[447] Hersch Lauterpacht, *The Problem of Jurisdictional Immunities of Foreign States*, 28 BRIT.Y.B.INT'L L. 220, 225 (1951).

[448] Jean Flavien Lalive, *L'immunité de juridiction des états et des organisations internationales*, 84 RCADI (1953-III), 209 ff., 258. (Translation mine). Then he continues that Weiss' proposition could be managed to be applied for the general practice, while the example that Weiss cites, that is, a warship, was without a doubt 'little satisfying'.

[449] H.R. Report, p. 16, 15 ILM 1398, 1406-1407 (1976).

[450] 448 F.Supp. 622 (S.D.N.Y. 1978), 17 ILM 1407 (1978), 63 ILR 63 (1982), conf'd 597 F.2d 314 (2d Cir. 1979), 63 ILR 137.

[451] 420 F.Supp. 954 (S.D.N.Y. 1976).

[452] 448 F.Supp. 622, 641.

[453] 336 F.2d 354 (2d Cir. 1964).

[454] 448 F.Supp. 622, 641.

[455] Id.

[456] Id.

[457] *Trendtex Trading Corp. Ltd. v. Central Bank of Nigeria*, [1977] 1 All E.R. 881, [1977] 2 W.L.R. 356, [1977] 1 Lloyd's Rep. 581 (C.A.), [1977] 1 Q.B. 529, 16 ILM 471 (1977), 64 ILR 111 (1983).

[458] 510 F.Supp. 309, 312.

[459] Id., p. 313. The default judgement previously obtained by the plaintiffs under §1608(e) FSIA had thus to be rendered void, 'for without subject matter jurisdiction the default judgment is a nullity.' 510 F.Supp. 309, 312.

[460] 443 F.Supp. 849 (S.D.N.Y. 1978).

[461] See Jowitt's *Dictionary of English Law (1977),* Vol. 1, 'Arrest', and *Ninth Decennial Digest (1976-1981),* Part I, Vol. 2, 'Arrest'.

[462] See Jowitt's *Dictionary of English Law (1977),* Vol. 1, 'Arrest', and *Words and Phrases (1969),* 'Arrest'.

[463] Sompong Sucharitkul, *Immunities of Foreign States Before National Authorities,* 149 RCADI (1976-I), 93, 122.

[464] *House Report,* p. 21, 15 ILM 1398, 1409 (1976). The problems of such admiralty actions were largely discussed in the literature and the solution under the FSIA was often criticized, if not authors were outright requiring an addendum to be made, or an 'admiralty sovereign immunities act' so be drafted, see for example Russell J. Pope, *Maritime Arrest Under the Foreign Sovereign Immunities Act: An Anachronism,* 62 TEXAS L.R. 511-535 (1983).

[465] *House Report,* p. 27, 15 ILM 1398, 1412 (1976).

[466] Georges R. Delaume notes that there are three major factors that determine the question of execution vel non: 'These factors relate to: (i) the personality of the borrower (since the rules applicable to foreign states may be different from those applicable to foreign public entities distinguishable from the state itself; (ii) the nature of the property sought to be attached or executed against (since execution is usually possible only against property used for commercial, as opposed to public, purposes; and (iii) the time at which execution is sought (since not all legal systems permit prejudgment attachment and the creditor's remedies may be limited to post-judgment execution.' (Transnational Contracts, Vol. II, Booklet 14, XII, Text pp. 1-2).

[467] We shall see this more in detail further down in the text. For the principle, it follows from statutory construction that the exceptions from the exceptions lead back to the rule (§1609), which is noteworthy, as this influences the allocation of the burden of proof.

[468] *House Report,* pp. 26-31, 15 ILM 1398, 1412-1415 (1976).

[469] 26 AJIL 453 (1932 Suppl.), Comment on Art. 22, p. 690.

[470] Id., p. 27, 15 ILM 1398, 1412-1413 (1976).

471 See, for example Sompong Sucharitkul, *State Immunities (1959)*, pp. 255-256, 347-368, citing the precedent *Duff Development v. Government of Kelantan*, [1924] A.C. 797, Jean-Flavien Lalive, *L'immunité de juridiction des Etats et des Organisations Internationales*, 84 RCADI (1953-III), 209, 272-273, Hersch Lauterpacht, *The Problem of Jurisdictional Immunities of Foreign States*, 28 BRIT.Y.B.INT'L L. 220-272, 241-243 (1951), Sompong Sucharitkul, *Immunities of Foreign States Before National Authorities*, 149 RCADI (1976-I), 89, 170, Ian Sinclair, *The Law of Sovereign Immunity. Recent Developments*, 167 RCADI (1980-II), 117, 220-223, Gamal Moursi Badr, *State Immunity (1984)*, pp. 117 ff.

472 *ILA Report of the Fifty-Ninth Conference held at Belgrade 1980*, pp. 219 ff, p. 329, note 45.

473 Id.

474 676 F.2d 47 (2d Cir. 1982), 21 ILM 618 (1982).

475 676 F.2d 47, 49, 21 ILM 618, 619.

476 Id.

477 Id.

478 532 F.Supp. 901 (S.D.N.Y. 1982), 21 ILM 1073 (1982), conf'd, 21 ILM 1066 (1982).

479 532 F.Supp. 901, 908-909, 21 ILM 1073, 1078-1079.

480 706 F.2d 411 (2d Cir. 1983).

481 26 U.S.T., T.I.A.S. N° 8159.

482 706 F.2d 411, 416-417.

483 See for a listing of the precedents, at pp. 417-418 of the judgment. In *Behring I*, already discussed, such an interpretation of the clause was expressly denied by the court, 475 F.Supp. 383, 392-393 (D.N.J. 1979).

484 *House Report*, p. 27, 15 ILM 1398, 1412-1413 (1976).

485 George R. Delaume, *Transnational Contracts*, Vol. II, Booklet 14, XII., §12.01, Text, p. 1. See also, specifically for the *State Immunity Act 1978*, of the United Kingdom, F. A. Mann, *The State Immunity Act 1978*, 50 BRIT.Y.B.INT'L L. 43, 62 (1979).

486 See, for example, Phipson and Elliott, *Manual of the Law of Evidence (1980)*, p. 54: 'The party who relies on an exception (or proviso) to some general rule imposing liability has the burden of proving that the exception applies to the case.'

487 475 F.Supp. 383, 395.

[488] The judge however refused to grand immunity to Iran because he saw an implicit immunity waiver in the *Friendship Treaty between the United States and Iran, of August 8, 1955*: 'With respect to the Treaty of Amity, my conclusions may be summarized as follows: First, it survives the Immunities Act. Second, the intent of the parties as of the time of the signing governs. Third, it is my task to determine that intent in accordance with ordinary rules of construction. Fourth, I believe that the parties intended that they be treated like any private person. Pre-judgment attachment of the property was proper. Defendants motion for the release of restraints is denied'. (Id., p. 396).

[489] Sompong Sucharitkul, *State Immunities (1959)*, p. 167. See, for example, *The Parlement Belge*, [1880] 5 P.D. 197, [1874-80] All E.R. 104 and *Juan Ismael & Co. v. Indonesian Government*, [1954] 3 All E.R. 236, [1955] A.C. 72, [1954] 3 W.L.R. 531, [1954] 2 Lloyd's Rep. 175. See also Article 3 of the *'Convention de Bruxelles pour l'Unification de certaines règles concernant les Immunités des Navires d'Etat',* of 10 April 1926, which stipulates: '§1. Les dispositions des deux articles précédents ne sont pas applicables aux navires de guerre, aux yachts d'État, navires de surveillance, bateaux-hôpitaux, navires auxiliaires, navires de ravitaillement et autres bâtiments appartenant à un État ou exploités par lui et affectés exclusivement, au moment de la naissance de la créance, à un service gouvernemental et non commercial, et ces navires ne seront pas l'objet de saisies, d'arrêtes et de détentions par une mesure de justice quelconque ni d'aucune procédure judiciaire 'in rem'.

[490] Id., p. 168.

[491] Charles Rousseau, *Droit International Public (1979)*, Tome IV, p. 19: 'On décèle dans la jurisprudence française une tendance à refuser le bénéfice de l'immunité d'exécution et de saisie lorsqu'il s'agit de biens situés en France mais détenus par l'État étranger à titre purement privé.'

[492] Hersch Lauterpacht, *International Law (1977)*, Vol. 3, p. 339.

[493] Id.

[494] Id.

[495] 28 U.S.C. §1610(a)(2) stipulates: '(2) the property is or was used for the commercial activity upon which the claim is based, … '.

[496] 28 U.S.C. §1610(b)(2) stipulates: '(2) the judgment relates to a claim for which the agency or instrumentality is not immune by virtue of section 1605(a)(2), (3), or (5), or 1605(b) of this chapter, regardless of whether the property is or was used for the activity upon which the claim is based.'

[497] Vol. II, Booklet 14, XII., Text, §12.03, pp. 13, 14.

[498] Id., p. 13

[499] Id.

[500] Idl, Note 2/ ad §12.03.

[501] 567 F.Supp. 1490 (S.D.N.Y. 1983).

[502] 567 F.Supp. 1490, 1498-1499.

[503] 567 F.Supp. 1490, 1498-1499.

[504] In addition, the question was, if the exception of §1610(a)(2) could be applied in the present case, 567 F.Supp. 1490, 1500-1503.

[505] 19 ILM 208, 212 (D.C.Cir. 1980)

[506] *Sutherland Statutory Construction (1975)*, §51.08.

[507] 19 ILM 208, 212.

[508] *Maxwell on the Interpretation of Statutes (1969)*, pp. 47, 48.

[509] See also *House Report*, p. 30, 15 ILM 1398, 1414 (1976).

[510] 19 ILM 208 (D.C.Cir. 1980).

[511] Id., p. 217.

[512] Notwithstanding the provisions of section 1610 of this chapter ...

[513] 'Section 1611exempts certain types of property from the immunity provisions of section 1610 relating to attachment and execution.' *House Report*, p. 30, 15 ILM 1398, 1414 (1976).

[514] 475 F.Supp. 383 (D.N.J. 1979), UN-MAT., p. 479, 63 ILR 261 (1982).

[515] 475 F.Supp. 383, 395, note 30. As the judge refers to note 16, regarding the burden of proof, I quote it here: 'Under the Immunities Act sovereign immunity is an affirmative defense which must be specifically pleaded. The burden is upon the foreign state to 'produce evidence of its claim of immunity', H.R. No. 94-1487, supra, at 17, [1976] U.S. Code Cong. & Admin. News, p. 6616.

[516] 475 F.Supp. 396 (D.N.J. 1979).

[517] Id., p. 405.

[518] The judge also examined the Treaty of Amity between the United States and Iran of August 8, 1955, but concluded that 'the treaty is silent with respect to whether certain types of property are subject to attachment.' (Id. p. 407).

[519] Id., p. 406, note 12.

[520] Id., pp. 407-408.

[521] 583 F.Supp. 320 (S.D.N.Y. 1984), 23 ILM 782 (1984).

[522] The fact of Banco de Guatemala's status as the central bank of that country was not contested.

523 583 F.Supp. 320, 321, 23 ILM 782, 784-785.

524 Id., p. 322, 23 ILM 782, 785. See also the article by Ernest T. Patrikis, *Foreign Central Bank Property: Immunity from Attachment in the United States*, 1982 U.ILL.L.REV. 265-287.

525 *House Report*, p. 31, 15 ILM 1398, 1414 (1976).

526 583 F.Supp. 320, 322, 23 ILM 782, 785.

527 Id.

528 Id., p. 321, 23 ILM 782, 784.

529 Id., p. 322, 23 ILM 782, 786.

530 Id.

531 Id. The court also referred to the before-mentioned article by Ernest T. Patrikis, *Foreign Central Bank Property: Immunity from Attachment in the United States*, 1982 U.ILL.L.REV. 265-287.

532 See also *Alcom Ltd. v. Republic of Colombia*, [1984] 2 Lloyd's Rep. 24 (H.L.), 23 ILM 719 (1984).

533 *Entwicklungstendenzen der Immunität ausländischer Staaten*, 40 ZaöRV 217 (1980). *Les tendances de l'évolution de l'immunité de l'État étranger*, in: *Droit international et droit interne (1982)*.